TOTAL QUALITY ENVIRONMENTAL MANAGEMENT

TOTAL QUALITY ENVIRONMENTAL MANAGEMENT

An ISO 14000 Approach

Vasanthakumar N. Bhat

QUORUM BOOKS
Westport, Connecticut • London

Library of Congress Cataloging-in-Publication Data

Bhat, Vasanthakumar N.
      Total quality environmental management : an ISO 14000 approach /
Vasanthakumar N. Bhat.
          p.   cm.
      Includes bibliographical references and index.
      ISBN 1–56720–097–4 (alk. paper)
      1. Production management—Environmental aspects. 2. ISO 14000
Series Standards. 3. Total quality management. 4. Industrial
management—Environmental aspects. 5. Environmental auditing.
      I. Title.
      TS155.7.B48   1998
      658.4'08—dc21   97–19761

British Library Cataloguing in Publication Data is available.

Library of Congress Catalog Card Number: 97–19761
ISBN: 1–56720–097–4

First published in 1998

Quorum Books, 88 Post Road West, Westport, CT 06881
An imprint of Greenwood Publishing Group, Inc.

Printed in the United States of America

The paper used in this book complies with the
Permanent Paper Standard issued by the National
Information Standards Organization (Z39.48–1984).

10 9 8 7 6 5 4 3 2 1

Copyright Acknowledgments

The author and publisher gratefully acknowledge permission to use the following:

Excerpts from International Chamber of Commerce. (1991). *The Business Charter for Sustainable Development*. Paris: International Chamber of Commerce.

Excerpts from International Chamber of Commerce. (1986). *Basic Steps of an Environmental Audit from the International Chamber of Commerce Position Paper on Environmental Auditing*. Paris: International Chamber of Commerce.

Excerpts from Coalition for Environmentally Responsible Economies. (1989). *Guidelines for Environmental Responsibility* (p. 1). Boston, MA: Coalition for Environmentally Responsible Economies.

Excerpts from J. Andy Smith, III. (1994). The CERES Principles and Corporate Environmental Accountability: A New Model of Partnership. In *GEMI '94 Conference Proceedings: Environmental Management in a Global Economy* (pp. 195–201). Washington, D.C.: Global Environmental Management Initiative.

Revised chapter from Vasanthakumar N. Bhat. (1996). "Life-cycle Assessment: Measuring Greenness." In *The Green Corporation: The Next Competitive Advantage* (pp. 52–66). Westport, CT: Quorum Books. An imprint of Greenwood Publishing Group, Inc., Westport, CT.

Contents

III: PRODUCT AND PROCESS ASSESSMENTS

IV: PERFORMANCE EVALUATION

V: IMPLEMENTATION

Illustrations

Preface

This book is a sequel to my earlier book, *The Green Corporation: The Next Competitive Advantage* (Quorum Books) that focused on reducing pollution and improving competitiveness. *The Green Corporation* dealt with green strategic planning, green design, green production, recycling, green marketing, green research and development, green auditing, total green management, green benchmarking, and so on. Rising environmental costs and a growing plethora of environmental laws have caused several managers to consider the environmental function a no-win proposition. Rising objections from industry and declining competitiveness have forced governments to go slow on environmental regulations. Rising unemployment and slow growth have reduced support for environmental issues in Europe and the Americas. In a provocative article, "It's Not Easy Being Green," in the May–June 1994 issue of *Harvard Business Review*, Noah Walley and Bradley Whitehead denounce win-win talk of environmentalists and assert that environmental initiatives are expensive and are destroying shareholder values of U.S. corporations. Walley and Whitehead, therefore, insist that environmental initiatives be based on shareholder values rather than on compliance, emissions, or costs. In an equally provocative article, "Green and Competitive: Ending the Stalemate," in the September–October 1995 issue of *Harvard Business Review*, Michael E. Porter and Class van der Linde argue that appropriate environmental regulations can spur innovations and reduce the total cost of a product. They argue that pollution means inefficiency, and, there-fore, environmental regulations have competitive implications. No matter who is right, every company has to improve environmental performance and comply with environmental regulations. Traditional strategies to force companies to satisfy environmental standards have been through rules and regulations or command and control approaches. The command and control approach achieves compliance through mandates and penalties. Although the command and control approach is compulsory for all, it is inefficient. The emphasis is on pollution control rather than pollution prevention. Moreover, it is bureaucratic, and companies have very little incentive to improve environmental performance. A market-based approach, which uses taxes, charges, and tradeable permits is more efficient and penalizes polluters. However, the effectiveness of market-based approaches is uncertain. The more recent trend is toward a partnership approach. Total quality management is their tool. Industry standards are their guidebooks. The emphasis is on employee involvement. Continuous improvement is their mantra. Environmental management system is their vehicle. This book discusses a total quality environmental management (TQEM) approach to carry out environmental programs in an organization.

This book is about TQEM and describes how TQEM can be applied to eliminate pollution and environmental degradation and to satisfy stakeholders. The elements of strategy are stakeholder focus, continuous improvement, teamwork, and management commitment. The continuous improvement technique involving the Plan-Do-Check-Act cycle is pervasive in all chapters of this book.

This book is divided into five parts. The first part deals with costs and benefits of pollution reduction and describes TQEM tools and techniques. Company assessment methodologies are explained in Part II. No company can improve its environmental performance without analyzing its products and processes, and the product and process assessment methodologies are described in Part III. Part IV focuses on the performance evaluation, and implementation strategies are discussed in Part V.

Rising environmental costs and worldwide increases in environmental regulations have changed the focus from pollution control to pollution elimination. Incentive-based systems of environmental regulations are replacing command and control regulations. In a market-based system of pollution reduction, the focus is on the environmental management systems. TQEM is the process. Chapter 2 discusses whether it makes sense to reduce pollution and analyzes some effects of pollution and waste generation.

In Chapter 3, we describe TQEM. After presenting various elements of TQEM, we present several tools with examples. Total quality management philosophies and principles are explained in this chapter.

In Chapter 4, our focus is on the environmental standards established by various industry associations. Such standards create an even playing field by reducing competitive disparities between companies in an industry because of different levels of environmental performance. Peer pressure forces companies to excel in environmental performance. Chapter 5 deals with environmental system standards, including ISO 14000, B.S. 7750, and the European Union's eco-management and audit scheme. Chapter 5 describes each of these standards and the differences between them. Environmental auditing is described in Chapter 6.

Chapters 7 and 8 deal with product and process assessment methodologies. Chapter 7 describes life-cycle assessment and its several variations, and environmental labeling is explained in Chapter 8.

Performance evaluation is a major element of environmental management systems. We present various environmental performance indicators in Chapter 9. Current accounting systems fail to provide accurate environmental costs. We present environmental accounting and project evaluation in Chapter 10. Chapter 11 focuses on environmental reporting within a TQEM framework.

Chapter 12 addresses training. Various approaches to setting up TQEM are described in Chapter 13. We also discuss various pitfalls in carrying out TQEM. Chapter 14 explains approaches adopted by various companies in starting TQEM. The bibliography includes a list of publications for further study.

The Atlanta Olympic Games was the final Olympics of this century. The next Olympics will be held in the twenty-first century. However, the results of the Atlanta Olympics convey a central lesson to all of us: if you want to be a world-class athlete, there is no substitute for discipline and practice. Continuous improvement requires continuous effort. Continuous improvement is the name of the game. For example, the 400-meter run took 54.20 seconds for Thomas Burke of the United States in 1896; Michael Johnson did it in 1996 in 43.49 seconds. The person who came in first and won a gold medal in 1980, just 18 years ago, would not even be among the top four runners. In other words, just to keep pace with progress, continuous improvement is a must. It is this spirit that underlies the new philosophy of TQEM.

I welcome your comments and suggestions about this book.

1

Introduction

The United States has made tremendous progress in combating the most unsightly and obvious effects of pollution. The quality of the air we breathe has improved significantly, and levels of most air pollutants have fallen dramatically since 1970. Emissions of lead in the air, for example, have decreased from 219.471 million short tons in 1970 to 4.885 million short tons in 1993.[1] By most available measures, water quality in the nation's rivers and streams has been improving steadily. Recycling programs and incineration have reduced the amount of solid waste being sent to landfills from 81 percent in 1980 to 66 percent in 1990. According to the 1992 Toxics Release Inventory Public Data Release, industrial release of toxic chemicals into the environment decreased by 35 percent from 4.85 billion pounds in 1988 to 3.16 billion pounds in 1992.[2] However, these achievements are not without cost. The United States currently spends more than $100 billion annually on pollution abatement and control. The compliance costs of U.S. industry from 1970 are estimated to be $1.4 trillion.[3] Studies show that environmental regulations reduce productivity. It is estimated that some small businesses are likely to spend $5,000 to $10,000 just to comply with toxic chemical handling and reporting, hazardous waste disposal, and underground storage tank regulations.[4] One in four Americans currently lives in an area where air pollution exceeds federal standards. More than $30 billion have been spent to clean up sites under the Superfund program. However, only 149 sites out of 1,275 have been cleaned so far. Some environmental programs have been downright inefficient. For example, the regulations relating to hazardous waste listing for wood preserving chemicals issued in 1990 will prevent one premature death at an estimated cost of $5.7 trillion.[5] It is estimated that the Atrazine/Alachlor Drinking Water Standard costs $92.070 billion per one premature death averted, Municipal Solid Waste Landfill Standards (proposed in 1988) cost $19.107 billion per one premature death averted, Hazardous Waste Land Disposal Ban (1st Third) costs $4.190 billion per one premature death averted, and so on.

Discharges into the air, water, and land were early methods of disposal of waste. The "end-of-the-pipe" pollution control was the strategy to improve compliance. About two-thirds of the plants in the United States were equipped for cleaning of exhaust gases as late as 1987. More than 66 percent of plants in metal mining, coal mining, mining and quarrying of minerals, heavy construction, food products, tobacco products, lumber and wood products, furniture and fixtures, chemicals, petroleum, stone, clay, glass and concrete, primary metal industries, electronic and electrical equipment, and transportation equipment were equipped for cleaning of exhaust gases according to a U.S. Environmental Protection Agency (EPA) special compilation.

Rising costs of controlling pollution by the end-of-the-pipe forced companies to initiate pollution prevention. Source reduction is the preferred method of pollution elimination. Green design and manufacturing are the future. ISO 14000 and industry standards are the tools. CERES Principles, the Business Charter for Sustainable Development, Responsible Care, ISO 14000, Environmental Leadership Programs, the Common Sense Initiative, and Project XL are the building blocks. Total quality environmental management (TQEM) is the process. This book describes effective implementation of environmental management programs using the TQEM approach.

CHANGING ENVIRONMENTAL LANDSCAPE

The quantity of toxic chemicals emitted by industry into the environment was 3.182 billion pounds in 1992. This reflects a 35 percent reduction in comparison with 1988 emissions. All industry groups except apparel, food, and tobacco showed a decrease in the total releases between 1988 and 1992. Industry groups including textiles, machinery, electrical, and measuring and photographic equipment showed more than 40 percent reduction in total releases from 1988 to 1992. Most emissions were into the air (58 percent) followed by underground injection (22.8 percent), land (10.6 percent), and surface water (8.6 percent). Chemicals, primary metals, paper, plastics, and transport equipment are the top five industries for total releases. Louisiana, Texas, Tennessee, Ohio, and Indiana are the top five states in total releases in the United States.

Growing environmental regulations are a serious concern for U.S. corporations. Federal, state, and local laws require companies to reduce emissions significantly, manage toxic and solid waste safely, stop using certain chemicals, and meet other requirements. States also are adopting their own laws. Clean air legislation in states like California, New York, and New Jersey mandates compliance with tougher standards. In addition, media-specific regulations focus on pollution released to each medium. Although these regulations have reduced emissions, they have encouraged end-of-the pipe pollution controls to manage waste rather than pollution prevention. In addition, different sets of mandates for air, water, and land discharges have increased cost of conformance and complexity of compliance. Therefore, integrated approaches to environmental management as alternatives to the traditional media-specific approach are being tried. Integrated approaches are likely to encourage pollution prevention, reduce compliance costs, and improve efficiency of regulations.

Increased scrutiny by stakeholders is changing the way the organizations operate. Environmental issues are affecting a variety of business decisions, including locations of new plants, selection of equipment, product development, and mergers and acquisitions. No wonder, according to a 1991 survey by McKinsey & Company, 92 percent of the 400 firms surveyed agreed with the statement "The environmental challenge is one of the central issues of the 21st century."[6] Strict and rigorous enforcement of environmental regulations is another concern to companies in the United States. Table 1.1 presents an enforcement and compliance summary of the period from August 10, 1990, to August 9, 1995, for selected industries. According to the EPA record of enforcement, more than 1,000 years of jail time and millions of dollars in fines and penalties have been imposed for violating environmental laws and regulations during the past 25 years. The number of cases initiated, defenders prosecuted, sentences, and fines imposed from 1990 to 1994 are as follows:

Fiscal Year	Cases Initiated	Defenders Prosecuted	Years of Incarceration	Fines ($ millions)
1990	112	100	75.3	5.5
1991	150	104	80.3	14.1
1992	203	150	94.6	37.9
1993	110	410	74.3	29.7
1994	123	525	99.0	36.8

Increasing costs of environmental protection are affecting the competitiveness of many industries. Pollution abatement and control expenditures rose from $60 billion in 1972 to $113 billion in 1992, in constant dollars, a massive 90 percent increase. In addition, EPA regulations are putting about 100 million hours of paperwork burden on Americans. Rising pollution abatement costs and paperwork burden can reduce productivity and increase costs of production. This can cost U.S. workers their jobs.

Intensive scrutiny by the public is another concern. About one in seven Americans is actively involved with environmental organizations. Several environmental organizations have grown significantly. These organizations are well-funded and have access to legal and environmental professionals. The memberships in 1990 and membership growth from 1970 for some environmental organizations are as follows:

Organization	Members in 1990	Percent Growth from 1970
National Wildlife Federation	5,800,000	123
Sierra Club	645,000	466
National Audubon Society	549,000	423
Wilderness Society	400,000	506
Environmental Defense Fund	220,000	2,100

Provisions for citizens' suits in the federal environmental laws have significantly increased the clout of these organizations. Any citizen can go to a federal court to prevent companies from violating the relevant federal laws or the permit terms and force companies to comply with them.

TABLE 1.1
Five-Year Enforcement and Compliance Summary, August 10, 1990, to August 9, 1995

Industry Sector	Facilities in Search	Facilities Inspected	Number of Inspections	Average Number of Months between Inspections	Facilities with One or More Enforcement Actions	Total Enforcement Actions	State-led Actions (%)	Federal-led Actions (%)	Enforcement to Inspection Rate
Metal mining	873	339	1,519	34	67	155	47	53	0.10
Non-metallic mineral mining	1,143	631	3,422	20	84	192	76	24	0.06
Lumber and wood	464	301	1,891	15	78	232	79	21	0.12
Furniture	293	213	1,534	11	34	91	91	9	0.06
Rubber and plastic	1,665	739	3,386	30	146	391	78	22	0.12
Stone, clay, and glass	468	268	2,475	11	73	301	70	30	0.12
Nonferrous metals	844	474	3,097	16	145	470	76	24	0.15
Fabricated metals	2,346	1,340	5,509	26	280	840	80	20	0.15
Electronics	405	222	777	31	68	212	79	21	0.27
Automobiles	598	390	2,216	16	81	240	80	20	0.11
Pulp and paper	306	265	3,766	5	115	502	78	22	0.13
Printing	4,106	1,035	4,723	52	176	514	85	15	0.11
Inorganic chemicals	548	298	3,034	11	99	402	76	24	0.13
Organic chemicals	412	316	3,864	6	152	726	66	34	0.19
Petroleum refining	156	145	3,257	3	110	797	66	34	0.25
Iron and steel	374	275	3,555	6	115	499	72	28	0.14
Dry cleaning	933	245	633	88	29	103	99	1	0.16

Source: U.S. Environmental Protection Agency, *Profile of the Fabricated Metal Products Industry*, EPA 310-R-95-007. (Washington, D.C.: U.S. Environmental Protection Agency, 1995), p. 107.

ENVIRONMENTAL CHALLENGES

AGENDA 21 adopted at the Earth Summit held in Brazil aptly summarizes the environmental challenges facing the world.[7] Some major themes of the summit were the quality of life on Earth, including poverty, changing resource consumption patterns, rising population, and health care needs; use of the Earth's natural resources, including land, water, energy, forests, deserts, and mountains; biological diversity and biotechnology; protection of global commons, including the atmosphere and the oceans; the management of human settlements; the management of wastes, including toxic chemicals, hazardous wastes, solid wastes, and radioactive wastes; and sustainable economic growth through international trade, environmental policies, and transfer of technology. The Rio Declaration on Environment and Development is reproduced in the Appendix to this chapter.

Environmental problems include population-related problems, such as distribution and mobility, health, education, and consumption; resources-related problems, such as soil degradation, water pollution, deterioration of the wetlands, drinking water pollution, groundwater contamination, agricultural productivity, deforestation, and pesticide residues in food; species decimation problems, such as wildlife destruction and ecosystem deterioration; energy depletion, including energy conservation and emissions into the atmosphere; industry-related problems, such as energy and raw material depletion, recycling, clean technologies, accidents, scarcity of landfills, accidental releases, oil spills, new toxic substances, workplace accidents, toxic waste generation, climate changes, global warming, and waste management; urban problems, such as air pollution, transportation, and traffic; multinational problems, such as ozone depletion, the greenhouse effect, air pollution, and acid rain; environmental knowledge explosion; and political problems.

The rising population is putting tremendous pressure on our planet. About 100 million people are inundating the earth every year. Rising disparities of incomes between and within nations; growing poverty, hunger, ill health, and illiteracy; and incessant disintegration of the environment are some effects of the rising population.

A sick environment jeopardizes health. More than 85 million Americans, or about one in three of our nation's population, breathe unhealthy air because millions of tons of pollutants are emitted into the atmosphere annually. The ozone layer, which protects the earth from solar ultraviolet radiations, is being destroyed by chemicals released on the Earth. Chlorofluorocarbons used in refrigeration and aerosols are the major culprits.

The depletion of the ozone layer can adversely affect agricultural production and human health. Each 1 percent reduction in the ozone layer can cause blindness in 100,000 people each year and 50,000 additional incidences of nonmelanoma skin cancer.

Dumping of wastes into the atmosphere is blocking infrared radiations from the earth, thus, raising its temperature. This phenomenon, called the greenhouse effect, can increase the earth's temperature and can cause worldwide changes in the global climate. Sulphur dioxide emitted by coal-burning power stations and nitrous oxides produced by automobiles can cause acidification of lakes and rivers. Acidic deposition, called acid rain, contaminates lakes, kills fish, damages trees, and destroys forests.

Human activities such as grazing, deforestation, and poor land management are destroying soil formed over thousands or millions of years. Land degradation is causing millions of people to leave the countryside and move into cities. Trees that cover more than a quarter of our Earth provide fuel, building materials, foods, medicine, and employment. However, human activities are destroying our forests. About 17 million hectares of tropical forests are disappearing each year. Increasing demand for forest products, pressures to increase agricultural production, rising population, and mismanagement of forests are some reasons for deforestation. The rising deforestation not only hastens desertification but also causes flooding and soil erosion.

More than 30 million species inhabit the earth, but only about 1.5 million have been described. The genetic variations in these species are a valuable source of genes that can be used to develop medicines and foods. However, rising human activities are destroying the species, and it is estimated that one in four species will be lost in the next 30 years.

Some 100,000 chemicals are currently produced commercially, and 1,000 to 2,000 new chemicals go into commercial production each year. These chemicals are released into the environment directly and indirectly as wastes. Some 338 million tons of hazardous wastes and 2 billion tons of solid wastes are produced each year worldwide.

Industry generates approximately 90 percent of sulfur dioxides, 50 percent of carbon dioxide and hydrocarbons, and 44 percent of nitrogen oxides and particulate matters that are generated by human activities. Industrial wastewater is responsible for two-thirds of the oxygen depletion of surface waters. Industries also cause accidents, and they are becoming frequent. As a result, industrial pollution is a subject of great concern.

According to Stuart Hart, major environmental challenges to sustainability of various economies are different.[8] For instance, developed economies face pollution-related challenges, such as greenhouse gases, toxic materials, and contaminated sites; depletion-related challenges, such as scarcity of raw materials and low levels of reuse and recycling; and poverty causing urban and minority unemployment. Emerging economies are confronted with pollution because of industrial emissions, water pollution, and lack of sewage treatment. Emerging economies overuse renewable resources and water for irrigation. Migration to cities, income disparities, and scarcity of skilled workers are poverty-causing challenges faced by emerging economies. Lack of sanitation, ecosystem destruction, and wood burning are major causes of pollution in survival economies. Deforestation, soil loss, and overgrazing are depletion-related environmental challenges, and rising population and dislocations are major causes for poverty in survival economies.

According to a survey of transnational corporations, the environmental challenges in relative importance to them are protection of the environment, management of toxic wastes, protection of water resources, protection of land resources, protection of the ocean, sound management of biotechnology, and conservation of biodiversity.[9]

ENVIRONMENTAL MANAGEMENT SYSTEM

In most organizations, environmental management systems evolved because of either regulatory requirements or community pressures. Accidents and serious environmental violations often force companies to set up environmental management systems. Environmental management systems are not legally required. However, companies feel the need for environmental personnel, operating procedures, reporting systems, good documentation, and audits to improve compliance and environmental performance, and these are the major elements of an environmental management system. Environmental management systems are voluntary in most countries. However, industry groups and standard organizations are developing codes and standards. Although most of these standards are voluntary, they have significant public relations value. In addition, by obtaining certification for meeting local standards, local manufacturers can create barriers to trade for foreign manufacturers. Governments and buyers can demand environmental certification for doing business, thus, creating a strong competitive advantage for local manufacturers. National standards may be formulated to make it easier for domestic manufacturers to get certification. To create a level playing field and reduce duplication, the International Standardization Organization has developed international standards for an environmental management system, which have several advantages. These standards help companies to transform their commitments to environmental excellence into reality. A single standard avoids duplication. Standards reduce the need for tough command-and-control regulations. They can show management commitment to environmental protection. Standards also help companies to improve their regulatory compliance. However, such standards should not end as trade barriers. They should not be very expensive. These standards should recognize the limitations of life-cycle analysis, environmental impact analysis, and environmental tools.

The purpose of a standard is to describe elements of an effective environmental management system. The standards should deal with environmental policy; goals, objectives, and targets; procedures; documentation systems; environmental metrics; measuring and monitoring; and reviewing environmental performance. Such standards should help a company to improve its environmental performance. Environmental standards should focus on the process rather than on performance. By following standards, a company should be able to improve its performance.

Environmental standards are growing exponentially. The United Kingdom's B.S. 7750, the U.S. Chemical Manufacturers Association's Responsible Care initiative, and the Global Environmental Management Initiative's Environmental Self Assessment Program are some examples of environmental standards.

Community pressure is another reason for growing adoption of standards among companies. With a view to responding to public concerns and the perception that businesses cannot be trusted, several companies are adopting standards to show environmental stewardship and accountability. Consumers are demanding more green products. However, many consumers are cynical about some claims made by the manufacturers. As a result, more companies are trying to lend credibility to their claims through third-party certification. Therefore, the national standards and codes are likely to grow in the future.

Government recognition of standards is likely to increase the popularity of standards. International standardization will dramatically reduce duplication of standards. Rising use of standards will reduce the need for command-and-control regulations, and this will help companies to attempt more cost-effective self-regulation.

A variety of stakeholders are concerned about environmental performance. Employees, shareholders, regulators, the public, environmental groups, consumers, and suppliers have different expectations about environmental performance. The companies with an environmental management system certified by a third party can provide to these stakeholders confidence that a company is doing everything to comply with regulations and to improve performance.

TOTAL QUALITY ENVIRONMENTAL MANAGEMENT

TQEM provides a process by which an organization can carry out a companywide program to eliminate pollution and improve environmental performance. This process can help to incorporate environmental concerns in day-to-day management decisions. The major elements of TQEM are stakeholder focus, continuous improvement, teamwork, and management commitment.

Stakeholder Focus

The TQEM philosophy originated from the total quality management (TQM) successfully used by companies to develop high-quality products and services. The focus of TQM is on customers who use products and services. Customers are of two categories: the internal customers, who are involved in the production of a product, and the external customers, who are end-users of a product. The focus of TQEM is on stakeholders. The stakeholders are those who feel the environmental impacts of products, services, and facilities of a company and include customers, shareholders, employees, competitors, local community, and society.

Continuous Improvement

The continuous improvement philosophy is based on the axiom, "no matter how good you are, you can always be better."[10] Inspection cannot incorporate quality into a product. Quality needs to be built into a product. This is achieved by continuously identifying causes of poor quality and eliminating them. Zero defect was the name of the game in TQM. Continuous improvement strategy reduces environmental impacts by identifying causes of environmental degradation and eliminating them. The traditional strategy of waste reduction was its cleanup. However, such a strategy costs money and resources. The goal of continuous improvement is to prevent the generation of waste in the first place. Zero waste is the name of the game in TQEM.

Teamwork

Environmental improvement projects require team effort. For instance, Monsanto has the eco-efficiency team to design efficiency metrics, the full-cost accounting team to formulate a methodology for environmental accounting, the index team to devise a corporate sustainability index, the new business/new products team to evaluate products and services that enhance sustainability, the water team to analyze global water needs, the global hunger team to develop strategies to reduce world hunger, and the communication and education team to examine training needs.[11] Environmental projects will be successful only if many people cooperate. Environmental projects typically are carried out by a team of employees from different departments. Japanese used quality circles to form teams to do work. It is not necessary to have a special purpose to form a team. Whenever two or more employees decide to be a team, a team is formed. One major ingredient of a TQEM process is that teams carry out environmental programs. TQEM mandates involvement of everyone to be active in environmental improvement.

Management Commitment

Successful TQEM programs require committed top managers. Top management sets the organization's goals and defines the organization's culture. It can eliminate any obstacles that prevent changes to the organization's mind-set. Top management commitment does not mean that senior executives should be involved in pollution elimination programs. However, top management must monitor progress of the implementation and take action to remove any barriers to pollution reduction. Management involvement will be higher for functional team structure than for cross-functional team structure. Similarly, management involvement will be lower if the goal is just cost reduction as compared with competitive advantage.

CONCLUSION

Changing environmental paradigms require new approaches to pollution reduction. Rising costs, public pressures, global competition, growing regulations, stringent enforcement, and increasing liabilities are changing the way that companies operate. Their focus is no longer just on profits but also includes environmental performance and its impact on stakeholders. Employee participation, environmental management systems, TQEM, and industry standards are some strategies that companies are employing to improve their environmental performance and satisfy stakeholders. The purpose of this book is to describe TQEM and effective ways to take advantage of it.

APPENDIX: THE RIO DECLARATION ON ENVIRONMENT AND DEVELOPMENT

The United Nations Conference on Environment and Development, having met at Rio de Janeiro, from 3 to 14 June 1992, reaffirming the Declaration of the United Nations Conference on the Human Environment, adopted at Stockholm on 16 June 1972, and seeking to build upon it, with the goal of establishing a new and equitable global partnership through the creation of new levels of co-operation among States, key sectors of societies and people, working towards international agreements which respect the interests of all and protect the integrity of the global environmental and developmental system, recognizing the integral and interdependent nature of the Earth, our home proclaims that:

Principle 1

Human beings are at the center of concerns for sustainable development. They are entitled to a healthy and productive life in harmony with nature.

Principle 2

States have, in accordance with the Charter of the United Nations and the principles of international law the sovereign right to exploit their own resources pursuant to their own environmental and developmental policies, and the responsibility to ensure that activities within their jurisdiction or control do not cause damage to the environment of other States or of areas beyond the limits of national jurisdiction.

Principle 3

The right to development must be fulfilled so as to equitably meet developmental and environmental needs of present and future generations.

Principle 4

In order to achieve sustainable development, environmental protection shall constitute an integral part of the development process and cannot be considered in isolation from it.

Principle 5

All States and people shall cooperate in the essential task of eradicating poverty as an indispensable requirement for sustainable development, in order to decrease the disparities in standards of living and better meet the needs of the majority of the people of the world.

Principle 6

The special situation and needs of developing countries, particularly the least developed and those most environmentally vulnerable, shall be given special priority. International actions in the field of environment and development should also address the interests and needs of all countries.

Principle 7

States shall cooperate in a spirit of global partnership to conserve, protect and restore the health and integrity of the Earth's ecosystem. In view of the different contributions to global environmental degradation, States have common but differentiated responsibilities. The developed countries acknowledge responsibility that they bear in the international pursuit of sustainable development in view of the pressures their societies place on the global environment and of the technologies and financial resources they command.

Principle 8

To achieve sustainable development and a higher quality of life for all people, States should reduce and eliminate unsustainable patterns of production and consumption and promote appropriate demographic policies.

Principle 9

States should cooperate to strengthen endogenous capacity-building for sustainable development by improving scientific understanding through exchanges of scientific and technological knowledge, and by enhancing the development, adaptation, diffusion and transfer of technologies, including new and innovative technologies.

Principle 10

Environmental issues are best handled with the participation of all concerned citizens, at the relevant level. At the national level, each individual shall have appropriate access to information concerning the environment that is held by public authorities, including information on hazardous materials and activities in their communities, and the opportunity to participate in decision-making processes. States shall facilitate and encourage public awareness and participation by making information widely available. Effective access to judicial and administrative proceedings, including redress and remedy, shall be provided.

Principle 11

States shall enact effective environmental legislation. Environmental standards, management objectives and priorities should reflect the environmental and developmental context to which they apply. Standards applied by some countries can be inappropriate and of unwarranted economic and social cost to other countries, in particular developing countries.

Principle 12

States should cooperate to promote a supportive and open international economic system that would lead to economic growth and sustainable development in all countries, to better address the problems of environmental degradation. Trade policy measures for environmental purposes should not constitute a means of arbitrary or unjustifiable discrimination or a disguised restriction on international trade. Unilateral actions to deal with environmental challenges outside the jurisdiction of the importing country should be avoided. Environmental measures addressing transboundary or global environmental problems should, as far as possible, be based on an international consensus.

Principle 13

States shall develop national law regarding liability and compensation for the victims of pollution and other environmental damage. States shall also cooperate in an expeditious and more determined manner to develop further international law regarding liability and compensation for adverse effects of environmental damage caused by activities within their jurisdiction or control to areas beyond their jurisdiction.

Principle 14

States should effectively cooperate to discourage or prevent the relocation and transfer to other States of any activities and substances that cause severe environmental degradation or are found to be harmful to human health.

Principle 15

In order to protect the environment, the precautionary approach shall be widely applied by States according to their capabilities. Where there are threats of serious or irreversible damage, lack of full scientific certainty shall not be used as a reason for postponing cost-effective measures to prevent environmental degradation.

Principle 16

National authorities should endeavor to promote the internationalization of environmental costs and the use of economic instruments, taking into account the approach that the polluter should, in principle, bear the cost of pollution, with due regard to the public interest and without distorting international trade and investment.

Principle 17

Environmental impact assessment, as a national instrument, shall be undertaken for proposed activities that are likely to have a significant adverse impact on the environment and are subject to a decision of a competent national authority.

Principle 18

States shall immediately notify other States of any natural disasters or other emergencies that are likely to produce sudden harmful effects on the environment of those States. Every effort shall be made by the international community to help States so afflicted.

Principle 19

States shall provide prior and timely notification and relevant information to potentially affected States on activities that can have a significant adverse transboundary environmental effect and shall consult with those States at an early stage and in good faith.

Principle 20

Women have a vital role in environmental management and development. Their full participation is therefore essential to achieve sustainable development.

Principle 21

The creativity, ideals and courage of the youth of the world should be mobilized to forge a global partnership in order to achieve sustainable development and ensure a better future for all.

Principle 22

Indigenous people and their communities, and other local communities, have a vital role in environment management and development because of their knowledge and traditional practices. States should recognize and duly support their identity, culture and interest and enable their effective participation in the achievement of sustainable development.

Principle 23

The environment and natural resources of people under oppression, domination and occupation shall be protected.

Principle 24

Warfare is inherently destructive of sustainable development. States shall therefore respect international law providing protection for the environment in times of armed conflict and cooperate in its further development, as necessary.

Principle 25

Peace, development and environmental protection are interdependent and indivisible.

Principle 26

States shall resolve all their environmental disputes peacefully and by appropriate means in accordance with the Charter of the United Nations.

Principle 27

States and people shall cooperate in good faith and in a spirit of partnership in the fulfillment of the principles embodied in this Declaration and in the further development of international law in the field of sustainable development.

NOTES

1. The Council on Environmental Quality, *Environmental Quality, The Twenty-fourth Annual Report of the Council on Environmental Quality*. (Washington, D.C.: U.S. Government Printing Office, 1993), p. 439.

2. United States Environmental Protection Agency, *1992 Toxics Release Inventory: Public Data Release*, EPA 745-R-94-001. (Washington, D.C.: U.S. Environmental Protection Agency, 1994), p. 3.

3. Peter Brimelow and Leslie Spencer, "You Can't Get There From Here," *Forbes*, July 6, 1992, p. 59.

4. U.S. Environmental Protection Agency, *The Small Business Sector Study: Impact of Environmental Regulations on Small Business*, EPA 230-09-88-039, September 1988. (Washington, D.C.: U.S. Environmental Protection Agency, 1988), p. 4-2.

5. *Budget for the United States Government, Fiscal Year 1992.* (Washington, D.C.: U.S. Government Printing Office, 1991), p. 448.

6. McKinsey & Company, "The Corporate Response to the Environmental Challenge," in *Transactional Environmental Law and Its Impact on Corporate Behavior,* edited by Eric J. Urbani, Conrad P. Rubin, and Monica Katzman. (Irvington-on-Hudson, N.Y.: Transnational Juris Publications, 1994), pp. 217–62.

7. Daniel Sitarz, *Agenda 21: The Earth Summit Strategy to Save Our Planet.* (Boulder, Colo.: EarthPress, 1993).

8. Stuart L. Hart, "Strategies for a Sustainable World," *Harvard Business Review,* 75 (January–February 1997): 70.

9. United Nations Center on Transnational Corporations, *Environmental Management in Transnational Corporations.* (New York: United Nations Center

on Transnational Corporations, 1993), p. 97.

10.   Global Environmental Management Initiative, *Total Quality Environmental Management: The Primer.* (Washington, D.C.: Global Environmental Management Initiative, 1993), p. 19.

11.   Joan Magretta, "Growth Through Global Sustainability: An Interview with Monsanto's CEO, Robert B. Shapiro," *Harvard Business Review*, 75 (January–February 1997): 79–88.

I

A NEW PARADIGM

2

Does It Pay To Be Green?

Most companies still think of environmental issues in terms of compliance. For them, dealing with the environment is a costly process. According to a recent General Accounting Office report, Americans spend more than 100 million hours on paperwork to comply with environmental regulations.[1] In a provocative article in the *Harvard Business Review*, "It's Not Easy Being Green," Noah Walley and Bradley Whitehead argue that highly profitable environmental projects have been identified and that companies will find it hard to come up with so-called win-win projects that will produce positive returns.[2] They also argue that environmental regulations are destroying market values of corporations, and, therefore, managers should consider shareholder values rather than compliance, emissions, or costs as a basis for making environmental decisions. In an equally provocative article, "Green and Competitive: Ending the Stalemate," Michael Porter and Class van der Linde argue that innovation and resource productivity caused by regulations will make companies more productive and competitive.[3] Green processes will increase yields, improve use of by-products, reduce material handling costs, make workplaces safer, and reduce waste disposal costs. Green products will reduce product costs, cut down packaging costs, and improve product resale and scrap values. However, this argument is not without flaws. Lower material usage often does not mean more efficient. For example, more wood was used by furniture manufacturers in the United States than in Europe during the colonial times. In Europe, labor was plentiful, whereas in the United States, wood was plentiful. Therefore, relative differences in prices led to the use of different proportions of wood and labor on two continents, and industries on both continents are efficient. In other words, efficiency does not mean factor efficiency.[4]

In a thought-provoking book, *The Environmental Protection Agency: Asking the Wrong Questions*, Marc Landy, Marc Roberts, and Stephen Thomas find faults with U.S. environmental policies.[5] They argue that the Environmental Protection Agency's (EPA) performance should be evaluated in terms of responsiveness, technical merits of the decisions, civic education, and capacity building. According to them, the EPA has failed miserably in public education. The miseducation has resulted in enormous spending on Superfund. Although environmental hazards are responsible for only a small portion of cancer cases, the EPA has failed to educate the public about it, and excessive focus on cancer has diverted attention from other serious environmental problems. Superfund, the Resource Conservation and Recovery Act, and steel enforcement programs have been badly designed. However, Gregg Easterbrook, in his book *A Moment on the Earth: The Coming Age of Environmental Optimism*, argues that environmental policies in the Western world have been a great success and environmental problems caused by human activities are small and almost solved.[6] In this chapter, we discuss various impacts of environmental decisions.

IMPACTS OF EMISSIONS

Product Costs

Lower emissions should mean lower costs. Wastes discharged consist of materials, labor, and equipment hours for which a company has paid. Waste management activities do not add value; instead, they add costs of handling, transportation, and disposal. Higher pollution typically means inefficient manufacturing process. Lower pollution improves process yields, enhances use of by-products, lowers energy consumption, makes workplaces safer, and ultimately reduces product costs. The product with higher quality, lower packaging, easy disposal, and higher safety secures higher market shares and premium prices. For example, chlorine-free papers secured an initial premium of about 25 percent and "green" refrigerators, 5 to 10 percent. Higher prices and lower costs should, therefore, offer higher profit margins to companies producing less pollution (Figure 2.1).

FIGURE 2.1
Relationship between Greenness and Profit Margins

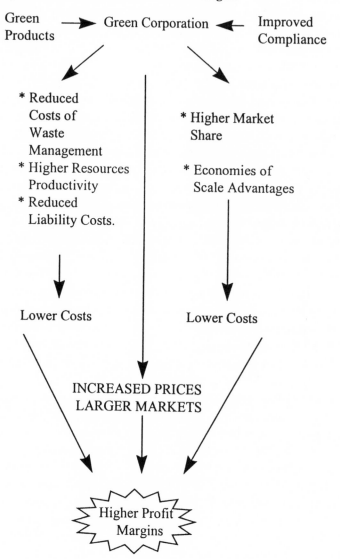

U.S. companies spend a significant amount of money on waste management. They consume raw materials, labor, and other resources to produce wastes and then squander resources to clean them up. In the process, many people get sick and die. From a company's point of view, there are four costs associated with pollution: direct, hidden, contingent liability, and intangible. Direct costs are those associated with a project, product, or process. Operating costs, such as those for materials, labor, and waste disposal, and capital costs, such as those for buildings, equipment, and project engineering, are examples of direct costs. Costs associated with compliance often are aggregated under the overhead and, as a result, are hidden from decision makers. Contingent liability costs include costs relating to liabilities arising out of accidental releases and legal damages for pollution. In addition, there are intangible costs such as costs associated with corporate image, customer acceptance, and goodwill. According to a recent study, some companies may be spending as much as 22 percent of their operating expenditures on environment-related activities.[7] The costs would have been much higher if costs borne by society were included. The current accounting system fails to consider total environmental costs. An example of road salt usage will illustrate this problem. Road salt is used to reduce driving risks on icy roads. A ton of road salt costs about $50 but causes about $1,400 in damages. Use of calcium magnesium acetate can avoid many damages caused by the road salt, but it costs about $650 per ton. So, a person who needs to decide what product should be used to reduce problems is likely to choose road salt rather than calcium magnesium acetate because he is looking for the most cost-effective solution from his point of view, not from society's point of view.[8] It is, therefore, obvious that society incurs much higher environmental costs than what is suggested by the compliance costs.

Companies that generate less waste will spend less on waste management. Such companies will have more money to invest, and, as a result, their growth rates will be higher. Because low-polluting companies have higher margins, their cash flows will be greater. Therefore, investors are likely to attribute much higher valuation to companies generating less pollution (Figure 2.1). In the 1980s, West Germany had some of the toughest environmental standards, but, according to a recent environmental damage accounting, pollution caused damage of more than 104 billion DM ($58 billion) in 1984 alone.[9] This represents approximately 6 percent of the West German gross national product. According to the Organization for Economic Cooperation and Development, it is possible for West Germany to reduce waste by 50 to 60 percent using low-level technologies.[10] Although many waste reduction strategies are simple, they need to be incorporated in the day-to-day working of the company to be successful.

Stock Market Values

We analyzed the link between market values of companies and emissions. Even though return on investments, return on equity, and sales growth are considered to measure performance of a company, it is the market value that determines its performance from the point of view of shareholders. We regressed stock market values of large companies belonging to the Standard and Poor 500 against growth rates, cash flows, risk, research and development (R&D) expenditures, logarithms of sales, and emissions per revenue. We find that emissions per revenue is inversely related to the market values based on the regression results of 250 observations; however, our confidence in this result is 0.88.[11]

Profit Margins

When logarithms of profit margins (sales revenue minus cost of goods sold) were regressed against logarithms of assets, labor, sales, and emissions per sales for the years 1988 to 1990, a negative relationship between emissions and profit margins was found, and this result is statistically significant at 0.98.[12]

Penalties

We analyzed the relationship between environmental penalties per sales and emissions per sales of 255 large companies belonging to Standard and Poor 500 for the years 1988 through 1990. The Spearman rank correlation provides statistical measure about the direct or inverse relationships between variables. We found that the Spearman rank correlation is 0.56, indicating a statistically significant (at the probability level of 0.95) relationship between emissions and penalties. In other words, companies with high emissions per sales are likely to have high penalties per sales.

We found a statistically significant relationship between sales and environmental penalties per sales. This does not mean that the extent of environmental violations by larger companies is more than that by smaller ones. This relationship is likely to mean that larger companies are scrutinized more often and more intensely.

Liability Risks

We use pollution abatement costs as percentage of output value for 1988 for 18 manufacturing industries as a measure of pollution intensity and product liability loss ratios for 1980–84 as a measure of liability risk. The Spearman rank correlation between the pollution abatement costs as a percentage of output value and bodily injury loss ratio is found to be 0.2946 and between the pollution abatement costs and property damage, 0.2640. Both of these relationships are not statistically significant at 0.95.

ENVIRONMENTAL STRINGENCY
AND INNOVATION RATES

Porter suggested that environmental regulations may have a positive impact on innovations.[13] Studies indicate positive relationships between environmental compliance expenditures and R&D expenditures and no statistically significant relationships between compliance expenditures and innovations measured by patent applications.[14] We analyzed environmental stringencies and innovation rates of various states. We used environmental control indicators developed by the Conservation Foundation for each state for the year 1983 as a measure of stringency of environmental regulations. These indicators are developed by taking the weighted average of a state's environmental efforts as judged by the staff of the Conservation Foundation.[15] The environmental indicators take into account factors such as congressional voting records, environmental impact statement process, state income-tax checkoff for wildlife and fisheries programs, per capita environmental quality control expenditures, hazardous waste program, protection of rivers, power plant siting laws, and so on. The innovation data is from the innovation citation database collected by the U.S. Small Business Administration and the Futures Group in 1982.[16] The innovation data was collected by the search of new product announcement sections of more than 100 trade journals and publications. Telephone interviews were used to collect additional information about innovations. Unlike patents, which denote new inventions, innovation citations represent introductions of commercially viable products. According to the survey, there were 4,200 manufacturing innovations in 1982. We also used the average number of patents obtained by each state normalized by the number of workers from 1972 through 1977, 1979, and 1981 as a measure of state innovative activity. The Spearman rank correlation coefficients between environmental stringency of states and innovative rates are given below.

	Patents per 100,000 Workers	Innovations
Environmental stringency indicator	0.6736	0.4838
Number of observations	29	43
Probability α	<0.005	0.005

Based on the Spearman rank correlation coefficients, we can say that there is a direct relationship between environmental stringency in each state and innovation rates and that this relationship is statistically significant at the 0.005 level.

We regressed the number of product introductions against the corporate R&D expenditures, university R&D expenditures, geographic coincident factors,[17] and environmental stringency indicators using state level data. All variables except geographic coincident factors and environmental stringency indicators are expressed in logarithms. The environmental indicators have a positive sign, indicating direct relationship between stringency of environmental regulations and innovative activity. When patents are regressed against population, corporate R&D expenditures, geographic coincident factors, environmental indicators, and liability insurance premiums using the state level data, we find that patents are directly related to environmental stringency indicators, again indicating a positive relationship between environmental regulations and innovative activity.

GREEN COMPANIES AND INNOVATION RATES

We analyzed the relationship between innovation performance and environmental performance at the company level. The analysis is based on 75 large companies belonging to the Standard & Poor 500. The innovation performance is measured in terms of patents per sales, current impact index, and technology cycle time. Typically, the higher the number of citations of a patent by other patents, the more significant is the patent. The citation indicator is called the current impact index. The current impact index is calculated by counting citations of patents granted to a company from 1986 to 1990 in new patents granted in 1991. These numbers are normalized by the average number of citations of all U.S. patents granted in 1991 by patents for the years 1986–91. The speed of innovations is measured in technology cycle times. The technology cycle time for 1991 is represented by the median age of the patents cited in the company's new patents granted in 1991.

The environmental performance of companies is measured in pounds of discharges into air, water, and land. The penalties under various environmental regulations also are used to measure environmental performance. These data are normalized using domestic sales. We use the average data for 1987 to 1989.

The Spearman rank correlation coefficients between innovation performance and environmental performance for companies are given below:

	Emissions per Sales Revenue	Penalties per Sales Revenue
Patents per sales	+0.3167*	−0.1637
Current impact index	−0.4025**	−0.3508*
Technology cycle time	+0.2005	+0.3729
Number of companies	75	75

*$\alpha < 0.05$
**$\alpha < 0.025$

Higher current impact reflects better R&D performance. Environmental performance measured in emissions and penalties positively affects R&D. Similarly, the lower the emissions and penalties, the lower the technology cycle time, again indicating positive relationships between environmental and R&D performance. The relationship between patents per sales and emissions and penalties per sales is not consistent. The patents per sales are positively related to emissions and negatively to penalties per sales. Two arguments could be given for this inconsistency. One could be that emissions per sales may not completely represent the environmental performance. Emissions are calculated by adding discharges irrespective of their risks to humans or the environment. Penalties may be better indicators of environmental damages than emissions because penalties typically reflect harm done to humans and the environment. The second argument is that penalties per sales revenue are higher for larger companies because they are scrutinized more often than smaller companies. Because of diseconomies of scale, the patents per sales revenue are smaller for large companies. This may be creating a negative relationship between penalties and patents.

To sum up, the R&D performance measured in terms of current impact index and technology cycle time are positively related to environmental performance measured in terms of emissions and penalties. However, relationships between patents per sales, emissions per sales, and penalties per sales are inconsistent.

ENVIRONMENTAL REGULATIONS AND JOBS

Firms try to maximize profits. When environmental restrictions are imposed, it increases the cost of a product. Higher product cost reduces its demand. Reduced sales reduce employment. In addition, industries move to areas where there are fewer environmental regulations. This reduces economic growth. Anecdotal evidence exists for loss of jobs as well as creation of jobs as a result of environmental regulations. However, anecdotal evidence is not an objective method of verifying a claim. The econometric studies are inconclusive when it comes to reaching a decision about the relationship between environmental regulations and jobs. Empirical studies indicate that environmental policies do not have negative effects on jobs.[18] There is no evidence of flight of industries to relocate to nations with the least stringent environmental policies.

In Figure 2.2, we present percentage reduction in emissions from 1988 to 1992 and the number of facilities in each industry group. For the apparel and food industries, both emissions and number of facilities have gone up. For tobacco, growth in number of facilities is negative; however, emissions have gone up. For paper, growth in number of facilities and emissions is negative. However, for most industries, numbers of facilities have increased and emissions have decreased. It is obvious from Figure 2.2 that a reduction in emissions has not resulted in a reduction in facilities.

CONCLUSIONS

Environmental policies and regulations have significant impact on the economy, jobs, and industry behavior. In this chapter, we present relationships between environmental issues and various factors. The relationships presented in this chapter are the associations identified by the statistical analysis and are not cause-and-effect relationships.

FIGURE 2.2
Emissions versus Facilities, 1988–92 by Standard Industrial Classification

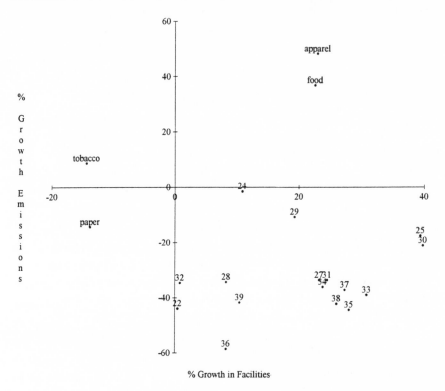

% Growth in Facilities

NOTES

1.   General Accounting Office, *Paperwork Reduction: Burden Reduction Goal Unlikely to be Met*, GAO/T-GGD/RCED-96-186. (Washington, D.C.: General Accounting Office, 1995), p. 16.

2.   Noah Walley and Bradley W. Whitehead, "It's Not Easy Being Green," *Harvard Business Review*, 72 (May–June 1994): 46–52.

3.   Michael E. Porter and Class van der Linde, "Green and Competitive," *Harvard Business Review*, 73 (September–October, 1995): 120–34.

4.   Nathan Rosenberg, *Technology and American Economic Growth*. (New York: Harper & Row, 1972).

5.   Marc K. Landy, Marc J. Roberts, and Stephen R. Thomas, *The Environmental Protection Agency: Asking the Wrong Questions, From Nixon to Clinton* (expanded ed.). (New York: Oxford University Press, 1994), pp. 310–14.

6.   Gregg Easterbrook, *A Moment on the Earth: The Coming Age of Environmental Optimism*. (New York: Viking, 1995).

7.   Daryl Ditz, J. Ranganathan, and R. D. Banks, *Green Ledgers: Case*

Studies in Corporate Environmental Accounting. (Washington, D.C.: World Resources Institute, 1995), p. 19.

8. Carl L. Henn and James A. Fava, "Life-cycle Analysis and Resource Management," in *Environmental Strategic Management,* ed. Rao V. Kolluru. (New York: McGraw-Hill, 1995), p. 575.

9. Earnest Callenbach, Frijof Capra, Lanore Goldman, Lutz Rudiger, and Sandra Marburg, *Ecomanagement.* (San Francisco: Barrett-Koehler, 1993), p. 4.

10. Organization for Economic Cooperation and Development, *The State of the Environment, Annual Report.* (Paris: Organization for Economic Cooperation and Development, 1991), p. 197.

11. V. N. Bhat, *The Green Corporation: Next Competitive Advantage.* (Westport, Conn.: Quorum Books, 1996), p. 251.

12. Ibid.

13. Michael E. Porter, "America's Green Strategy," *Scientific American,* 264 (April 1991): 168.

14. Adam B. Jaffe and Karen Palmer, *Environmental Regulation and Innovation: A Panel Data Study,* Working Paper 5545. (Washington, D.C.: National Bureau of Economic Research, 1996).

15. Christofer J. Duerkson, *Environmental Regulation of Industrial Plant Siting.* (Washington, D.C.: The Conservation Foundation, 1983), pp. 224–25.

16. Maryann P. Feldman, *The Geography of Innovation.* (Boston, Mass.: Kluwer Academic, 1994), pp. 120–21.

17. Adam B. Jaffe, "Real Effects of Academic Research," *American Economic Review,* 79 (December 1989): 957–70.

18. Robert Repetto, *Jobs, Competitiveness and Environmental Regulation: What are the Real Issues.* (Washington, D.C.: World Resources Institute, 1995).

3

Total Quality Environmental Management Tools and Techniques

Emissions into air, water, and land were the early methods of getting rid of waste. End-of-pipeline waste treatment was the strategy to comply with laws and regulations. However, increasing pollution control costs and growing regulations forced companies to come up with better methods to improve compliance. Public pressures, growing regulations, shareholder expectations, and international competition are forcing companies to reduce environmental impacts of their products and services. In response to the pressures for reducing pollution, a number of companies are adopting a new management practice called total quality environmental management (TQEM). TQEM is a novel approach to the art of pollution reduction. Its goal is to reduce pollution and increase stakeholder satisfaction by transforming existing management practices. TQEM needs to be tailor-made for each organization. Even though TQEM is hard to define, there are attributes common to all TQEM adopted by various organizations.

TQEM is stakeholder driven. This means that the stakeholders are the final arbiters of environmental performance of a company. In other words, environmental results are judged by the stakeholders. The characteristics of products, services, and processes that generate a perception of greenness on the part of stakeholders will increase their satisfaction and, ultimately, increase profits. Stakeholder focus of TQEM requires knowledge of what a stakeholder wants and needs, which may be learned from market research, focus groups, and questionnaires.

TQEM requires strong leadership. TQEM practices may be new to company employees and managers. Strong leadership with clear focus on pollution prevention will be needed to bring about changes and achieve pollution reduction goals.

Continuous improvement is a hallmark of TQEM. TQEM assumes that all products, processes, and services can be improved to reduce wastes. Continuous improvement requires a new management philosophy that stimulates innovations to improve. Even without external pressures, continuous improvement is called for, because environmental costs constitute a significant part of costs of sales.

TQEM involves planning, doing, checking, and acting. TQEM requires continuous monitoring and corrective actions to reduce wastes. TQEM requires actions based on facts, data, and analysis.

TQEM demands employee involvement. All employees are trained in the TQEM tools and techniques that are required to reduce wastes. One of the tenets of TQEM is that employees closest to the process are in the best position to understand and reduce wastes.

Lower pollution affects a company in a variety of ways. Figure 3.1 presents a model of TQEM. According to the model, TQEM should enhance employee relations, improve operating procedures, increase stakeholder satisfaction, and raise financial performance.

According to Global Environmental Management Initiative, basic elements of TQEM include identification of stakeholders, continuous improvement, doing the job right the first time, and taking a systems approach.[1] Customers could be internal, such as other departments, and external, such as stockholders, consumers, regulators, community groups, and environmental groups. A recent Aetna advertisement, "The pencil costs 14 cents. The eraser, millions," highlights the need for doing the job right the first time. Pollution reduction across functional areas needs to be done to take full advantages of interactions between functions and their effects on waste generation.

QUALITY PHILOSOPHY

With a view to helping companies to successfully implement total quality management (TQM), quality experts have suggested various strategies. Edward Deming, Joseph Juran, Philip Crosby, and Genichi Taguchi stand out among quality experts. Deming has suggested 14 points to improve quality;[2] these as modified for TQEM are as follows:

FIGURE 3.1
Total Quality Environmental Management Model

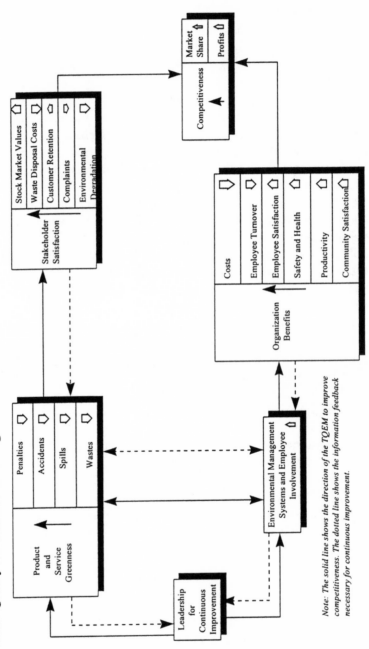

Note: The solid line shows the direction of the TQEM to improve competitiveness. The dotted line shows the information feedback necessary for continuous improvement.

Source: Adapted from General Accounting Office, *Management Practices: U.S. Companies Improve Performance through Quality Efforts*, NSIAD-91-190. (Washington, D.C.: General Accounting Office, 1991), p. 15.

1. Management must develop an environmental mission statement and express its commitments to it. This represents a long-term perspective and dedication to pollution prevention.

2. Management must promote a new philosophy of pollution elimination. Management must make it clear that pollution is unacceptable.

3. The purpose of pollution reduction should be to reduce costs, improve stakeholder satisfaction, and remain competitive. Management should never plan for pollution levels but should focus efforts on improving process efficiencies and increasing yields.

4. Purchasing decisions should involve both price and environmental performance. The purchasing decisions should be based on broad-based criteria including environmental results. The management should replace the traditional purchasing criterion of lowest prices by broad-based measures of long-term success.

5. Pollution elimination should focus on "cradle-to-grave." Reducing emissions to one medium, such as air, water, or land, is not pollution reduction. The goal should be to reduce the total of all pollution to all media. In other words, a systems approach to reduce pollution is needed.

6. Training in pollution reduction is essential. Training should emphasize source reduction. The goal should be to help employees make decisions based on facts and numbers.

7. Leadership is essential for pollution reduction. Pollution reduction involves changes. Therefore, empowerment of employees is essential.

8. Keep an open communication channel. Employees must not fear to question current practices and come up with ideas for improvements.

9. An interdisciplinary multimedia approach to pollution reduction should be adopted. Decisions made in one department have impact on the environmental performance of other departments; therefore, the whole company should work as a single entity.

10. Eliminate numerical goals for pollution reduction. The targets, slogans, and exhortations asking employees for reduced pollution are counterproductive. However, the organization should have a clear focus on pollution reduction.

11. There should be no numerical goals for pollution reduction. Instead, a company should adopt a philosophy of continuous improvement. Numerical goals are counterproductive because they lead to higher costs. In addition, performance of one department can adversely affect the environmental results of another department.

12. Avoid pollution reduction by objectives. Pollution reduction by objectives may reduce pollution, but it may result in increased costs, lower morale, and adverse consequences.

13. Introduce training programs for supervisors and employees. Training programs increase employee skills and also lead to cost-effective pollution reduction.

14. Be proactive in eliminating pollution. Management should encourage reducing pollution and following the previous 13 points.

According to Deming, lack of constancy in objectives and goals, short-term perspective, management by objectives, job-hopping among top management, and excessive indirect costs are some major obstacles for TQM.

To implement TQM successfully, Crosby recommends a clear definition of TQM, a commitment to improve quality, and a performance metric that focuses on the improvement process. According to Crosby, five phases of a quality system include uncertainty, awakening, enlightenment, wisdom, and certainty. Crosby's 14 points to implement TQM, modified for TQEM, are as follows:[3]

1. Top management commitment is essential for TQEM.

2. There should be a pollution reduction team to implement a continuous improvement program.

3. There should be an accounting system to accurately show pollution problems.

4. Costs of pollution should include costs to a company and society.

5. There should be environmental awareness programs to raise the personal concern toward environmental degradation.

6. TQEM should include methods to eliminate pollution.

7. "Zero-emission" planning should begin with management's commitment to pollution elimination.

8. Employee training should include pollution elimination and reduction.

9. Zero-Emission Day should represent the company's and employees' commitment to pollution elimination.

10. Goal setting translates individual actions into the reduction of pollution.

11. Error-cause removal helps employees to identify problems for achieving zero emission.

12. There should be a reward system for those who achieve goals.

13. TQEM councils should meet regularly to discuss pollution problems.

14. Continuous improvement involves doing it over and over.

Juran suggests a trilogy involving quality planning, quality control, and quality improvement to implement TQM.[4] Quality planning involves identification of stakeholder needs, quality control emphasizes identification of deficiency between actual performance and stated goals, and quality improvement focuses on identification of the symptoms and their solution.

Taguchi introduced the concept of robust design.[5] Variations in product characteristics are directly related to lack of quality. Every product is exposed to several disturbing factors. The disturbing factor could be outer disturbances (such as variations in temperature), inner disturbances (including wear and tear of a product because of its operation), and manufacturing variations (including variations between different units). What a product is trying to deliver is called the signal. Noise is disturbance that is degrading the signal. Robustness is measured in terms of signal-to-noise ratio. By choosing the best design, effects of disturbing factors on product performance can be reduced. This is called a robust design. Taguchi suggests the use of statistical design of experiment methodology to choose designs. His quality philosophy includes:

Quality losses are caused by product failures after sales. Product design, rather than on-line quality control, is the major determinant of product failures.

Products with robust design will generate strong performances irrespective of disturbances.

Robust designs can be produced by reducing the average of the square of deviations for combined components averaged over the possible disturbances caused by customer use.

Overall quality loss is proportional to the square of deviations from the target value.

It is better to be on target than to be within specifications.

Consistent production should be the goal of designs.

Consistency will reduce variances, which, in turn, will reduce variances in the production system as a whole.

Quality investments may be chosen based on the deviations from the target values.

The Deming Prize, established by the Union of Japanese Scientists and Engineers to recognize individuals and organizations, uses such factors as policies, organization and its management, education and training, information collection and its use, analysis, standardization, control, quality assurance, business results, and future plans to evaluate potential candidates.[6]

The Malcolm Baldrige National Quality Award, instituted to recognize companies in the United States, uses the leadership system, strategic planning, customer and market focus, and human resource development and management to evaluate potential candidates.[7]

The U.S. General Accounting Office, which analyzed Baldrige Award finalists, identified attributes such as managerial leadership, customer focus, employee participation, open corporate culture, fact-based decision making, and cooperation with suppliers for successful implementation of TQM.[8]

TOTAL QUALITY ENVIRONMENTAL MANAGEMENT TOOLS FOR NUMERIC DATA

Data collection, histograms, Pareto charts, Ishikawa diagrams, stratification, scatter plots, run charts, flow charts, matrix data analysis, and control charts are some TQEM tools that can be used to develop alternatives to reduce pollution. A unique feature of these tools is that they can be used by teams.

Data collection is the first step in any program to reduce pollution. Teams must use data to make effective pollution reduction decisions. Data collection involves asking what the pollution problem is and identifying information that needs to be collected to answer the problem.

Histograms are useful to analyze large quantities of data. The histogram is a frequency diagram displaying causes on the x-axis and their frequency on the y-axis. Histograms can show variations in product or process characteristics, and they display data, making it easy to analyze data.

The Pareto chart is a bar chart drawn with causes on the x-axis and frequency on the y-axis. The Pareto chart helps to concentrate on the significant few rather than the insignificant many. Causes are ranked by frequency. The Pareto chart is based on the notion called "the vital few and the trivial many." It is also known as the 80–20 rule or the ABC analysis. Often, however, it is not the frequency of causes that determines the remedial actions, it is the extent of consequences. In these instances, Pareto charts should be drawn based on consequences rather than frequency. DuPont has used the Pareto principle extensively to identify waste reduction alternatives. According to its experience, 80 percent of the environmental benefits possible from all projects come from the first 20 percent of costs.[9]

The Ishikawa diagram, also known as a fishbone or a cause-and-effect diagram, helps to identify the root causes of a problem. Causes can be categorized into management, labor, process, material, machine, testing instrument, or operating environment. The first step in the development of an Ishikawa diagram is to identify the problem. The next step is to develop various causes. These causes are then categorized into various groups, such as management and labor. The Ishikawa diagram is drawn showing various causes.

Stratification can help identify causes, particularly when data relate to different sources. Some examples of stratification include classifying materials by suppliers, machines by age and make, operators by experience and shift, time by season and day or night, and operating environment by temperature.

If data stratified based on various causes are continuous, then the scatter plot is an excellent tool to identify causes.

Run charts display data over time or in the sequence in which they are generated and indicate variations in data over time.

Flow charts display how a process or system operates. Flow charts, along with material balance, are extremely useful for developing pollution reduction strategies.

The matrix data analysis uses a statistical technique called "principal component analysis" to analyze data. It is particularly useful for analyzing vast quantities of data. Principal components are analyzed, and the significant principal components are plotted on a graph.

Every process has variations, and control charts keep track of them. However, if a process is going through random fluctuations, the variations should lie between statistically determined upper and lower limits. If there are some assignable causes, then the process variations are likely to fall outside these limits. Therefore, intervening in the process whenever process variations fall outside the limits is an effective way to prevent waste generation. Often, waste discharges are monitored with control charts to ensure that the discharges do not deviate from normal levels. Figure 3.2 summarizes TQEM tools for numeric data.

TOTAL QUALITY ENVIRONMENTAL MANAGEMENT TOOLS FOR NONNUMERIC DATA

TQEM tools for nonnumeric data include affinity diagrams, relation diagrams, matrix diagrams, process decision program charts, and arrow diagrams.

FIGURE 3.2
Total Quality Environmental Management Tools for Numeric Data

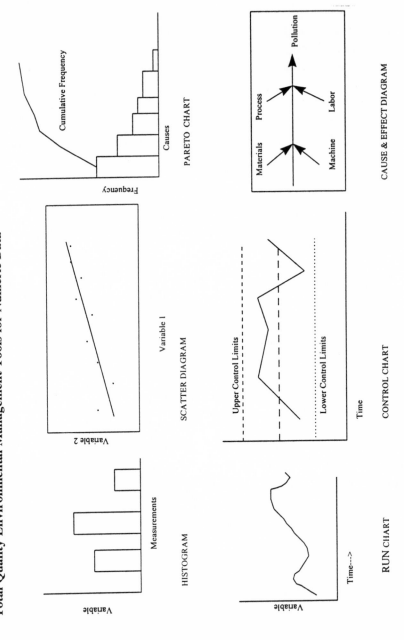

The affinity diagram is an excellent tool for organizing, grouping, and reducing large quantities of verbal data, such as customer needs, ideas, and opinions, based on their similarities. The emphasis of affinity diagrams is association rather than logical connections. The first step in the preparation of an affinity diagram is definition of subjects. The next step is brainstorming to gather data regarding the subject matter, followed by organizing data into groups in hierarchical order. Each higher order group should represent the sum of the members in the lower order groups.

The purpose of the relation diagram is to display the logical relationship between a proposal, idea, problem, or question and various data. The affinity diagram could be used to generate data. The relation diagram is useful when it is difficult to show relations between verbal ideas and when it is necessary to indicate steps sequentially.

Tree diagrams illustrate the categorization of problems, ideas, needs, and proposals in subgroups. The tree diagram is useful for defining problems in terms of well-defined subproblems. Such a breakdown allows all components of a problem to be analyzed.

Matrix diagrams organize large quantities of data and graphically display logical connections between different attributes.

The process decision program chart is a flow chart that displays actions and decisions in the sequential order to reach a desired outcome. It is useful for new plans and plans whose purpose is to avoid catastrophe.

The arrow diagram is a useful tool for planning. It can be used to display relationships between various activities. The Gantt chart and critical path methods are types of arrow diagrams.

RISK MANAGEMENT TOOLS

Increased safety and substantial cost reductions are possible by appropriate allocation of resources based on risk criteria. The purpose of risk assessment is to estimate the probability of occurrence of an adverse effect and the magnitude of consequences. Risk assessment can be financial risk analysis to estimate liability or property risk, safety hazard analysis to evaluate low probability–high consequence events, health risk assessment to examine human health risks, and environmental risk analysis to understand interactions among people and the ecosystem. Risk assessment involves problem identification, probability estimation, analysis of consequences, and, finally, risk characterization. Typical outputs include number of deaths, injuries, cancer risks, economic risks, and so on. Checklists, rough analysis, and "what if?" analysis are overview methods of risk analysis. Failure mode and effects analysis (FMEA) and fault tree analysis are two commonly used techniques to identify failures in a system.

FMEA is a useful tool to identify failures in a system. FMEA is a systematic analysis of a product or process, its functions, and failure causes and consequences. In FMEA, lower component failures are identified, and their effect on local as well as system-level consequences are analyzed. One of the prerequisites for an effective study of FMEA is a thorough understanding of the functions of the components and their relationship to the function of the whole system. The goal of FMEA is to identify potentials for failures and actions to avoid them. Therefore, FMEA can be used in the design stage to develop products with least potential catastrophes and also can be used to analyze manufacturing systems and develop suitable process control systems. FMEA can be used in the current operating systems to identify possibilities for failures and their consequences. A FMEA analysis consists of system definition, depth of analysis, analysis of the function of the system, analysis of the function of the components, determination of potentials for failures, determination of potential consequences of failures, methods to detecting failures, restricting failures from spreading, assessing seriousness of failures, identifying failure causes, identifying relationships between various failures, and documentation. FMEA can be extended by quantifying likelihood of failure, seriousness of consequences of failures, and probability of detection.

The fault tree analysis displays connections between failures in a system and causes of these failures on lower system levels. The drawing of a fault tree can lead to better understanding of the system and its potential for failures. The drawing of a fault tree starts with the definition of a failure and identification of various causes. The relationships between causes and failures are identified using or-gate, and-gate, and so on.

TOTAL QUALITY ENVIRONMENTAL MANAGEMENT PROGRAMS

Most successful companies use a variety of techniques to encourage TQEM programs. Written source reduction policy, leadership, TQEM goals, formal TQEM programs, material tracking system, material balance audit, full cost accounting, and employee participation methods are some unique features of TQEM programs.

Several companies publish explicit written policies promoting source reduction as the primary waste reduction strategy. Others consider source reduction as one of several waste reduction options including recycling, treatment, and disposal.

Companies assign monitoring of waste reduction activity to a top level line manager or to an environmental or safety manager. This manager's effectiveness can be affected by his or her level in the organizational structure.

Companies set goals for reduction of wastes. Goals could be for specific chemicals or a group of chemicals defined by various statutes.

An effective material tracking system can easily uncover sources of material wastes. A good tracking system will record inputs and outputs of all processes. A full accounting system will keep track of both chemical specific and multimedia (solid, liquid, or gas) inputs and outputs. There are several inventory programs for tracking materials.

The material balance audit is a simple yet underutilized tool for identifying sources of material wastes. The material balance principle, which is based on the first law of thermodynamics, states that mass input should be equal to mass output plus mass accumulated. Frequently, the material balance can provide more accurate estimates of wastes than direct measurements of wastes. The material balance principle also can be used to develop estimates for historical emissions data.

A full cost accounting system records pollution costs of each process rather than lumping them as overheads. Companies with accounting systems that capture costs by processes can easily identify potential sources of wastes. Such an accounting system also can help companies to come up with waste reduction projects that reduce costs (see Chapter 10).

There are a variety of ways to involve employees in TQEM programs. Idea solicitation, suggestion programs, training programs, and reward systems are some ways to encourage employee participation. TQEM circles, in which a small group of employees discuss different problems and develop suggestions for waste reduction, also can increase employee participation.

State and federal government technical assistance programs, trade association–industry technical assistance programs, and vendor assistance are other sources of TQEM programs.

INCORPORATING ENVIRONMENTAL FACTORS INTO PRODUCTS

One major goal of TQEM is to translate stakeholder wants and expectations to reality. There are only a few methods that can translate stakeholder environmental needs into product and process characteristics. One such method is quality function deployment (QFD).[10]

QFD can help to convert stakeholder needs to design attributes, which in turn can be translated into part attributes. These part attributes can be used as the basis for process requirements and also production requirements. QFD is an excellent tool for communication among professionals from different functions. Therefore, QFD encourages concurrent engineering. Product development traditionally was done in a series of steps; each step was performed in isolation, and changes in design resulted in dramatic cost overruns. Therefore, companies are employing concurrent engineering in which multifunctional teams work together early in the design process with clear objectives and concurrent decision making. Because product development steps are done in parallel, concurrent engineering reduces design changes and cuts product development time significantly.

Development of QFD includes identification of stakeholder needs and wants; analysis of competitors' products, processes, and services to determine their ability to satisfy stakeholder needs and wants; establishment of critical attributes for products, processes, and services; and incorporation of these attributes through proper product development.

Figure 3.3 outlines a step-by-step process by which stakeholder needs and desires can be incorporated into components, processes, production, and, ultimately, products. First, needs and wants are translated into product characteristics, and then parts are designed to satisfy product characteristics. Processes then are identified that can meet parts requirements, and production requirements are developed from these processes. A concept of different parts of QFD is shown in Figure 3.4.

BENCHMARKING

Benchmarking is a process of improving performance by copying the best practices of other organizations. Benchmarking accomplishes performance improvement by comparing a company's performance in terms of products, processes, methods, organization, and practices with companies that excel in these areas. Competitive intelligence gathering focuses on competitions. The goal of benchmarking is to identify performance shortfalls in comparison with companies that excel in a particular function and to take corrective actions to outperform them. Benchmarking achieves this by comparing and copying operations, products, and services both within and outside the company's primary industry.

Benchmarking helps companies to develop performance goals. It exposes companies to different operations, products, and services and provides ways to improve their own performance. The detailed steps in the benchmarking process are as follows:[11]

FIGURE 3.3
Quality Function Deployment Process

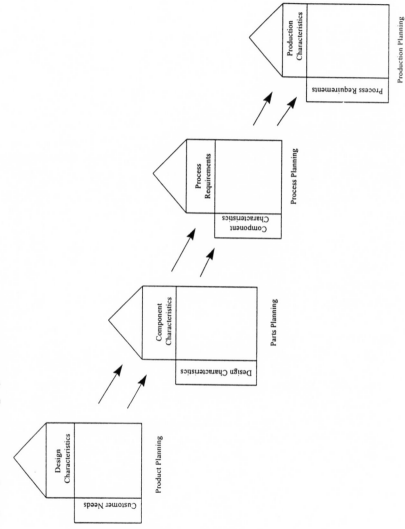

FIGURE 3.4
House of Quality

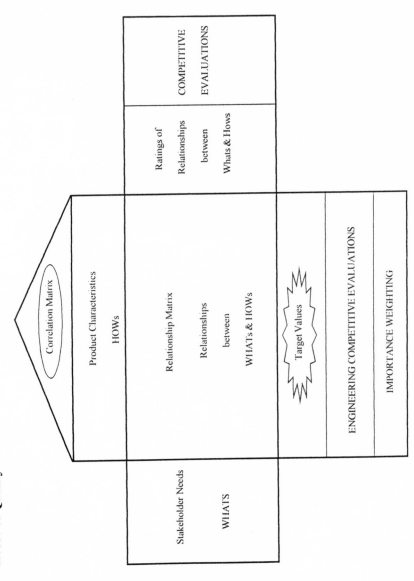

obtain top management commitment for benchmarking,

form a top management committee for benchmarking,

identify functions to benchmark,

form a mini-team to benchmark that function,

train team members in benchmarking methodology,

identify the best-in-the-class company in that function,

select key performance measures (see Chapter 9) for that function and establish current levels of performance,

collect data,

compare the performances and set goals to achieve,

discuss the findings with the top management committee,

develop and implement action plans, and

audit the implementation.

The major elements of benchmarking include documenting the existing system, researching for organizations with best practices, selecting the organizations, gathering data, identifying pros and cons, and developing recommendations and implementing the improved system.

The first step in benchmarking is documenting the existing system. This step will help not only to understand the process but also to identify the opportunities for improvement. Flow diagrams, flow charts, material and energy balance, and other tools can be used during this step. Researching to identify organizations excelling in a particular function include literature search, study of industry trends, and discussions with consultants, trade groups, and so on. Various directories and databases also can be used to identify potential benchmarking candidates. According to the environmental indicators in the *1995 Corporate Environmental Profiles Directory* published by the Investor Responsibility Research Center, the companies excelling in various industry groups in emissions per dollar of domestic revenue are:[12]

Aerospace-Defense	Lockheed Corporation
Aluminum	Alcan Aluminum Limited
Automobile	Chrysler Corp.
Beverages (soft drinks)	PepsiCo Inc.
Chemicals	Praxair Inc.
Diversified chemicals	FMC Corp.
Speciality chemicals	Sigma-Aldrich
Household products	Clorox Co.

Diversified machinery	Caterpillar Inc.
Diversified industrial manufacturing	Johnson Control Inc.
Domestic integrated oil	USX-Marathon Group
International integrated oil	Chevron Corp
Paper and forest products	Mead Corp.
Steel	Worthington Industries Inc.

It is not necessary to use a consultant to do benchmarking. The cost of performing benchmarking can be reduced by using consortium studies done by International Benchmarking Clearinghouse of the American Productivity and Quality Center. This clearinghouse also provides on-line databases covering business practices, benchmarking studies, company screening, and so on. Industrial Technology Institute's Performance Benchmarking Service can provide a ranking of performance measures of a facility against more than 25 companies in the same industry and with similar operations.

According to the U.S. Environmental Protection Agency Toxics Release Inventory Database for 1993, average releases and transfers per facility in pounds are:[13]

Stone, clay, and concrete	46,000
Lumber and wood products	24,000
Furnitures and fixtures	148,000
Printing	147,000
Electronics and computers	133,000
Rubber and miscellaneous plastics	104,000
Motor vehicles, bodies, parts, accessories	369,000
Pulp and paper	706,000
Inorganic chemical manufacturing	450,000
Petroleum refining	3,088,000
Fabricated metals	123,000
Iron and steel	1,825,000
Nonferrous metals	1,349,000
Organic chemical manufacturing	1,052,000

Once researching for potential candidates is done, the next step is to identify a manageable number of organizations to visit. Before visiting companies, it is a good idea to prepare a list of questions in order to gather comparable information about organizations. The next step is to identify pros and cons of various processes in the organizations. While comparing processes, organizational culture, regulatory requirements, and so on should be considered.

Some potential areas for benchmarking include waste reduction, waste accounting, legal compliance, training, environmental information system, environmental performance measurement and reporting system, recycling, auditing, employee policies, injury and illness minimization, energy consumption, waste transportation, public relations, communications, and emergency planning.

PRINCIPLES FOR EFFECTIVE TOTAL QUALITY ENVIRONMENTAL MANAGEMENT

In this section, we will briefly review some of the principles that can enhance the effectiveness of a TQEM program.

Top Management Support

TQEM must have the commitment of top management if it is to be effective. The chief executive officer must be the champion of TQEM and should develop the plan of action to implement TQEM. All personnel must understand that their company takes TQEM seriously. Putting TQEM in writing, designating a "czar" at the highest management level to coordinate the program, introducing incentive systems, allocating adequate resources, and training employees are some ways to show top management support for TQEM.

Pollution Prevention

Although U.S. companies incur only a small fraction of revenue on environmental capital and operating expenditures, studies show that as much as 20 percent of their operating expenditures are environmentally related costs. In other words, U.S. companies spend a lot of money on raw materials, labor, and other resources to produce wastes and then clean them up. In the process, many people get sick, many die, and many lawyers get rich. Companies must prevent waste generation in the first place, and emphasis must be placed on pollution prevention rather than pollution control.

Receptive Culture

For an effective TQEM, the corporate culture must be in harmony with the TQEM principles. Corporate culture should accept the axiom that, for a business to be successful in a highly competitive market, it must understand and respond to the needs of the stakeholders. If a company fails to satisfy the needs of its stakeholders, eventually it will fail.

Stakeholder satisfaction is essential for a company to prosper and requires careful definition of stakeholders, accurate determination of their needs, and focused organization to fulfill these needs. Before the environment became an issue, most stakeholders were concerned only about financial performance. However, environmental impacts of products, processes, and services have caused employees, communities, investors, and others to consider environmental aspects.

An effective TQEM requires a holistic view of the business. This forces management to think business in life cycles rather than as an aggregation of functions. A life-cycle approach requires viewing the business across functions and focusing on stakeholder needs. This change in organization's perspective has to be implanted in the management.

Another aspect relating to management culture is communication. Management must communicate and explain the importance of pollution reduction to employees at all levels. Communication is essential to reduce employee skepticism. Although environmental plans may result in changes, management must try to get employee commitment to the changes.

Training is essential to change culture and make TQEM effective. Working across functions and implementing changes require negotiation and conflict resolution skills. Therefore, training programs should be developed to support TQEM.

Incentives and rewards are required to internalize the new culture. A performance measurement system should emphasize the new culture. The employees should be evaluated for identifying and solving problems. The management should continuously monitor that employees apply what they have learned.

To sum up, successful TQEM involves the ability of an organization to rethink the values and aspirations shared by its members. Management emphasis should be on not only economy and efficiency but also stakeholder satisfaction. TQEM strategy requires increased focus on the needs of stakeholders. A performance measurement system that involves measurement and reporting of results should deal with indicators relating to stakeholder satisfaction. Finally, TQEM includes incentives and reward systems for managers.

Mission Changes

Effective TQEM requires radical changes in product design, manufacturing processes, distribution systems, use, and disposal. Such changes cannot be done overnight. Therefore, successful TQEM mandates reexamination and modification of mission. The aim is to link organizational goals, objectives, information, and strategies to meet the mission needs. Strategic planning often is used to make operational plans consistent with strategic goals. The goal of the planning should be to allow employees to make environmental decisions about products, processes, training, personnel, and improvements based on today's and tomorrow's needs. Strategic planning also could be used to identify cause-and-effect relationships among priorities, goals, and future actions.

Cross-Functional Teams

Engineering design, manufacturing, finance, sales, and marketing are separate "stovepipes" in most organizations. As a result, design function ignores critical product attributes like customer satisfaction, disposal requirements, and so on. However, pollution crosses functions. Therefore, effective pollution reduction requires cross-functional teams. This is the new logic of TQEM.

Life-Cycle Approach

Pollution is not reduced when waste discharges into one medium are shifted into another medium. Therefore, reducing emissions into the atmosphere is not pollution reduction if it increases discharges into water or land. Similarly, if waste generation is reduced during manufacturing but increases during other phases of a product life cycle, this does not constitute waste reduction. Waste is reduced if and only if the effects of all wastes generated during the life of a product are reduced. In short, pollution elimination efforts should be directed toward all phases of a product's life, not just a singular phase.

The maximum pollution reduction can be achieved by focusing on the life cycle of a product, rather than just one or two phases of a product. Decisions made in various phases of a product are interrelated. For example, design decisions have significant cost and environmental impacts on manufacturing, distribution, use, and disposal. Therefore, designs should be evaluated in terms of their impacts during their entire life cycles rather than functional stovepipes. Typically, redesign of a product and processes can yield benefits several times as large as attempts to optimize one functional area.

Organizational Restructuring

Organizational restructuring, including partnering and decentralization, needs to be introduced to ensure that authority and responsibility are delegated to achieve pollution reduction in the most efficient manner. Partnering involves teamwork and commitment between departments to achieve a common goal. Partnering helps to eliminate adversarial or confrontational relationships between departments. Authority in organizations can be decentralized through delegation and empowerment. The purpose of delegation is to move administrative function from one part to another part of an organization. Empowerment involves giving employees the authority and tools they need to do their jobs.

Performance Measurement System

Performance measurement system involves establishment of goals, selection of means to achieve goals, implementation of means, measurement of progress, and corrective action. An organization needs a performance measurement system to assess progress toward goals. For a performance measurement system to be effective, performance indicators should be related to the mission.

Full Cost Accounting

Current accounting systems fail to consider total environmental costs and instead aggregate many environmental costs under the category of overhead. This results in the selection of wrong product mix, inaccurate pricing of products, and inappropriate choice or rejection of pollution reduction alternatives. Full accounting is a prerequisite for both understanding the total costs of environmental degradation and achieving pollution reduction.

Stakeholder Involvement

Pollution reduction requires involvement of stakeholders, including employees, suppliers, and consumers. Companies need to encourage stakeholder participation using TQEM philosophy. TQEM tools, benchmarking, concurrent engineering, performance metrics, life-cycle assessment, and environmental auditing are some tools to encourage stakeholder involvement.

CONCLUSIONS

TQEM is a novel approach to implement pollution reduction programs in organizations. In addition to stimulating employee participation, TQEM produces a formalized management structure to plan, organize, and implement environmental programs. It provides a useful framework to incorporate environmental issues into day-to-day management decisions. However, all companies are not successful in reaping full advantages of TQEM. Among all causes that obstruct successful implementation of TQEM in companies, lack of top management commitment stands out.

NOTES

1. Global Environmental Management Initiative, *Total Quality Environmental Management: The Primer*. (Washington, D.C.: Global Environmental Management Initiative, 1993).

2. W. Edward Deming, *Out of the Crisis*. (Cambridge, Mass.: MIT, Center for Advanced Engineering Study, 1986), pp. 23–24.

3. P. B. Crosby, *Quality is Free*. (New York: McGraw Hill, 1979), pp. 176–259.

4. J. M. Juran, *Juran on Planning for Quality*. (New York: Free Press, 1988).

5. Genichi Taguchi and Don Clausing, "Robust Quality," *Harvard Business Review*, 68 (January–February 1990): 65–75.

6. Francis X. Mahoney and Carl G. Thor, *TQM Trilogy*. (New York: American Management Association, 1994), pp. 58–60.

7. *1997 Application Guidelines, Malcolm Baldrige National Quality Award*. (Gaithersburg, Md.: National Institute of Standards and Technology, 1996).

8. General Accounting Office, *Management Practices: U.S. Companies Improve Performance Through Quality Efforts*, GAO/NSIAD-91-190. (Washington, D.C.: General Accounting Office, 1991).

9. H. Dale Martin, "Environmental Planning: Balancing Environmental Commitments with Economic Realities," in *Environmental Management in a Global Economy, GEMI '94 Conference Proceedings*. (Washington, D.C.: Global Environmental Management Initiative, 1994), pp. 57–65.

10. John R. Hauser and Don Clausing, "House of Quality," *Harvard Business Review*, 66 (May–June 1988): 63–73.

11.   V. N. Bhat, *The Green Corporation: The Next Competitive Advantage.* (Westport, Conn.: Quorum Books, 1996), p. 225.

12.   Investor Responsibility Research Center, *1995 Corporate Environmental Profiles Directory.* (Washington, D.C.: Investor Responsibility Research Center, 1995).

13.   U.S. Environmental Protection Agency, *1994 Toxics Release Inventory,* Public Data Release EPA-745-R-96-002. (Washington, D.C.: U.S. Environmental protction Agency, 1996).

II

COMPANY ASSESSMENTS

4

Industry Environmental Standards

With a view to helping companies develop environmental policies and guidelines, several industry associations have developed their own codes of business practices. The purpose of these codes is to demonstrate to the public that businesses do care about environmental excellence. By persuading companies in an industry to follow a set of principles, these codes try to reduce competitive distortions between companies caused by differences in environmental performance. The international nature of these codes helps companies to prevent passage of stringent command-and-control regulations. From policymakers' points of view, these standards are likely to accelerate the development of environmentally conscious products, processes, and services. Chemical Manufacturers Association's (CMA) Responsible Care program, International Chamber of Commerce's Business Charter for Sustainable Development: Principles for Environmental Management, American Petroleum Institute's Strategies for Today's Environmental Partnership (STEP) program, and American Forest and Paper Association's Sustainable Forest Management Initiative are some examples of industry standards. The Occupational Safety and Health Administration (OSHA), the American Society for Testing and Materials, NSF International, and the American National Standards Institution have established standards that a company can adopt to improve its environmental performance.

BUSINESS CHARTER FOR
SUSTAINABLE DEVELOPMENT

The Business Charter for Sustainable Development: Principles for Environmental Management developed by the International Chamber of Commerce is a voluntary code consisting of 16 principles, which are as follows:

1. Corporate priority

    To recognize environmental management as among the highest corporate priorities and as a key determinant to sustainable development to establish policies, programs and practices for conducting operations in an environmentally sound manner.

2. Integrated management

    To integrate these policies, programs and practices fully into each business as an essential element of management in all its functions.

3. Process of improvement

    To continue to improve corporate policies, programs and environmental performance, taking into account technical developments, scientific understanding, consumer needs, and community expectations, with legal regulations as starting point; and to apply the same environmental criteria internationally.

4. Employee education

    To educate, train and motivate employees to conduct their activities in an environmentally responsible manner.

5. Prior assessment

    To assess environmental impacts before starting a new activity or project and before decommissioning a facility or leaving a site.

6. Products and services

    To develop and provide products or services that have no undue environmental impact and are safe in their intended use, that are efficient in their consumption of energy and natural resources, and that can be recycled, reused, or disposed of safely.

7. Customer advice

    To advise, and where relevant educate, customers, distributors and the public in the safe use, transportation, storage and disposal of products provided and to apply similar considerations to the provision of services.

8. Facilities and operations

    To develop, design and operate facilities and conduct activities taking into consideration the efficient use of energy and materials, the sustainable use of renewable resources, the minimization of adverse environmental impact and waste generation, and the safe and responsible disposal of residual wastes.

9. Research

To conduct or support research on the environmental impacts of raw materials, products, processes, emissions and wastes associated with the enterprise and on the means of minimizing such adverse impacts.

10. Precautionary approach

To modify the manufacture, marketing or use of products or services or the conduct of activities, consistent with scientific and technical understanding, to prevent serious or irreversible environmental degradation.

11. Contractors and supplier

To promote the adoption of these principles by contractors acting on behalf of the enterprise, encouraging and, where appropriate, requiring improvements in their practices to make them consistent with those of the enterprise; and to encourage the wider adoption of these principles by suppliers.

12. Emergency preparedness

To develop and maintain, where significant hazards exist, emergency preparedness plans in conjunction with the emergency services, relevant authorities and the local community, recognizing potential transboundary impacts.

13. Transfer of technology

To contribute to the transfer of an environmentally sound technology and management methods throughout the industrial and public sectors.

14. Contributing to the common effort

To contribute to the development of public policy and to business, governmental and intergovernmental programs and educational initiatives that will enhance environmental awareness and protection.

15. Openness to concerns

To foster openness and dialogue with employees and the public, anticipating and responding to their concerns about the potential hazards and impacts of operations, products, wastes or services, including those of transboundary or global significance.

16. Compliance and reporting

To measure environmental performance; to conduct regular environmental audits and assessments of compliance with company requirements, legal requirements and these principles and periodically to provide appropriate information to the board of directors, shareholders, employees, the authorities and the public.

Using the principles of this code as a basis, the Global Environmental Management Initiative has developed an environmental self-assessment program to help a company to evaluate and improve its environmental performance.[1] Following the Global Environmental Management Initiative's self-assessment program, the 16 principles can be categorized into planning, organizing, implementing, and controlling (Figure 4.1).

Planning

Planning consists of corporate priority, prior assessment, products and services, and precautionary approach. Management must accord the highest priority to environmental management and establish policies and programs for environmental excellence. Management should evaluate environmental consequences of its new businesses, projects, divestitures, and plant closings. The products and services principle requires management to evaluate products, services, and distribution systems to ensure that these do not undermine the environment. Products and services should be energy and resource efficient and easy to recycle, reuse, or dispose of. The precautionary approach principle requires that changes of processes, products, and services should avoid serious environmental degradation.

Organizing

Organizing consists of integrated management, facilities and operations, research, and emergency preparedness principles. The integrated management principle requires incorporation of environmental considerations in all functional areas of a business. The facilities and operations principle addresses requirements of production facilities, which should have operating standards to reduce pollution. Management also should try to reduce energy consumption, cut down pollution, improve employee health, and reduce risk at its facilities. Research should reduce wastes by focusing on raw material procurement, products, processes, emissions, and wastes. Hazard and incident assessment, emergency response plans, product safety, and employee training are some requirements of emergency preparedness.

Implementing

Employee education, customer advice, contractors and suppliers, transfer of technology, and contributing to the common effort make up the implementing phase. Employee training should include awareness programs; environmental, health, and safety training; and skills training. The

FIGURE 4.1
Business Charter for Sustainable Development as a Framework for Environmental Management

PLANNING
Corporate Priority
Prior Assessment
Products and Services
Precautionary Approach

ORGANIZING
Integrated Management
Facilities and Operations
Research
Emergency Preparedness

FRAMEWORK FOR ENVIRONMENTAL MANAGEMENT

CONTROLLING
Process Improvement
Openness to Concerns
Compliance and
Reporting

IMPLEMENTING
Employee Education
Customer Advice
Contractors and Suppliers
Transfer of Technology
Contributing to the
Common Effort

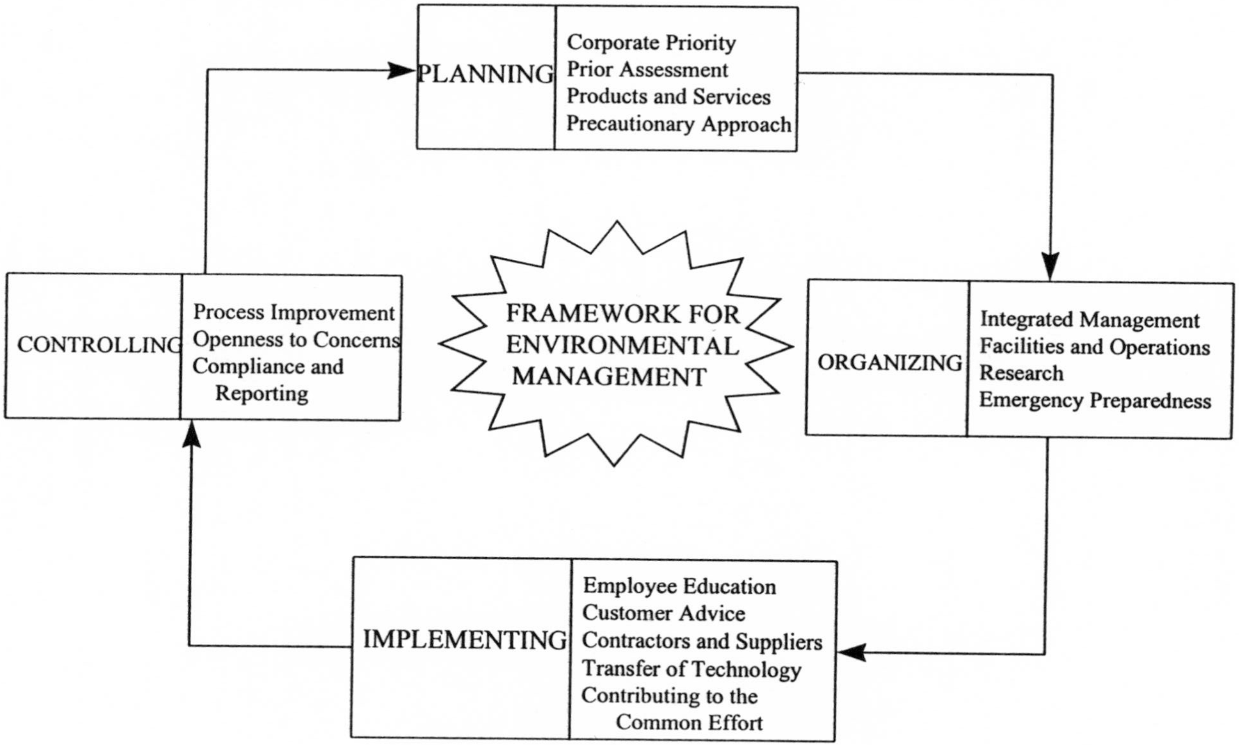

goal is to increase environmental awareness among employees and motivate them to improve environmental performance on a continuous basis. Product stewardship is the heart of the customer advice principle. Customers, distributors, and the public should be informed about the safe transportation, storage, use, and disposal of products. Contractors and suppliers also should be involved in improving environmental performance. Procedures to transfer technology and management methods to partners, customers, distributors, suppliers, and business units should be reviewed from time to time. Companies also should strive for rational public policy and should take initiatives to improve environmental awareness in the public.

Control

Control involves monitoring performance and taking corrective actions. Process of improvement, openness to concerns, and compliance and reporting are principles that make up the control phase. The improvement process involves study of technical developments, new research studies, and current environmental performance with a view to improve policies, programs, products, and environmental performance. A company should be sensitive to concerns of employees, customers, and the community. A company should put in place procedures to measure compliance continuously and report these measures to stakeholders. Environmental audits should be a part of such procedures.

RESPONSIBLE CARE INITIATIVE

Bhopal, Love Canal, and other chemical industry–related environmental disasters forced the chemical industry to launch the Responsible Care initiative to respond to public concerns about its poor environmental records. The CMA requires all its members to follow its Responsible Care program. In addition, the public is involved in developing program elements through a public advisory panel. Figure 4.2 presents an overview of this comprehensive industry initiative that consists of:

ten guiding principles to improve environmental performance,

six codes of management practice to help develop an effective environmental management system and improve performance, public advisory panel to receive inputs from the public and develop plans to respond to public concerns,

member company self-evaluations of management practices to track and report progress in the implementation of the Responsible Care program,

executive leadership groups to exchange experience and monitor the progress of implementation,

membership requirement of commitment to Responsible Care initiative,

performance measurement system to define measures for all codes,

partnership program to help affiliated associations to develop similar initiatives,

mutual assistance program to help members carry out the initiative, and

public outreach program to publicize the initiative.

Ten Guiding Principles

A commitment to the initiative is a requirement to become a member of the CMA. The guiding principles provide a company with a framework to manage its environmental responsibilities in the conduct of its business. The guiding principles require companies to respond to community concerns about chemicals; develop and produce chemicals that can be handled safely; incorporate health, safety, and environmental issues in product and process development; report hazards and take corrective actions promptly; train customers in the safe handling of chemical products; ensure safe operation of plants and facilities; advance environmental knowledge through research; resolve past environmental problems; actively participate in public policymaking; and share experiences with others.

Six Codes of Management Practices

The six codes of management practices provides a series of objectives to ensure implementation of guiding principles. They are community awareness and emergency response, process safety, pollution prevention, distribution, employee health and safety, and product stewardship.

The purpose of the community awareness and emergency response code is to maintain open communication channels between a chemical company and its local communities. With a view to maintaining and improving community relations, the community awareness and emergency response code of management practices focuses on community outreach and emergency response and preparedness. It requires companies to train key employees in communications, educate employees about

FIGURE 4.2
An Overview of the Responsible Care Program

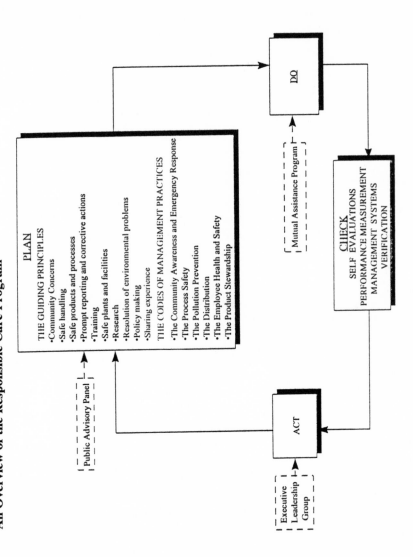

emergency response plans and safety, and have continuous dialog with employees about their concerns. An outreach program to inform the public about the emergency response program to respond rapidly to emergencies is also a critical part of this code. This code also deals with the equity and fairness issues relating to emission reduction to hiring.

The pollution prevention code encourages waste reduction to improve safety and to protect human health and the environment. The goals of this code include reduction of emissions, continuous improvement, and better management of wastes generated. Key elements of this code focus on management commitment; inventory of wastes generated; evaluation of environmental impacts of releases; education; establishment of priorities; goals to reduce wastes; priority in the order of source reduction, recycle-reuse, and treatment; communication with employees; design of new facilities, processes, and products to reduce wastes; and review of contractor-supplier waste reduction practices.

The process safety code emphasizes prevention of fires, explosions, and accidental chemical releases. It demands sound engineering practices, operations, and maintenance to make a facility safe. Because process safety requires interdisciplinary effort, the code suggests practices in management leadership, technology, facilities, and personnel. The code requires senior management leadership; clear accountability; measurement of performance; environmental audits; investigation of fires, explosions, and accidental chemical releases; transfer of safety knowledge to others; and community involvement in the design of a facility's process safety systems. Technologic aspects of the safety code require complete documentation and periodic review. Safety reviews; sound engineering practices; consideration of safety aspects in new, expanded, and modified facilities; and documentation of maintenance are some management practices that deal with facilities. Training, procedures and work practices, and identification of skills and knowledge to perform jobs are issues that are addressed under personnel aspects of the code.

The product stewardship code is intended to make health, safety, and environmental protection an integral part of a product throughout its entire life. It requires leadership, accountability, and adequate resources from management. This code demands that a company make available information on health, safety, and environmental hazards of its product and, using this information, characterize existing and new products with respect to their risk. Risk management; consideration of health, safety, and environmental impacts during product and process development; employee education; evaluations of contractors and suppliers based on health, safety, and environmental performance; and risk management information dissemination are some other key elements of this code.

Employee and safety code of management practices focuses on employee health and safety issues at company work sites. This code protects and promotes employee health and safety by focusing on program management, identification and evaluation of health and safety hazards, prevention and control, and communication and training. Top management commitment; documentation; procedures for identifying and evaluating health and safety hazards; health and exposure assessments; occupational medical surveillance programs; preventive maintenance programs; timely investigation of illnesses, injuries, and incidents; prompt correction actions; and communication of health information are major requirements of the employee health and safety code.

The distribution code of management practices is intended to reduce the risk of damage caused by distribution of chemicals by risk management, compliance review and training, carrier safety evaluations, better handling and storage, and emergency preparedness. Improved risk management through periodic risk evaluations, risk reduction, and monitoring and reporting are major elements of this code. Regular review of regulations and training are major elements of compliance. This code demands that all carriers be evaluated for their fitness to transport chemicals. In addition, documented procedures for handling and storage are requirements of this code.

Public Advisory Panel

The public advisory panel is a unique feature of the Responsible Care initiative. This panel, consisting of 15 citizens, meets five times a year and identifies issues that are of concern to the public. They were actively involved in the development of the six codes of management practices.

Member Self-Evaluation

Another significant feature of the Responsible Care initiative is the self-evaluation of environmental performance by members. Every member has to indicate extent of implementation using the six levels. The six levels based on the various stages of implementation are no action, evaluating company practices, developing implementation plan, implementing action plan, management practice in place, and reassessing implementation. This reporting system is a strong self-motivator to improve performance, because the evaluations are made by companies themselves, not by outsiders. Every code has a self-evaluation form that a company uses in measuring progress in implementing the code. These forms are submitted to the CMA, which, in turn, publishes aggregate progress to the public.

Executive Leadership Groups

Executive leadership groups are like mentors. They monitor each company's continual progress and suggest ways to quicken the implementation process. They also review the code of management practices requirements and suggest improvements.

Obligation of Membership

Every company should provide a written commitment to the Responsible Care initiative by signing the guiding principles to be a member of the CMA. Employees should be informed about the commitment, and a good-faith effort should be made to implement the guiding principles and codes of management practices.

Performance Measures

The Responsible Care initiative includes a performance measurement system. The performance in the pollution prevention code is measured by U.S. Environmental Protection Agency's Toxics Release Inventory (TRI) releases and off-site transfers. Employee health and safety code performance is measured using injury and illness records required to be maintained by OSHA. Process safety code performance is measured by requiring facilities to inform the CMA of reportable incidents.

SUSTAINABLE FORESTRY INITIATIVE

With a view to ensure that "future generations of Americans will have the same abundant forests that we enjoy today,"[2] the American Forest & Paper Association has launched a sustainable forestry initiative. The major elements of this initiative include five principles of sustainable forestry, an action plan with 12 guidelines, and performance indicators. The principles of sustainable forestry, in summary form, consist of land stewardship ethic by managing forests better, environmentally responsible forestry practices, protection of forests from damages, management of forests that takes into account their unique features, and continuous improvement of forestry practices and their continuous monitoring and reporting.

With a view to translating these five principles into actual practices, an action plan has been drawn up with the following guidelines:

actively practice sustainable forestry,

reforest promptly,

protect water quality,

improve wildlife habitat,

consider visual impact when harvesting,

protect special sites,

encourage biodiversity,

improve wood use,

use chemicals carefully,

teach others the practice of sustainable forestry,

inform the public about the progress, and

raise public awareness about the sustainable forestry practices.

To measure the progress of implementation of the Sustainable Forestry Initiative, every member must submit annual reports. These reports will contain key indicators about environmental performance such as harvest method, research funding, reforesting timetables, trained loggers, and share of raw materials delivered.

STRATEGIES FOR TODAY'S ENVIRONMENTAL PARTNERSHIP PROGRAM

STEP is an initiative of the American Petroleum Institute to help oil and gas companies improve their environmental, health, and safety performance. The significant elements of STEP include:

safe operation of plants and facilities;

priority for safety, health, and environmental factors in planning, product, and process development;

timely disclosure of safety, health, and environmental hazards and prompt corrective actions;

training customers, transporters, and others about safe handling, transportation, and use of materials;

conservation of natural resources and energy;

research on the environmental impacts on materials, products, and wastes;

commitment to reduce emissions and waste generation;

commitment to resolve environmental problems;

working with government and others for responsible public policy and regulations; and

promotion of these principles and helping others to improve their environmental performance.

Environmental performance measurement is done by reporting environmental performance and progress in implementing management practices in annual Petroleum Industry Environmental Performance Report and annual Self-Assessment Report, respectively.

ENVIRONMENTAL PROTECTION AGENCY'S INITIATIVES

The U.S. Environmental Protection Agency (EPA) has several voluntary programs to promote pollution reduction and environmental compliance. Design for the Environment in collaboration with stakeholders in specific industries assesses the risks, costs, and performance of various products, processes, and technologies. The Environmental Accounting Project in collaboration with business, trade associations, and academia encourages the use of environmental accounting and capital budgeting practices. The Green Lights program is intended to prevent pollution, recognize environmental leadership, and encourage the use of energy efficient lighting in buildings. Energy Star Computers and hardware equipment power down when they are not in use, reducing electricity consumption. Climate Wise, a joint EPA and Department of Energy program, encourages effective strategies to cut down energy consumption, reduce greenhouse gases, and increase profits. Water Alliances for Voluntary Efficiency tries to reduce water consumption. PEST SMART Pesticide Environmental Stewardship program is designed to reduce the use and risk of pesticides by working with pesticide users. The WasteWi$e program is intended to reduce municipal solid waste generation by large businesses.

Common Sense Initiatives

The Common Sense Initiative (CSI) is a joint effort between EPA and private industry to develop cost-effective environmental protection strategies. The goals of the CSI are to bring together representatives from federal, state, and local governments; industry; environmental organizations; and labor organizations and try to come up with industry-specific solutions to environmental problems in automobile manufacturing, computers and electronics, iron and steel, metal finishing, petroleum refining, and printing. The representatives, after studying the industry as a whole, will develop solutions to environmental problems. The solutions will focus on pollution prevention, rather than end-of-pipe controls. These solutions, which will be completed based on a consensus, will be tailor-made for each industry. Currently, the CSI is considering ways to reduce reporting requirements, improve permit procedures, foster community involvement, reduce obstacles to pollution prevention, and find ways to offer regulatory flexibility to achieve environmental results.

Project XL

The purpose of Project XL is to provide pollution reduction flexibility to a regulated entity in return for an enforceable commitment to achieve better environmental results than what would have been achieved through full regulatory compliance.[3] The criteria to select projects include environmental performance, cost savings, paperwork reduction, stakeholder support, project innovativeness, transferability of expertise to other facilities, feasibility, reporting procedures, and consistency with environmental justice criteria.

Environmental Leadership Program

The purpose of the Environmental Leadership Program (ELP) is to promote and recognize environmental leadership and encourage pollution elimination in manufacturing industries. The major elements of the original program published in the *Federal Register*[4] included a corporate statement of environmental principles and a model facility program. In view of tremendous support from the industry for a voluntary program to recognize environmental excellence, the EPA decided to go for a few voluntary, facility-based pilot projects.[5]

Even though the original ELP proposal was not implemented, it had several interesting features that a company can emulate. The purpose of the original ELP was to recognize companies with chief executive officer–level commitment to environmental excellence. Such a recognition system will encourage companies to go beyond compliance. Demonstration of environmental excellence through a statement of corporate commitment, openness, compliance records, and a reduction in environmental degradation can promote comprehensive environmental programs in other companies. Such a program can lead to model environmental management systems that go beyond compliance by incorporating pollution prevention into all functions of a company, including design, purchasing, engineering, manufacturing, marketing, and distribution.

The original ELP was based on several assumptions. The criteria for recognition should be stringent to make the program credible with the general public. At the same time, the criteria should be practical to encourage several companies to volunteer. The companies selected should have excellent environmental records. Pollution prevention and sustainability will be the critical components of this program. The emphases of the program will be goals and results rather than processes. The states will be involved in the program. The program will set measurable goals to make the program accountable to the general public. Consistent and objective standards to evaluate potential facilities will be established to cut red tape.

The basic elements of the ELP will include a corporate statement of environmental principles and a model facility program. The company selected under the ELP will incorporate these environmental principles into design, production, distribution, and marketing functions. The company will show its commitment publicly to the principles. In addition, the company will state its intentions to abide by the principles through a letter to the EPA. Companies interested in having their plants recognized as model facilities should indicate their intention to abide by the principles.

The plants must meet high standards to be recognized as a model facility. The company should have a strong environmental record and should abide by the statement of environmental principles. The application will be reviewed by experts on pollution elimination approaches. The states will be involved in the program. The recognition of a model facility will be for a period of two or three years, and a company can reapply for it. Third-party review of application, multiple layers of recognition, special provisions for small business, and so on also are being considered for incorporation into the ELP.

Criteria that will be used to evaluate plants include risk reduction goals, measures, and public accountability; planning; green business practices; community participation; and legal compliance. The TRI provides a basis for setting risk reduction goals and measuring progress. High-risk pollutants are the potential targets of pollution elimination. In addition to high-risk pollutants, energy and greenhouse emissions may be targeted for reduction and elimination.

The ELP program will require companies to submit additional data and concrete reasons for significant changes in the level of emissions. The data collection will involve facilities located outside the United States. Each model facility will submit aggregate waste and emissions data for TRI and non-TRI releases. The model facility also may be required to submit data about consumptions of energy, water, and raw materials and about generation of nonhazardous solid waste.

Top management support is essential for environmental excellence. Therefore, ELP will require companies to publish a plan of pollution prevention that top management has supported. The plan will emphasize source reduction, recycling, treatment, and disposal (in descending order of preference) as pollution reduction approaches. The company will commit to making waste elimination a priority; cutting down the use of water, energy, and other natural resources; reducing emissions into all media; and promoting high environmental management practice. Each model facility will prepare a pollution elimination plan that uses strategies such as product redesign, process changes, and energy and water conservation to reduce pollution. Environmentally sound business practices include consideration of environmental factors in product development and material and process selection, adoption of environmental accounting, and use of progressive labor policies, including employee incentives. Design for environment can help to reduce pollution by helping to develop safer products. Life-cycle analysis can help reduce the environmental impacts of a product at all stages of its life. Full cost accounting and total cost accounting can help a company to identify the "true" environmental costs of a product.

Employee participation is essential for improved environmental performance. Many studies show that employee participation can play a significant role in reducing pollution and improving compliance. Corporate environmental leaders also recognize that community involvement is an essential element of environmental strategy. OSHA's Hazard Communication Standard and the EPA's Emergency Planning and Community Right to Know Act mandate disclosure requirements to employees and communities. ELP suggests that companies should go beyond the disclosure requirements of OSHA and the Emergency Planning and Community Right to Know Act. Each model facility will require employees to be active in training and maintaining compliance. Outreach programs and their effectiveness in terms of policy changes should be essential elements of community and employee involvement.

Each company should institute an effective environmental compliance management system. Environmental auditing should be a part of such a system. In addition, companies should reveal all enforcement actions, including penalties, fines, and TRI emissions data. Each model facility should have a comprehensive compliance management system that includes a self-evaluation program for identifying deficiencies and taking corrective actions.

In response to the public comments on the original proposal, the EPA and states decided to ask facilities to volunteer to show new approaches to environmental management compliance. The EPA selected 12 facilities belonging to the Gillete Company, the Duke Power Company, the John Roberts Company, Puget Sound Naval Shipyard, McClellan Air Force Base, and so on. The principles that will be demonstrated include environmental management systems, community outreach and employee involvement programs, and a multimedia compliance program (Table 4.1).

THE OCCUPATIONAL SAFETY AND HEALTH ADMINISTRATION'S VOLUNTARY PROTECTION PROGRAMS

The voluntary protection programs of OSHA are a cooperative effort of government, industry, and labor to improve worker safety and health in the workplace.[6] This program, which recognizes qualified employers and removes them from periodic inspections, emphasizes management commitment, worker involvement, work site analysis, hazard prevention and control, and training. It recognizes participants as Star, Merit, and Demonstration work sites. Star is bestowed on work sites with a safety performance better than the industry's national average; these sites are evaluated every three years, with annual injury rate reviews. Merit is bestowed on work sites with potential to achieve Star qualifications; they are evaluated yearly. The purpose of Demonstration work sites is to display alternative methods of achieving Star quality results in industries for which OSHA needs more experience or information. These work sites are inspected yearly and may receive Star recognition. The voluntary protection program recognizes about 198 participants with Star, 40 participants with Merit, and 2 with Demonstration.

CONCLUSIONS

In this chapter, we describe various industry codes to improve environmental performance. Each code has its own advantages and disadvantages. However, they provide guidelines that a company can copy to

TABLE 4.1
Goals of the Environmental Leadership Program

Arizona Public Service, Deer Valley Facility
   Consolidation of environmental guidance documents,
   Development of guidance to establish environmental objectives and critical success
      factors,
   Implementation of environmental best management practices,
   Definition of qualitative and quantitative measures, and
   Development of vocabulary for environmental reporting.

Ciba-Geigy St. Gabriel
   Environmental Management Systems for waste management, integrated environmen-
      tal policies and procedures, and environmental planning,
   Development of program elements for environmental auditing to improve environ-
      mental results, and
   Development of program elements for environmental education and outreach pro-
      grams.

Duke Power Company
   Environmental Management Systems
      Use of Business Process Improvement to define EMS processes,
      Identification of environmental impacts to processes and departments,
      Definition of benchmarks for environmental performance, and
      Development of structure for process ownership and implementation.
   Environmental Auditing
      Auditor exchange program to analyze, network and benchmark environmental
         auditing,
      Quality control system for self audit, and
      Improvement of audit.
   Community and Employee Involvement
      Development of curriculum for pollution prevention and ecosystems,
      Education of the public and employees, and
      Development of site-based environmental projects.

The John Roberts Company
   Environmental mentoring program for small business, and
   Publicizing experiences with the environmental auditing as a compliance verification
      tool.

Source: U.S. Environmental Protection Agency, *Environmental Leadership Program, Pilot Project Fact Sheets*. (Washington, D.C.: U.S. Environmental Protection Agency, 1996).

improve its performance. Although it is hard to gauge the impacts of these codes on environmental results of companies, they push companies to improve performance. In addition, these codes force companies to consider environmental impacts beyond compliance. Rising peer pressure and stricter monitoring through these industry codes will coerce companies to set up improved environmental management systems. Reporting requirements will force management to evaluate their decisions in terms of environmental impacts. Management commitment will increase environmental awareness among employees.

APPENDIX: THE INTERNATIONAL CHAMBER OF COMMERCE'S BUSINESS CHARTER FOR SUSTAINABLE DEVELOPMENT

Elements to Be Reviewed

Corporate Priority

Corporate mission statement
Top management commitment
Allocation of adequate resources
Communication with stakeholders
Effective environmental management system
Management structure

Integrated Management

Environmental planning
Management reporting and control system
Management information system for performance evaluation

Process of Improvement

Monitoring of technical development
Improvement of policies, programs and products
Revisions of performance goals
Establishment of procedures to carry out change

Employee Education

Environmental awareness programs
Evaluation of employee training and its improvement
Training of personnel in environmental health and safety

Empowerment and motivation of employees to improve environmental performance

Prior Assessment

Evaluation of environmental impacts before business acquisition, product introductions, and so on
Planning for site closing

Products and Services

Environmental impacts of products and services
Energy and resource efficient products and services
Product stewardship
Waste reduction and safe disposal

Customer Advice

Dissemination of information about products and services to customers and distributors
Training of distributors and transporters about safe handling of products
Communication with the public about product safety

Facilities and Operations

Manufacturing practices with emphasis on waste minimization
Pollution elimination
Waste treatment and disposal
Energy conservation program
Natural resources productivity
Safety and health program
Accident reduction program

Research

Research on environmental impacts of materials
Research on environmental impacts of products
Research on processes
Research on waste elimination and reduction

Precautionary Approach

Monitoring of changes in scientific and technical advancements
Process changes to reduce environmental impacts
Marketing changes to reduce environmental impacts

Product or service changes to reduce environmental impacts
Activity changes to reduce environmental impacts

Contractors and Suppliers

Encouraging contractors to adopt pollution elimination
Using environmental performance to select a contractor or supplier

Emergency Preparedness

Hazard evaluation and identification
Preparation of emergency response plans
Ensuring product safety
Training of employees to respond to emergencies

Transfer of Technology

Development of technology for pollution elimination
Training companies in the rudiments of an effective environmental
    management system
Training the public sector in environmentally effective technology and
    management expertise

Contributing to the Common Effort

Helping to develop sound public policy
Encouraging environmental protection programs
Encouraging environmental educational programs

Openness to Concerns:

Stakeholder identification
Responding to stakeholder needs and expectations

Compliance and Reporting

Environmental audits
Environmental performance measurements
Environmental reporting

Elements of Responsible Care Program

Guiding Principles

Community concerns
Safe management of chemicals

Incorporation of health, safety, and environmental issues in new product and process development

Communication of environmental hazards

Training customers and distributors in safe handling of chemicals

Safe and healthy plant and facilities

Research on environmental, health, and safety effects of products, processes, and wastes

Resolution of problems caused by past disposal of wastes

Encouragement of sound environmental public policy

Sharing of knowledge with others

Codes of Management Practices

The community awareness and emergency response code

The pollution prevention code

The process safety code

The distribution code

The employee health and safety code

The product stewardship code

Occupational Safety and Health Administration Voluntary Protection Program Check List

Management Leadership and Employee Involvement

Managerial commitment

Top management involvement

Integration of safety and health concerns in planning

Management of safety and health protection on the same footing as productivity and quality

A written safety and health program

A performance-based safety and health policy

Clear assignment of health and safety responsibilities

Assignment of authority

Allocation of adequate resources

Contract employees receive the same protection as company's own employees

Employee involvement

Annual evaluation of safety and health programs with reports, corrective actions, action plans, and verification procedures

Work Site Analysis

A method to identify existing and potential work hazards
A preuse analysis to ensure safe processes, materials, and equipment
Continuous monitoring of toxic substances and noise
Periodic inspection
Routine hazard analysis
A written hazard reporting system
Documentation of accident investigations
Documentation of all hazards that need to be controlled or eliminated
Analysis of accident and illness trends

Hazard Prevention and Control

Availability of certified safety and health professionals
Adequate engineering and engineering oversight
Written safety rules and procedures
A consistent disciplinary system for all violators of procedures
Written procedures for use and maintenance of personal protective
    equipment
Written procedures to respond to emergencies
Clear procedures to correct hazards
Medical and emergency services within reach in short time
Availability of first-aid and cardiopulmonary resuscitation trained per-
    sonnel all times
Engagement of health professionals to perform hazard analysis
Continuous monitoring and maintenance of workplace equipment

Safety and Health Training

Health and safety training
Personal protective equipment training
Emergency preparedness training
Documentation of training

Review

Availability of written safety and health programs and all docu-
    mentation for review by the Occupational Safety and Health
    Administration

Concurrence

Support for the program from any collective bargaining agents
Employee support for the program

Source: Occupational Safety and Health Administration Voluntary Protection Program brochure.
(Washington, D.C.: U.S. Department of Labor, Occupational Safety and Health Administration).

NOTES

1. Global Environmental Management Initiative, *Environmental Self-Assessment Program*. (Washington, D.C.: Global Environmental Management Initiative, 1994).

2. *Sustainable Forestry for Tomorrow's World: First Annual Report on the American Forest & Paper Association's Sustainable Forestry Initiative*. (Washington, D.C.: American Forest & Paper Association, Inc., 1996), pp. 5–6, 9.

3. *Federal Register*, FRL-5197-9, dated May 22, 1995.

4. *Federal Register*, FR 4802, dated January 15, 1993.

5. *Federal Register*, FR 36062, dated June 21, 1994.

6. *Federal Register*, FR 26339, dated July 12, 1988.

5

Environmental System Standards: ISO 14000

An effective environmental management system (EMS) is essential for superior cost-effective compliance. Environmental management evolved because of community pressures and regulations. Environmental regulations forced corporations to organize personnel to establish operating procedures, monitor their implementation, respond to their noncompliance, take action to correct deficiencies, document environmental activities, evaluate environmental performance, and perform environmental audits. However, there is no legal requirement to establish an EMS in an organization. If companies comply with the law, nobody cares whether an organization has an EMS or not. However, several countries are setting up voluntary standards, including third-party certification, to enhance the effectiveness of environmental management. Even though these standards are voluntary, community pressure makes it necessary for companies to adopt them. Pressures from buyers and public relations value also encourage their adoption. Although command-and-control regulations have achieved a significant improvement in environmental results, this has been accomplished at a high cost. The emphasis of regulations on pollution control rather than pollution prevention has resulted in expenditures of more than $100 billion on litigation, bureaucracies, and unnecessary procedures in the United States. Governments all over the world have come to realize that command-and-control pollution control regulations should be replaced by voluntary pollution prevention. This change in emphasis has produced environmental standards such as European Union's Eco-Management and Audit Scheme (EMAS), BS 7750, and ISO 14000. In this chapter, we briefly describe ISO 14000 and compare it with other standards.

OVERVIEW OF ISO 14000

The ISO 14000 series are international EMS standards established to improve the environmental performance of companies. These standards are intended to achieve improved environmental results by a management process rather than by coercion from regulations. The elements of the ISO 14000 series standards provide an effective framework to integrate environmental decision making into day-to-day company operations. The third-party certification process ensures their consistent implementation. International acceptance of these standards reduces duplication and creates a level playing field. Therefore, these standards improve international trade by reducing trade barriers.

The International Standardization Organization (ISO), consisting of national standard bodies from 118 countries, develops product standards for all except electrical and electronic industries. Since 1979, the ISO has developed organizational standards such as the ISO 9000 series for quality management and quality assurance. The success of ISO 9000 series standards encouraged the ISO to develop the 14000 series to address organizational needs to respond to impacts of products, processes, and services on the environment.

ISO standards on environmental management do not deal with test methods for pollutants, standards for pollutants, environmental performance, and product standards. The ISO 14000 series consists of organization and process standards (EMS, environmental performance evaluation, and environmental auditing), product oriented standards (life cycle assessment [LCA], environmental labeling, and environmental aspects in product standards; and terms and definitions (Figure 5.1).

Two types of ISO 14000 series documents include specification standards and guidance standards. A specification standard describes requirements against which a facility will be audited for registration-certification purposes. A guidance standard offers instructions to implement EMS and its relationships with other systems. Although documents concerning ISO 14000 series are several, an applicant will be audited only against the requirements of ISO 14001, the EMS, to be certified. Other documents guide implementation of the system or the analysis of product attributes. ISO 14001 provides a framework for the management system that helps

FIGURE 5.1
ISO 14000 Environmental Management System Overview

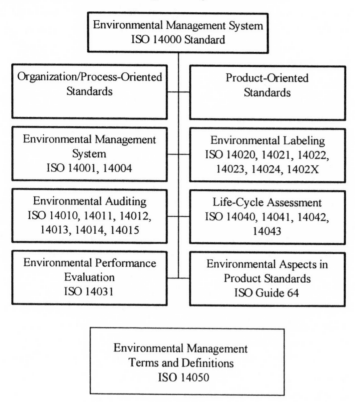

an organization to satisfy its environmental performance requirements. The EMS represents a management structure that deals with environmental impacts of products, processes, and services. It provides a framework based on which an organization performs its environmental management functions, including allocation of resources, assignment of tasks, and improvement of procedures and processes. The EMS elements include environmental policy, planning, implementation and operation, checking and corrective action, and management review.

ISO 14010, ISO 14011, and ISO 14012 describe general principles of environmental auditing, guidelines to audit EMS, and qualification requirements for environmental auditors. ISO 14011 presents audit guidelines to evaluate the performance of EMS, find out whether processes put in place to improve compliance are working, and verify the efficacy of the management reviews in capturing the effectiveness of EMS. The auditor only evaluates the processes, not outcomes. The responsibility for outcomes rests with the management, according to the ISO 14001.

Performance evaluation is a key feature of EMS. It is essential for the management to monitor performance from time to time and ensure that policy goals, objectives, and targets are met. ISO 14031 presents performance indicators.

The environmental labeling and LCA focus on product characteristics that impact the environment. LCA guidelines deal with measurements of environmental consequences of a product during various stages of its life. LCA guidelines are used to develop labeling standards and are likely to be used for environmental rating of products and marketing.

The environmental aspects of product standards guide emphasizes life-cycle thinking in product standards involving environmental aspects. This standard will consist of various designs for the environment strategies. The goal is to increase the awareness that product design can significantly affect the environmental impacts of a product and that LCA and various design strategies need to be adopted to develop environmentally friendly products.

Terms and definitions describes the technical terms used in various 14000 environmental standards. Because many environmental terms used in the standard are used in everyday language, misunderstanding of various terms appearing in different standards is likely. In addition, many of these terms may be wrongly translated into other languages. This standard, therefore, will avoid such ambiguities and ensure uniform understanding of technical terms throughout the world.

THE ISO 14001 STANDARD

The ISO develops standards in stages. The technical management board, consisting of 12 members from national organizations, decides whether a standard needs to be developed. A technical committee, consisting of voting and nonvoting members, does the technical work relating to a standard. The technical committee forms subcommittees and working groups to speed up its work. Standards are developed through a consensus process. Adoption of standards is voluntary, and, therefore, standards try to satisfy industries and customers. The initial draft of a standard typically progresses through a final working draft, a committee draft, a draft international standard (DIS), and a final international standard. The ISO 14001 and ISO 14004 series are final international standards. The following description of the ISO 14001 and 14004 are based on the ISO DIS 14001 and 14004 respectively.

ISO 14001 and 14004 deal with the EMS. ISO 14001 deals with requirements for third-party registration and is the specification standard. However, ISO 14004, which describes various suggestions to design and implement an EMS, is a guidance standard.

The purpose of the ISO 14001 standard is to take a company beyond compliance. The entire EMS will help to build a management process to achieve excellence. A good compliance system by itself will not help a company to avoid catastrophic accidents. However, a good management process can prevent tragedies and reduce day-to-day environmental accidents. Regulations only require companies to comply with them; they do not require companies to implement effective and efficient management processes to avert environmental mishaps. The purpose of ISO 14001 is not only to take stock of environmental aspects of operations, products, and services but also to implement management processes to improve environmental results. The ISO 14000 series consists of the following major elements: environmental policy, legal aspects, objectives and goals, environmental management programs, management and employee commitment, environmental planning, emergency preparedness and response, operational control and maintenance program, environment system procedures and documentation, environmental audit, and communication.

Environmental audits, reviews, and other activities may be adequate to achieve the compliance goals of an organization. However, systematic management process coordinated with other management tasks is essential to make EMS effective. Therefore, the purpose of the EMS is to provide elements of a management system that can be meshed with other management functions and achieve superior goals. Because these standards are international, they are likely to create a level playing field for international trade. ISO 14001 presents requirements of such an international standard. Because environmental standards focus on management process, not on performance goals, two organizations that have adopted the ISO 14001 management system may have different performance levels. ISO 14000 excludes issues relating to occupational health and safety management. There are similarities between ISO 9000 and ISO 14000; however, unlike ISO 9000, which focuses on customer needs, ISO 14000 deals with several parties affected by the environment.

The ISO 14001 EMS is founded on the total quality management concept of continual improvement (Figure 5.2). W. Edwards Deming's "Plan-Do-Check-Act"[1] cycle is its tool. The EMS is initiated with the definition of an environmental policy. The environmental policy will be a public document that will widely circulate the management commitment to continual improvement, prevention of pollution, compliance with environmental laws and regulations, and creating a framework for setting objectives and targets. The next step is planning. Planning will focus on environmental aspects of activities, products, and services; legal requirements; objectives and targets; and programs to achieve objectives and targets. Implementation will include allocation of adequate human, technological, and financial resources; training; communication; documentation of the environmental system; document control; and emergency preparedness and response. Checking and corrective action (the check phase) deals with procedures to monitor and evaluate environmental results of operations and activities regularly. The procedures to respond to nonconformance are an essential feature of this step. Procedures to identify, maintain, and dispose of environmental records, including those relating to training, auditing, and management reviews, are essential for successful checking and corrective action. Periodic environmental audits to find out whether the EMS satisfies ISO standards and has been carried out properly is another requirement of this step. The EMS ends with a top management review. ISO 14001 also contains annexes with useful information about the standard.

To sum up, ISO 14001 provides a structure for the management to carry out EMS. It is flexible and can be used by any company of any size. It is a voluntary standard and encourages a total quality management approach to address environmental problems. It encourages total employee involvement. It is neither a product nor a performance standard. It focuses on the management process and does not mandate any performance level.

ISO 14001 includes several definitions. Continual improvement focuses on enhancing the EMS to achieve improvements. Improvements should be consistent with the organization's environmental policy. The improvements need not take place in all areas simultaneously. The environment refers to surroundings, including air, water, land, natural resources, flora, fauna, and humans and their interrelation. Environmental aspect refers to an element of products, services, or activities that can affect the environment. Environmental impact represents any change to the environment caused by activities, products, or services (Figure 5.3). Environmental change can be adverse or beneficial. The purpose of EMS is to develop, implement, achieve, review, and maintain the environmental policy. It includes organization structure, planning activities, responsibilities, practices, and so on. The EMS audit objectively and systematically tries to examine whether the EMS conforms to the audit criteria and informs the management of the results. Environmental objectives represent an organization's overall environmental goal that should be consistent

FIGURE 5.2
ISO 14001 Environmental Management System Model

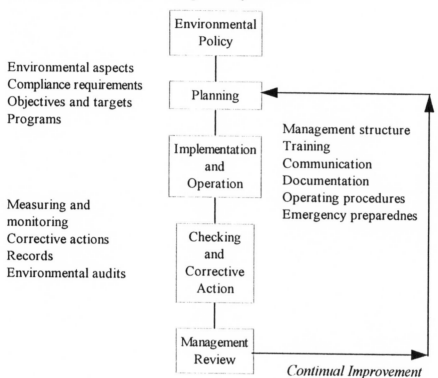

with the policy. Environmental performance should be based on policy, objectives, and targets.

Launching ISO 14001

ISO 14001 requires enormous documentation and costs a great deal. Every manager should, therefore, thoroughly examine the need for ISO 14001. ISO 14001 registration provides a single uniform standard for plants in several countries for a multinational company. Often, small adjustments can bring a plant to ISO 14001 requirements. ISO registration is also an excellent selling tool. In addition, if a company has been registered under ISO 9000, there are significant overlaps with ISO 14000. Uniform standards in all plants make technology transfer and pollution prevention easy. Government incentives, happy stakeholders, and improved environmental results are some reasons for smaller companies

FIGURE 5.3
Identification of Environmental Impacts

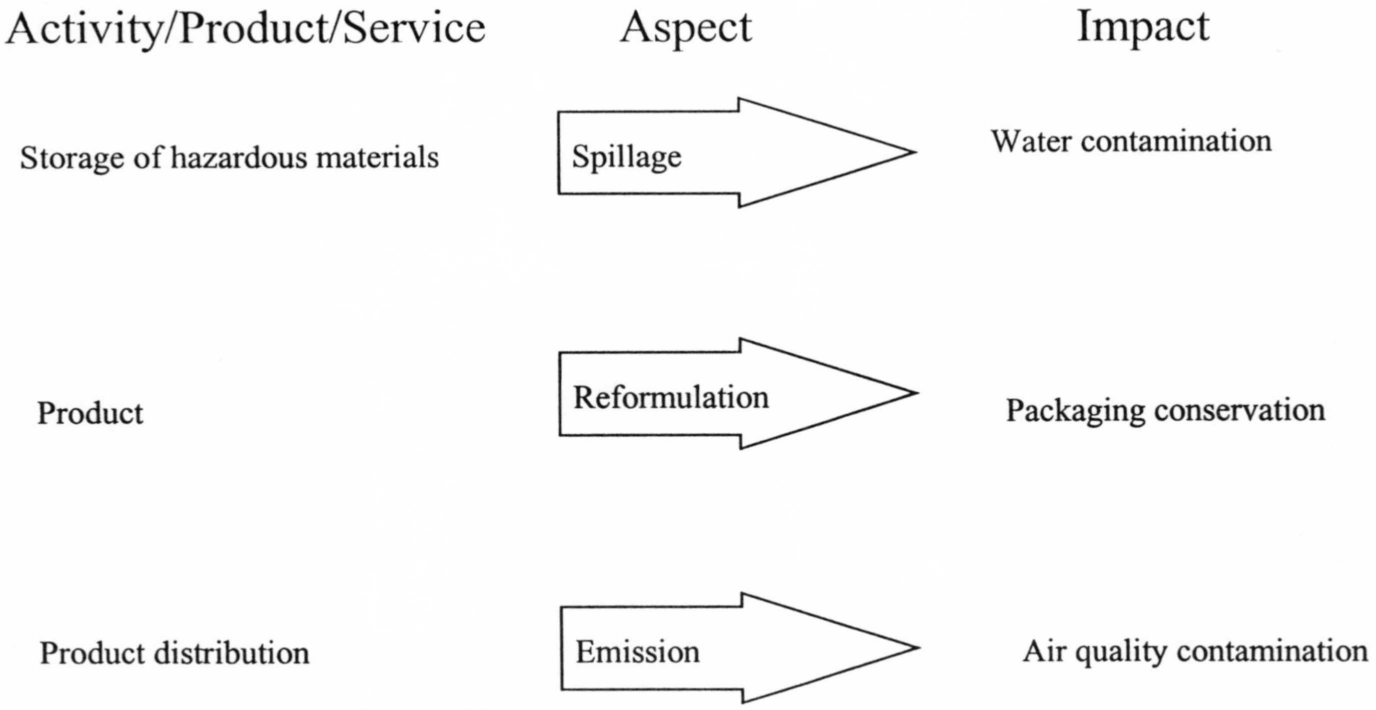

Activity/Product/Service Aspect Impact

Storage of hazardous materials

Spillage → Water contamination

Product

Reformulation → Packaging conservation

Product distribution

Emission → Air quality contamination

to go for ISO 14000 registration. Once reasons for going for ISO 14001 are identified, the next step is defining expected outcomes and identifying differences between the current system and what needs to be done to conform to ISO 14001 requirements.

Data on various elements of the ISO 14001 standard can be collected through questionnaires, interviews, checklists, examination of records, inspections, and benchmarking. Other sources of information include government agencies, databases, industry associations, and handbooks. This process of assessing the differences between the current system and ISO 14001 EMS is called a gap analysis. The worksheet given in the Appendix can help in identifying gaps in the current system. The next step is to commit to launch ISO 14001. Like ISO 9001, ISO 14001 registration can be obtained at any level. However, to reduce logistical problems, it is a good idea to achieve registration for each site. In addition, a company should be willing to provide enough resources to implement the system. Because ISO 14001 affects multiple functions, top management support is essential for its effective implementation.

The ISO DIS 14004 EMS guidelines on principles, systems, and supporting techniques offer procedures to implement and continually improve EMS. According to these guidelines, key principles in implementing EMS include:

high corporate priority for environmental management;

effective communication with internal and external stakeholders;

identification of environmental impacts of activities, products, and services;

commitment to environmental protection;

environmental planning for all phases of a life cycle of a product or process;

establishment of processes to accomplish goals;

allocation of adequate resources;

evaluation of environmental performance against policy, goals, and objectives;

continual improvement through environmental auditing; and

encouragement of contractors and suppliers.

Once a company decides to go ahead with the ISO 14001 implementation, its first task to develop environmental policy. Environmental policy provides an overall direction to a company's efforts to reduce the effects of its activities, services, and products on the environment. A company can use the guiding principles developed by various industry groups discussed in Chapter 4 to develop environmental policy. Environmental policy should involve mission, vision, core values and beliefs; communication requirements with stakeholders; continual improvement; pollution prevention; coordination with other policies; local conditions; laws and regulations; industry attributes; life-cycle approach; integrated approach; education and training; technology transfer; monitoring and control; and top management commitment.

Once the environmental policy is developed, the next step is to plan to achieve the goals set in the environmental policy. Planning should focus on environmental impacts, legal requirements, internal performance metrics, objectives, and management projects.

Identification of environmental aspects and their impacts is a major part of planning. Environmental aspects represent the causes, and impacts represent the effect. Aspects could be associated with a product, service, or activity and could be a spill, discharge, emission, reuse, or noise. Impact could be adverse or beneficial and should be evaluated for its effects on the environment and business. The various dimensions of environmental impact could be the scale, the severity, the likelihood of the happening, and the duration. Legal exposure, cost, effect on the stakeholders, and public image are some business impacts.

Planning should deal with establishment of procedures to identify legal requirements. Federal, state, and local governments; industry associations; legal databases, such as Lexus; and environmental attorneys are excellent sources of legal information. Laws could relate to media, industry, product, packaging, and the general environment.

What cannot be measured cannot be evaluated. Developing criteria to evaluate environmental performance is, therefore, essential. Some environmental performance criteria include emissions, product stewardship, environmental accidents, risk reduction, and spills (Chapter 9).

It is impossible to go anywhere unless you know where you want to go; therefore, objectives are essential. Objectives should be consistent with the environmental policy and should be based on environmental aspects and legal requirements. Objectives should be specific, well-defined, measurable, and achievable. A manager should be willing to allocate adequate resources to achieve them. In addition, employees affected by the objectives should be involved in the target-setting process. Some objectives include reduction of waste, new designs, reduction in impact of packing materials, reduction of accidents, and reduction of emissions into air.

An environmental management program is necessary to achieve objectives. The program should be meshed with the corporate long-range planning. The environmental management program should deal with periodic discussions, allocation of resources, measurement and review, and development of action plans to make up for any deficiencies.

Once a company has developed an environmental policy, identified legal requirements, developed internal performance criteria, established environmental objectives, and put in place an environmental management program, the next step is its implementation. Implementation involves ensuring adequate human, physical, and financial resources; integrating EMS with existing corporate management; assigning responsibility for EMS; motivating employees; training; communicating; documenting; developing operational and control procedures; and establishing procedures for emergency preparedness.

The organization should identify training requirements. Employees doing tasks involving significant impacts upon the environment must be targeted for appropriate training. The training programs should emphasize the importance of compliance with the requirements of the EMS. The training programs should highlight the advantageous effect of improved personal performance on the environment. The ultimate goal should be ensuring that employees working on tasks involving significant environmental impacts are competent, based on education, training, and experience.

An organization should formulate procedures to improve internal communication. Procedures are required to receive communication from stakeholders regarding environmental aspects and the EMS. The management also should consider the processes for external communication.

The organization should maintain documentation on the core elements of the EMS. Procedures to find documentation relating to the EMS should be available. The documentation should be reviewed periodically and revised if necessary. The organization also should ensure that current versions of documents relating to the operations involved in the effective functioning of the EMS are available at all locations. There should be procedures to remove obsolete documents and retain them if these documents are required for legal purposes.

Operations and activities with significant impact on policy, objectives, and targets should be identified, and their proper functioning should be ensured. In addition, the organization should establish procedures to identify the potential for and respond to accidents and emergencies. Review of emergency preparedness and response procedures should be done periodically. To ensure effective implementation, the organization should measure, evaluate, and take corrective actions. For this purpose, management should set up systems for measuring and monitoring actual performance against goals. Comprehensive documentation on legislative and regulatory mandates, permits, environmental impacts, environmental audits, and so on should be maintained.

The final step in the implementation is review and improvement. One key element of EMS is continual improvement. Review should focus on the identification of shortfalls and on methods to improve the EMS.

Advantages and Disadvantages

According to the initial indications, ISO 14000 will be accepted worldwide. Some countries, including Austria, have adopted ISO 14000 as their national standard. According to a recent survey of 115 companies with sales of more than $1 billion a year, 62 percent strongly believe that ISO 14000 certification will be essential to business success, 61 percent believe that it is a competitive advantage in certain markets, and more than one in three believes that it can reduce cost and improve quality.[2]

The ISO 14000 standard demands employee involvement. It requires organizations to establish elaborate documentation. This may result in increased costs without commensurate benefits. In addition, increased documentation may open companies to undiscovered violations and subject them to millions of dollars in fines. Unlike ISO 9000 certification, which can be obtained for a company or a product line, ISO 14000 is site specific, and managers, therefore, have to make decisions regarding sites to be certified. The focus of ISO 14000 is on the process, not on outcomes. This may increase an activity-oriented management process rather than the result-oriented management process currently practiced in many organizations. This also may reduce the significance of legal compliance among employees. In addition, standards may make regulators complacent in enforcing environmental laws. Organizations may use ISO registration as a symbol of superior environmental performance, although ISO registration does not represent environmental excellence. All that registration does is to convey to the public that the organization has an EMS that meets requirements given in the ISO 14001. Currently, companies that perform environmental auditing according to the Environmental Protection Agency guidelines, disclose violations discovered, and take corrective action are subject to reduced penalties. Companies that implement ISO 14001 also are likely to get reduced penalties if regulators are willing to accept the significance of ISO 14001 standards. Customers are likely to perceive companies in a favorable light if they obtain ISO 14001 registration. An effective EMS conveys the top management commitment for environmental protection to customers. It also helps a company to improve its relationship with the public and community. Companies with lower emissions have lower risks. This encourages people to invest in the company, enhancing the company's access to capital. Lower liability risk reduces insurance costs. A company with superior environmental records is perceived favorably by the public. Lower emissions reduce material and energy requirements and, thus, reduce costs.

RELATED DEVELOPMENTS

The management standards developed by ISO share certain common elements, including setting policies, identification of gaps in performance, allocating resources, monitoring, and management review. Therefore, development of a common management standard with a guidance document explaining implementation in different areas such as quality, environment, and health and safety is possible. Occupational health and safety are other likely areas for standard development. The BS 8750 standard, Guide to Occupational Health and Safety Management, developed in the United Kingdom, and ISO 20000 are examples of such standards. Another trend is the development of sector-specific management standards. The big three automakers have developed QS-9000 standards, which include ISO 9001 standard requirements and additional requirements unique to the auto manufacturers. ISO will be less likely to support such standards, because they will destroy the very foundation of a universal consensus standard. However, ISO will encourage development of such sector-specific standards in the form of industry guidelines or codes of management practices. Consequently, a recent attempt to develop ISO 14001 in the forestry sector for sustainable forest management was prevented.

THE ECO-MANAGEMENT AND AUDIT SCHEME

With a view to harmonizing different national standards, the European Union (EU) promulgated *E.U. Regulation 1836/93, Allowing Voluntary Participation in an Eco-Management and Audit Scheme*, (EMAS) for companies to improve their environmental performance and provide information to the public. EMAS requires formal EMS and auditing and reporting of independently audited environmental performance. It describes procedures to register a facility on an EU-authorized list of participating sites and to use an EU-approved statement of participation and emblems to promote its participation. EMAS regulations consist of 21 articles and 5 annexes. Although EMAS is voluntary, it is likely to become mandatory. EMAS is applicable to industrial companies and companies in electrical, gas, steam, and waste disposal sectors and will be extended to other sectors soon. Public pressures, EMAS requirement for public procurement, and lower enforcement costs likely will force rapid adoption of EMAS by companies in Europe. If a company meets EMS requirements under national, European, or any international standards, then such a company is deemed to have satisfied the EMS requirements for EMAS.

The company environmental policy and the EMS program should be in writing and should be available to the public. The environmental policy should be based on the following principles:

creation of environmental awareness among employees;

evaluation of environmental impacts of activities, products, and services;

monitoring activities on local environment;

actions to reduce pollution;

actions to eliminate accidental emissions;

implementation of procedures to verify compliance;

revision of procedures in the light of noncompliance;

cooperation with public authorities;

environmental reporting;

advice to customers about the handling and disposal of products; and

ensuring equivalent EMS at the contractors' sites.

The environmental policy, program, and audits must deal with evaluation and reduction of environmental impacts, energy savings, raw material savings, waste prevention, noise reduction, new processes and process changes, product planning, environmental performance of contractors and suppliers, prevention of environmental accidents, emergency preparedness, training, and environmental reporting.

Environmental review should examine adherence to these principles. Changes to products, processes, and activities must involve objectives, means to achieve them, procedures to implement them, and mechanisms to correct any errors.

Environmental objectives should include continual improvement of environmental performance. The major elements of an EMS program, according to EMAS are:

Environmental policy with a focus on
    legal compliance and
    continuous improvement of environmental performance

EMS with emphasis on
> responsibilities and authorities of environmental personnel,
> management personnel with responsibility for implementation,
> employee awareness program about the importance of EMS,
> training programs,
> documentation system,
> register of significant environmental effects,
> planning and control procedures for activities that affect the environment,
> work procedures for employees,
> procurement and contracting procedures,
> measurement and control of process characteristics,
> documentation of activities,
> investigation and rectification of noncompliance,
> examination of preventive mechanisms,
> documentation of policies, objectives, and programs,
> records of compliance,
> environmental audits

Verification of EMS by an external auditor

Publication of environmental statement

Registration.

A unique feature of EMAS is a requirement to maintain a register of environmental effects, such as emissions to atmosphere, discharges to water, use of natural resources, and discharge of energy or noise. Environmental auditing and continual improvement are requirements of EMAS. The environmental statement with the site description, significant environmental issues, pollution data, environmental performance, and other information should be prepared after a site is audited. Verification and validation of EMS by an accredited verifier are essential. When a site meets regulatory and compliance requirements, it can be registered.

To sum up, the EMAS scheme starts with the definition of an environmental policy, followed by environmental review, objectives, program introduction, environmental effects register, auditing program, verification and validation by an accredited agency, and site registration.

BRITISH STANDARD 7750

The purpose of the BS 7750, the British Standard for EMS, is intended to complement rather than replace EMAS. This standard, which is similar to BS 5750 for quality management, intends to achieve objectives of improved environmental performance through formal, documented management systems and procedures. This standard requires companies to develop policies and objectives after doing an extensive review of significant environmental effects. This policy should be made publicly available. The organization should develop an environmental plan with objectives and targets and methods to accomplish them. In addition, the organization should maintain a register of all environmental regulations, legislation, and industry codes that apply to the company. The responsibility for EMS should clearly be assigned. The impacts on the environment must be evaluated, and environmental targets for each individual employee must be assigned. Training is an essential requirement of this standard. Continuous improvement in performance also is required. Documentation about achievement of objectives and targets should be maintained. Environmental audits and periodic review of EMS and its compliance with the standard should be done.

MAJOR DIFFERENCES AMONG EMAS, BS 7750, AND ISO 14000

EMAS is intended for industrial activities, whereas ISO 14001 and BS 7750 are for both industrial and nonindustrial activities. In contrast to ISO 14001, EMAS and BS 7750 call for an extensive review of the environmental impacts before environmental policies are developed. EMAS and BS 7750 are concerned about environmental impacts, whereas ISO 14001 is about "aspects." Every company can compile information about its inputs and outputs. However, it is very hard to collect information about the environmental impacts of inputs and outputs. Therefore, implementation of EMAS and BS 7750 will be affected by what a company decides are impacts of inputs and outputs. However, this dilemma is overcome in ISO 14001 by considering only aspects that are environmental inputs and outputs. ISO 14001 and BS 7750 apply to the whole or part of an organization, whereas EMAS is site specific. Both EMAS and BS 7750 require compilation of a register of environmental effects and compliance requirements. ISO 14001 emphasizes environmental aspects of activities, products, and services and obligations under regulations and industry codes. EMAS and BS 7750 mandate more public information than does ISO 14001. For example, BS 7750 participants should compile a register of environmental aspects and their consideration in the EMS. A BS 7750 company should publicize its objectives and targets and steps taken to achieve them. EMAS requires publication of a verified environmental statement containing details about EMS and environmental performance.

ISO 14000 IMPLEMENTATION

The following is a checklist for planning and implementing ISO 14001.

Deciding whether to go for ISO 14000
  Identify expectations and outcomes
  Find out advantages and disadvantages
  Decide whether to certify or only implement ISO 140001
  Decide level or boundaries (process, plant, division, and so on) seeking certification (scoping)
  Review current EMS
  Design a preliminary system
  Do a gap analysis
  Estimate resources required
  Make a commitment

Planning
  Form a team and appoint a champion
  Hire a consultant
  Publicize goals and action plans
  Establish organizational relationships
  Involve everyone
  Develop environmental policy
  Allocate resources
  Train team members
  Communicate
  Gain stakeholder approval

Implementation
  Identify environmental aspects
  Identify legal requirements
  Set environmental targets consistent with the policy
  Implement environmental management programs
  Issue new procedures
  Train personnel on appropriate environmental subjects
  Communicate internally and externally
  Document EMS
  Establish an emergency preparedness and response plan

Checking and taking corrective action
  Monitor and measure results
  Identify nonconformance
  Keep records
  Perform environmental audits
  Focus on improvements
  Register

Management review
   Monitor and identify deficiencies
   Improve, improve, improve, improve, improve.

CONCLUSIONS

According to an Investor Responsibilty Research Center survey of manufacturing companies, four in ten subscribe to one or more voluntary environmental codes. Among Standard and Poor's 500 companies, 43 subscribe to the Responsible Care initiative, 42 subscribe to the Business Charter for Sustainable Development, nineteen subscribe to Strategies for Today's Environmental Partnership, 7 subscribe to Global Environmental Management Initiative, and 6 subscribe to Sustainable Forestry Principles.[3] Rising costs of environmental compliance will accelerate the move from command-and-control legislation to market-based approaches to environmental management. Globalization and international trade will force convergence toward global standards for environmental management systems. Incentives for governments for lax enforcement of environmental laws will encourage third-party verification systems and more reporting of environmental information. Use of environmental auditing as a compliance tool will increase. Industry codes of management practices and standards of EMS will likely rise as governments provide more incentives of reduced enforcement actions and penalties. Continual public pressures and need for third-party verified environmental information will persuade companies to obtain registration.

APPENDIX: WORKSHEET

The following is a worksheet to help assess the status of the ISO 14001 implementation in your organization.

1. Environmental Policy

    Formulation of environmental policy

       o Needs improvement   o Complies with the standard   o Worldclass

    Appropriateness of the policy to the nature, scale, and environmental impacts of the products and services

       o Needs improvement   o Complies with the standard   o Worldclass

    Policy incorporates continual improvement

       o Needs improvement   o Complies with the standard   o Worldclass

Policy commits to pollution prevention

o Needs improvement   o Complies with the standard   o Worldclass

Policy commits to comply with laws and regulations

o Needs improvement   o Complies with the standard   o Worldclass

Policy commits to comply with industry codes

o Needs improvement   o Complies with the standard   o Worldclass

Policy describes procedures for setting and reviewing environmental goals and targets

o Needs improvement   o Complies with the standard   o Worldclass

Policy documentation

o Needs improvement   o Complies with the standard   o Worldclass

Communication of policy to all employees

o Needs improvement   o Complies with the standard   o Worldclass

Availability of the policy to the public

o Needs improvement   o Complies with the standard   o Worldclass

2. Planning

Plan formulation

o Needs improvement   o Complies with the standard   o Worldclass

Procedures to identify environmental aspects and their significant impacts on the environment

o Needs improvement   o Complies with the standard   o Worldclass

Procedures to identify legal and industry standard requirements concerning environmental aspects of a company's products and services

o Needs improvement   o Complies with the standard   o Worldclass

Environmental objectives incorporate significant impacts

o Needs improvement   o Complies with the standard   o Worldclass

Environmental objectives incorporate legal and other requirements

o Needs improvement   o Complies with the standard   o Worldclass

Environmental objectives consider technological options, financial and business requirements, and views of stakeholders

o Needs improvement   o Complies with the standard   o Worldclass

Setting objectives and goals for functions and various levels of the organization

o Needs improvement   o Complies with the standard   o Worldclass

Establishment of programs to achieve objectives and targets

o Needs improvement   o Complies with the standard   o Worldclass

Objectives and goals are consistent with environmental policy

o Needs improvement   o Complies with the standard   o Worldclass

Objectives and goals are consistent with pollution prevention

o Needs improvement   o Complies with the standard   o Worldclass

3. Implementation

Documentation and communication of roles, responsibilities, and authorities of employees in carrying out an environmental program

o Needs improvement   o Complies with the standard   o Worldclass

Allocation of resources, including human and specialized skills, technology, and financial resources

o Needs improvement   o Complies with the standard   o Worldclass

Appointment of specific management representatives to carry out environmental management functions

o Needs improvement   o Complies with the standard   o Worldclass

Identification of training needs and training of employees

o Needs improvement   o Complies with the standard   o Worldclass

Training of employees about the importance of conformance with the EMS

o Needs improvement   o Complies with the standard   o Worldclass

Training of employees about the significant environmental impacts and the benefits of pollution reduction

o Needs improvement   o Complies with the standard   o Worldclass

Establishment of roles and responsibilities of employees in realizing compliance with the EMS

o Needs improvement   o Complies with the standard   o Worldclass

Establishment of procedures to inform employees about the potential consequences of violating operating procedures

o Needs improvement   o Complies with the standard   o Worldclass

Assuring that employees are competent based on education, training, and experience to do tasks involving significant environmental impacts

o Needs improvement   o Complies with the standard   o Worldclass

Establishment of procedures for internal communication between the different levels and functions of the organization

o Needs improvement   o Complies with the standard   o Worldclass

Establishment of documentation procedures for external communication about environmental aspects and EMS

o Needs improvement   o Complies with the standard   o Worldclass

Documentation of EMS

o Needs improvement   o Complies with the standard   o Worldclass

Establishment of procedures for document control

o Needs improvement   o Complies with the standard   o Worldclass

Procedures for periodic review, revision, and approval of document control system

o Needs improvement   o Complies with the standard   o Worldclass

Location of current versions of documents

o Needs improvement   o Complies with the standard   o Worldclass

Removal of obsolete documents

o Needs improvement   o Complies with the standard   o Worldclass

Retention of obsolete documents for legal purposes

o Needs improvement   o Complies with the standard   o Worldclass

Establishment of procedures for creating and revising various types of documents

o Needs improvement   o Complies with the standard   o Worldclass

Identification of operations and activities associated with significant environmental aspects

o Needs improvement   o Complies with the standard   o Worldclass

Establishment of documented procedures concerning situations where lack of documents can lead to violations of environmental policy, objectives, and goals

o Needs improvement   o Complies with the standard   o Worldclass

Establishment of procedures relating to significant environmental aspects of goods and services provided by suppliers

o Needs improvement   o Complies with the standard   o Worldclass

Communication of relevant procedures to suppliers

o Needs improvement   o Complies with the standard   o Worldclass

Establishment of procedures to identify the potential for and response to accidents and emergencies

o Needs improvement   o Complies with the standard   o Worldclass

Establishment of procedures for emergency preparedness and response strategies

o Needs improvement   o Complies with the standard   o Worldclass

Periodic testing of emergency preparedness and response procedures

o Needs improvement   o Complies with the standard   o Worldclass

4. Checking and Corrective Action

Procedures to monitor and measure performance of operations and activities with significant impact on the environment

o Needs improvement   o Complies with the standard   o Worldclass

Documentation of information about performance, operational controls, and compliance with objectives and targets

o Needs improvement   o Complies with the standard   o Worldclass

Calibrations of equipment and their documentation

o Needs improvement   o Complies with the standard   o Worldclass

Periodic review of compliance with laws and regulations

o Needs improvement   o Complies with the standard   o Worldclass

Establishment of procedures for investigating nonconformance, taking actions to reduce the consequences of nonconformance, and initiating corrective actions

o Needs improvement   o Complies with the standard   o Worldclass

Assignment of responsibility and authority to investigate nonconformance; take actions to reduce consequences and initiate corrective actions

o Needs improvement   o Complies with the standard   o Worldclass

Appropriateness of corrective action to the potential impact of the nonconformance

o Needs improvement   o Complies with the standard   o Worldclass

Maintenance of records to show the changes in the documented procedures in the light of corrective or preventive action

o Needs improvement   o Complies with the standard   o Worldclass

Establishment of procedures for the identification, maintenance, and disposition of environmental records

o Needs improvement   o Complies with the standard   o Worldclass

Identification, maintenance, and disposition of records, including training and audit review and results records

o Needs improvement   o Complies with the standard   o Worldclass

Legibility, identifiability, and traceability of records of the activity, product, or service

o Needs improvement   o Complies with the standard   o Worldclass

Maintenance and storage of records make it easy to retrieve and protect them from damage and deterioration

o Needs improvement   o Complies with the standard   o Worldclass

Documentation of retention of records

o Needs improvement   o Complies with the standard   o Worldclass

Maintenance of records to show compliance with the standard

o Needs improvement   o Complies with the standard   o Worldclass

Programs and procedures to perform periodic EMS audits

o Needs improvement   o Complies with the standard   o Worldclass

Effectiveness of the audit in determining whether the EMS is consistent with the internal requirements and the standard

o Needs improvement   o Complies with the standard   o Worldclass

Effectiveness of the audits in determining whether EMS has been implemented and maintained properly

o Needs improvement   o Complies with the standard   o Worldclass

Presentation of audit results to management for review

o Needs improvement   o Complies with the standard   o Worldclass

Inclusion of audit scope, frequency, and methodologies and of responsibilities and requirements for performing audits and reporting results in audit procedures

    o Needs improvement   o Complies with the standard   o Worldclass

5.   Management Review

Periodic reviews of the EMS by top management for suitability, adequacy, and effectiveness

    o Needs improvement   o Complies with the standard   o Worldclass

Collection of information for evaluation by top management

    o Needs improvement   o Complies with the standard   o Worldclass

Evaluation by management for the need for changes in environmental policy, objectives, and the EMS based on audit results, changing conditions, and the commitment to continual improvement

    o Needs improvement   o Complies with the standard   o Worldclass

NOTES

1.   W. Edwards Deming, *Out of the Crisis*. (Cambridge, Mass.: MIT Center for Advanced Engineering Study, 1986), pp. 23–24.

2.   Kara Sissell and Rick Mullin, Fitting in ISO 14000: A Search for Synergies, *Chemical Week*, November 8, 1995, p.42

3.   Investor Responsibility Research Center, *1995 Corporate Environmental Profiles Directory*. (Washington, D.C.: Investor Responsibility Research Center, 1995), p. 85.

6

Environmental Auditing

Environmental auditing involves an exhaustive inspection of a plant or facility to identify noncompliance with laws and regulations and verify the effectiveness of environmental management systems. It involves evaluation of risks of operations. It is a powerful tool to monitor environmental compliance and reduce risks of noncompliance. Still, environmental auditing is not mandated by any law. However, community pressures, strict enforcement of environmental laws, increasing tort liabilities, and accidents like those of Bhopal and Chernobyl force U.S. companies to go for environmental auditing to improve compliance with federal and state laws. Exponential growth of environmental regulations (from 300 pages of Code of Federal Regulations in 1975 to about 12,500 pages in 1995) accompanied by rising jail times and fines and penalties for noncompliance made it essential for corporate management to set up systems to ensure improved environmental performance. The actions of the Securities and Exchange Commission against U.S. Steel in 1977, Allied Chemical in 1979, and Occidental Petroleum in 1980, requiring companies to disclose the true magnitude of their environmental liabilities, forced the practice of environmental auditing among large companies. The Environmental Auditing Policy Statement issued by the U.S. Environmental Protection Agency (EPA) in 1986 encouraged several companies to embark on environmental auditing. Prosecutorial guidelines issued by the U.S. Department of Justice and Organizational Sentencing Guidelines promulgated by the U.S. Sentencing Commission, both in 1991, giving favorable treatment for companies with audit programs, motivated companies to establish auditing programs to shield themselves from potential environmental costs. In addition, the codes of management practices such as the Coalition for Environmentally Responsible Economies principles and the International Chamber of Commerce's (ICC) Business Charter of Sustainable Development (see Chapter 4) require signatories to perform environmental auditing. The development of the Eco-Management and Audit Scheme in Europe accelerated the use of environmental auditing as a tool to achieve environmental performance beyond compliance. Declining competitiveness forced companies to develop cost-effective methodologies to improve environmental results. The enactment of the Comprehensive Environmental Response, Compensation and Liability Act of 1980, which deals with cleanups of hazardous waste sites and corrective action requirements of the Resource Conservation and Recovery Act, also forced corporate managers to take environmental auditing seriously. The purpose of this chapter is to discuss environmental auditing programs suggested by various organizations.

U.S. ENVIRONMENTAL PROTECTION AGENCY ENVIRONMENTAL AUDITING

The EPA has promulgated two significant policy statements on environmental auditing. The first one, promulgated in 1986, encourages the use of environmental auditing.[1] The second one, issued in 1995, presents incentives for companies that voluntarily discover, disclose, and correct environmental law violations.[2] According to the EPA, environmental auditing "is a systematic documented periodic and objective review of regulated entities (private firms and public agencies with facilities subject to environmental regulations) of facility operations and practices related to meeting environmental requirements."[3] The purpose of environmental auditing is to ensure compliance, assess the effectiveness of environmental activities, and evaluate risks from materials and practices. It is a quality assurance tool. However, it is not a substitute for activities (such as continuous emissions monitoring) that are required by laws, regulations, and permits.

Environmental auditing serves several purposes. It improves environmental results, and it helps top management to get reliable information on facility compliance status. Because auditing quality depends on top management commitment, the EPA has no intention of mandating environmental auditing; however, the EPA encourages its use.

Even though the EPA has authority to call for relevant information on the environmental compliance status of a regulated entity, with a view to encourage auditing, it would not routinely ask for such audit reports. It would decide to ask for audit reports on a case-by-case basis. However, auditing does not change monitoring, reporting, or recording requirements imposed on regulated entities under various statutes.

The EPA does not want to provide any incentives, such as reduced inspections or enforcement actions, to encourage environmental auditing. Consequently, the EPA will continue its regulatory oversight. However, the EPA will inspect facilities with poor environmental records more often. In addition, it will fine-tune its regulatory responses to violations based on a company's genuine efforts to improve compliance. The EPA also may use auditing provisions in consent decrees and other settlement negotiations if auditing may reduce recurring violations. The EPA also will encourage federal agencies to go for environmental auditing.

The EPA will encourage states to develop environmental policies that are consistent with the basic policies. The regulated entities must report or record compliance information under existing regulations, even if information is obtained through an audit. The regulatory agency should not reduce enforcement responses or inspections. Inspection priorities should take into account compliance performance. In addition, states will follow minimum oversight requirements under the statutes and will not establish precise form and structure for auditing programs.

According to the EPA, effective elements of environmental auditing include:

top management support,

independence of auditing function from audited activities,

adequate number of competent auditors,

specific objectives, scope, resources, and frequencies for auditing,

well-documented data collection, analysis, and interpretation of audit,

prompt audit reports indicating violations, corrective actions, and schedule for implementation, and, finally,

quality assurance to ensure accuracy and completeness of audits.

Environmental auditing may address problems beyond compliance, such as:

environmental policies,

training,

communication with employees,

communication with government and the public,

third-party environmental practices,

assignment of personnel to perform emergency procedures,

incorporation of environmental factors in operating procedures,

application of best management practices,

preventive and corrective maintenance systems to reduce potential environmental accidents,

use of best process and control technologies,

documentation,

analysis of past environmental accidents and actions to prevent their recurrence,

use of source reduction techniques, and, finally,

substitution of materials by least hazardous ones.

Incentives for Self-Policing: Discovery, Disclosure, Correction and Prevention of Violations Final Policy Statement issued in 1995 by the EPA, provides reduction in civil penalties and waiver of criminal prosecution when a regulated facility discloses and corrects violations of environmental requirements. One significant feature of this policy statement is that the EPA will forego gravity-based penalties, which represent the punitive portion of a penalty that is in excess of the economic benefit, for violations satisfying specified conditions discovered through environmental audits and corrected promptly. The gravity-based penalties for violations discovered voluntarily and corrected promptly will be reduced by 75 percent to encourage self-policing. In addition, the EPA will not recommend criminal prosecution for violations discovered through audits or due diligence if they are rectified promptly. However, this waiver will not apply if the violation represented a substantial risk to human health or the environment, is a repeat violation, or is an individual or corporate criminal act. The nine conditions to take advantage of reduction of gravity-based penalties include:

1. Violation must have been discovered through an audit or due diligence.
2 Violation must be discovered voluntarily.
3. Violations are reported within ten days of their discovery.
4. Violation must have been discovered and disclosed before government or third-party actions.
5. Violations are corrected promptly.

6. The regulated entity takes actions to prevent the recurrence of violations.

7. Violation is not a repeat violation.

8. Violations do not involve actual harm or substantial risk to public health or the environment.

9. Violator discloses violations fully and cooperates with the EPA.

INTERNATIONAL CHAMBER OF COMMERCE ENVIRONMENTAL AUDITING

According to the ICC, self-regulation is more effective, and excessive regulation is counterproductive. Therefore, the ICC's strategy to combat environmental degradation is an appropriate dose of legislation and voluntary programs. One of its 16 principles of the Business Charter for Sustainable Development states, *"Compliance and reporting.* To measure environmental performance; to conduct regular environmental audits and assessments of compliance with company requirements, legal requirements and these principles and periodically to provide appropriate information to the Board of Directors, shareholders, employees, the authorities and the public." The ICC has, therefore, issued a position paper indicating the meaning, benefits, and practical methodology of environmental auditing. The ICC defines environmental auditing as "a management tool comprising a systematic, documented, periodic and objective evaluation of how well environmental organization, management and equipment are performing with the aim of helping to safeguard the environment by: (i) Facilitating management control of environmental practices; (ii) Assessing compliance with company policies, which would include meeting regulatory requirements."[4]

Advantages of audits include comparison between facilities, increased employee awareness, cost reduction, better training programs, data collection for emergency response system, enhanced environmental database, improved performance measurement system, good public relations, and lower risk.

The major elements of an effective environmental auditing, according to the ICC, include management commitment, impartial audit team, competent audit team, structured audit procedure, well-documented written reports, quality control of audit system, and follow-up.

The ICC suggests a three-phase environmental auditing program consisting of pre-audit activities, at-site activities, and post-audit activities (Figure 6.1). Pre-audit activities focus on the preparation of the audit. Selection of facilities to audit, formation of audit teams, development of

FIGURE 6.1

Basic Steps of an Environmental Audit

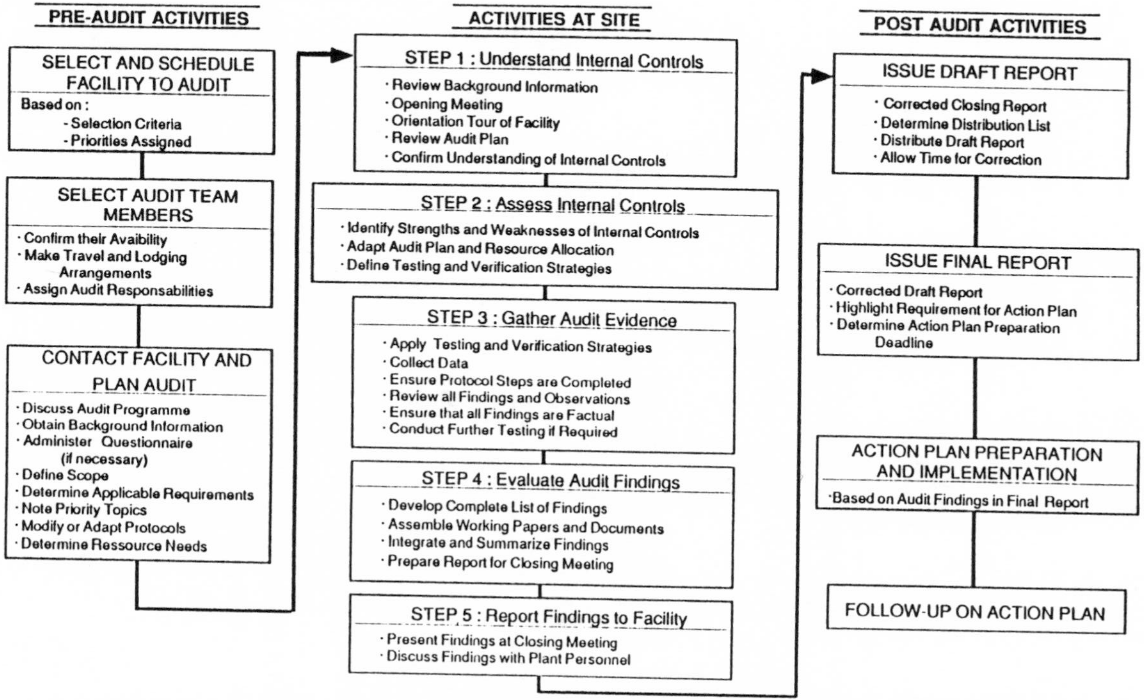

PRE-AUDIT ACTIVITIES

SELECT AND SCHEDULE FACILITY TO AUDIT

Based on :
· Selection Criteria
· Priorities Assigned

SELECT AUDIT TEAM MEMBERS

· Confirm their Availability
· Make Travel and Lodging Arrangements
· Assign Audit Responsabilities

CONTACT FACILITY AND PLAN AUDIT

· Discuss Audit Programme
· Obtain Background Information
· Administer Questionnaire (if necessary)
· Define Scope
· Determine Applicable Requirements
· Note Priority Topics
· Modify or Adapt Protocols
· Determine Ressource Needs

ACTIVITIES AT SITE

STEP 1 : Understand Internal Controls

· Review Background Information
· Opening Meeting
· Orientation Tour of Facility
· Review Audit Plan
· Confirm Understanding of Internal Controls

STEP 2 : Assess Internal Controls

· Identify Strengths and Weaknesses of Internal Controls
· Adapt Audit Plan and Resource Allocation
· Define Testing and Verification Strategies

STEP 3 : Gather Audit Evidence

· Apply Testing and Verification Strategies
· Collect Data
· Ensure Protocol Steps are Completed
· Review all Findings and Observations
· Ensure that all Findings are Factual
· Conduct Further Testing if Required

STEP 4 : Evaluate Audit Findings

· Develop Complete List of Findings
· Assemble Working Papers and Documents
· Integrate and Summarize Findings
· Prepare Report for Closing Meeting

STEP 5 : Report Findings to Facility

· Present Findings at Closing Meeting
· Discuss Findings with Plant Personnel

POST AUDIT ACTIVITIES

ISSUE DRAFT REPORT

· Corrected Closing Report
· Determine Distribution List
· Distribute Draft Report
· Allow Time for Correction

ISSUE FINAL REPORT

· Corrected Draft Report
· Highlight Requirement for Action Plan
· Determine Action Plan Preparation Deadline

ACTION PLAN PREPARATION AND IMPLEMENTATION

·Based on Audit Findings in Final Report

FOLLOW-UP ON ACTION PLAN

Source: International Chamber of Commerce, *Position Paper on Environmental Auditing.* (Paris: International Chamber of Commerce, 1989).

audit plans, and collection of background information are some of the activities during this phase. The purpose of pre-audit activities is to collect enough information to perform the audit at the highest performance level. The audit team may include members from the site being audited. Some advantages of including members from the site are accessibility for the audit team to a member who is familiar with the site and increased credibility with the local workforce. On the other hand, actual or perceived reduction in objectivity caused by an insider on the audit team should be considered. The lack of internal expertise in smaller companies can be balanced by using outside consultants.

Activities at the site include five basic steps — familiarizing with management control system, evaluating internal control system, collecting data, evaluating data, and reporting. The first step in at-site environmental auditing is learning about current management control systems through questionnaires, observations, and interviews. This step will focus on the major elements of internal controls, including documentation and procedures, by which an organization responds to accidental releases, inspection programs, and so on. The next step is to evaluate how well the current system is meeting its goals. During this step, the auditing team will focus on compliance. The third step is data collection, which involves verification of whether the control systems perform as planned. Compliance with the regulatory limits, training records, purchasing department records, and so on are inspected to ensure compliance with internal procedures and legal requirements. Once the data are collected, the audit team will analyze data from the overall performance of the control system. The final step includes the preparation of an audit report and formal discussions with the site management. The audit report will contain significant findings and their effect on the internal control systems.

Post-audit activities consist of two steps — preparation of the final audit report and a plan for corrective actions. The final report will be evaluated by the site management and audit teams for accuracy and presented to the appropriate management. The audit does not serve its primary purpose of correcting deficiencies unless facility personnel come up with action plans and schedules to rectify weaknesses in the system. Therefore, follow-up is an essential part of the post-audit activities.

Essential elements of environmental auditing include top management support, trust between auditors and auditees, going beyond compliance, management should not restrict auditing processes, public should be involved, auditing team should not surprise auditees, and auditing frequency should be related to the degree of hazard.

ISO 14000 — ENVIRONMENTAL AUDITING

The purpose of environmental auditing is to improve compliance, reduce liability, meet management's fiduciary responsibility, develop data on compliance, and ensure future compliance. Environmental auditing programs are the only formal system to ensure improved environmental results. ISO 14001 extends the environmental management system beyond regulatory requirements by broadening the management commitment to industry standards. This has expanded the focus of environmental auditing programs from compliance with regulatory requirements to compliance with internal management systems.

ISO 14001, Section 4.4.4, deals with the environmental management system audit. The purpose of an environmental audit is to ensure proper implementation and maintenance of environmental management systems. The audit frequency should be based on the environmental risk of the activity and the results of earlier audits. The audit procedures should include scope, frequency, and procedures to conduct audits. Audits should ensure proper implementation and maintenance of environmental management systems and should provide feedback to management. The audit focus should be on the system put in place to ensure compliance rather than on the compliance status of the organization. Similarly, environmental auditing is not conformity assessment process done to issue the certificate of registration. Environmental auditing is performed for the management to help determine implementation of the environmental management system. On the other hand, conformity assessment process is done for the registrar to ensure conformance with ISO 14001 guidelines. Environmental audits can also be used to "self-declare" adherence with ISO 14001 requirements.

With a view to helping companies to develop effective auditing systems, the International Standardization Organization (ISO) has issued the following publications:

ISO 14010 – *Guidelines on Environmental Auditing — General Principles on Environmental Auditing,*

ISO 14011 — *Guidelines on Environmental Auditing — Audit Procedures — Auditing Environmental Management Systems,* and

ISO 14012 — *Guidelines on Environmental Auditing — Qualification Criteria for Environmental Auditors.*

ISO 14010 deals with scope, definitions, audit requirements, and general principles of environmental auditing. ISO 14011 focuses on audit procedures, including objectives and audit teams and their responsibilities. ISO 14012 describes qualifications of auditors, training requirements, and educational standards.

According to the ISO auditing standards, the main goal of environmental auditing is verification. The focus is on conformance with standards, rather than performance. Auditing can be done by either internal or external audit teams. The external auditors have experience in several organizations and, therefore, have broader knowledge. Internal teams are familiar with the organization and facilities, operations, and processes; however, to ensure objectivity, members should not be from the facility, operation, or process being audited. In addition, members should neither report to nor receive performance evaluations from the managers of facilities, operations, or processes being audited. The auditing team should not include members who had the responsibility to implement the environmental management system. In addition, to demonstrate the independence of internal audit teams, external experts may be included in the audit team. The management should ensure that the audit team has adequate resources to perform internal audits.

The lead auditor should be a qualified person to perform and manage an environmental audit. Auditors should have a secondary education and have relevant experience and training in environmental science and technology, environmental law and regulations, environmental management, environmental auditing, and facility operations technology. In addition, the environmental auditor should have excellent writing and interpersonal skills. He or she should be objective, independent, and sensitive; should be able to make decisions based on evidence; and should have the ability to execute an audit. Including an attorney in the audit team is a good idea. Auditing should be done in a structured fashion. To ensure accuracy of results, quality assurance policies should be followed throughout the audit.

Auditing Procedures

Auditing is done in four phases: audit initiation, audit planning, audit execution, and audit reporting and recording (Figure 6.2).

Audit initiation involves deciding the boundaries of the audit and evaluating availability of documents. Audit planning involves assignment of work to audit teams and audit documentation. Audit execution deals with the opening meeting, data collection, development of findings, and the closing meeting. The fourth phase, audit reporting and recording, includes report preparation and distribution and document retention.

FIGURE 6.2
Environmental Auditing Procedure According to ISO 14011

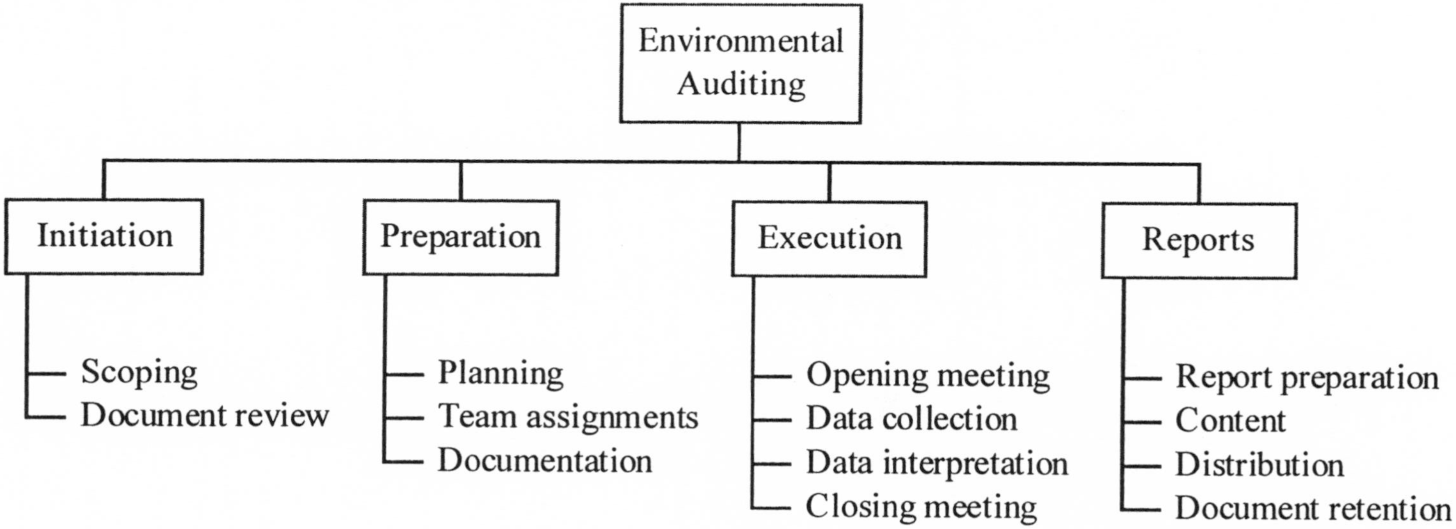

Environmental auditing begins with the establishment of audit boundaries. During this step, the audit team should decide the objectives and develop criteria for evaluating the environmental management system.

Audit preparation is an essential part of an audit. The audit plan involves pre-audit activities such as determining the adequacy of documentation, resources, and audit team assignments. To protect an organization from regulatory actions, procedures need to be established to keep documents from disclosure, to report violations, and to ensure implementation of corrective actions. There should be a structured procedure for keeping complete records of an audit.

The purpose of an environmental audit is to make sure that the environmental management system performs as planned. The site audit begins with an opening meeting. The purpose of the opening meeting includes meeting site personnel, ensuring cooperation, describing audit methodology to site personnel, discussing the audit schedule, and making sure that adequate resources are available. To ensure conformance of environmental management systems to ISO 14001 and internal management control systems, the audit team should collect data. Data collection will include interviews, reviews of documents, inspection of operations and processes, and measurements and tests. Any nonconformance with audit criteria should be recorded. In addition, corrective action required should be identified. Once data are collected, they should be reviewed with a site manager. The data collection ends with a closing meeting, the purpose of which is to reconcile differences and collect any missing data or information.

The final phase of environmental auditing is report preparation. Audit reports should be objective, written in a clear and concise manner. In addition, all data collected during an audit should remain confidential and should be retained for future use.

The European Union's Eco-Management and Audit Scheme requires verification of environmental audit of a company by an external accredited ecoauditor. The environmental audit can be done by an internal auditor or an external auditor. However, an accredited environmental auditor who is independent of the company auditor must verify the audit. Companies also are required to publish a full environmental audit statement every three years and simplified statements in other years. The audit frequency has to be decided by the senior management, based on the problems, emissions, and complexity. A company is required to set targets for improving environmental performance based on the audit results and using the best available technology. It also is required to update its environmental policy based on audit results and technological progress. An accredited auditor should be familiar with auditing methodologies, management processes, environmental issues, relevant regulations, and technical knowledge about the plant.

AMERICAN SOCIETY FOR TESTING AND MATERIALS STANDARD FOR ENVIRONMENTAL COMPLIANCE AUDITS

The purpose of the American Society for Testing and Materials (ASTM) Standard for Environmental Compliance Audits is to help organizations comply with U.S. regulations. Because ISO 14000 standards are intended to be used internationally, they do not address regulatory compliance of a company. To correct this deficiency, ASTM standards focus specifically on U.S. legal issues associated with audits and describe requirements for audits, auditor qualifications, and how compliance audits differ from other types of environmental audits.

ASTM standards require that auditors should be independent of the activities they audit. To assure freedom from interference, the internal auditor should receive clear support from the board of directors. In addition, there should be a written charter clearly describing the purpose, authority, and responsibility of the auditor. An external auditor should not have any relationship with the company. He or she should attest to strict confidentiality and demonstrate a commitment to professional and ethical standards.

The environmental audit team should be proficient in management information systems, engineering, control systems, management systems, accounting, finance, statistics, and law. Environmental auditors should have excellent interpersonal, communication, organizational, and analytical skills.

The environmental audits should verify whether environmental goals will be met and whether the management system is performing as intended. The audits should examine systems, operations, and programs and their reliability and integrity. The major elements of environmental audits include:

written environmental policy statement,

well-defined authority and responsibility for personnel involved in environmental management programs,

comprehensive procedures for environmental management programs,

appropriate placement of internal auditor in the organization, adequate resources,

management commitment,

training,

use of risk assessment methodologies,

reporting procedures, and

quality assurance of environmental management.

The audit plan should be in writing and include audit objectives and criteria to evaluate the management systems. Results of the audit work should include descriptions, data, and audit findings along with a statement affirming conformance to generally accepted environmental auditing standards, a statement attesting management responsibility for the environmental management system, and a statement saying that the audit does not evaluate compliance with specific laws or regulations. A quality assurance program to evaluate the work done by the environmental audit is a must. In addition, corrective actions for any deficiencies should be an essential part of an audit.

ENVIRONMENTAL AUDITING ROUNDTABLE STANDARDS FOR ENVIRONMENTAL AUDITS

The purpose of Environmental Auditing Roundtable's Environmental, Health and Safety (EHS) audits is to provide bare minimum criteria for the performance of an EHS audit, which involves evaluation of the EHS status of an organization or site against specific criteria.[5] The focus of these guidelines is the process of an audit. An auditor must be proficient in auditing processes, management system analysis, legal requirements, environmental technologies, plant operations, and environmental impacts. He or she should have excellent interpersonal, planning, and analytical skills. An auditor must perform audits accurately, consistently, and objectively and should be independent. Every audit must have well-defined objectives. There should be well-defined plans and procedures for audit preparation, fieldwork, and reporting. Audit fieldwork must be supervised effectively. In addition, there should be quality assurance built into the auditing process to ensure accuracy and continuous improvement. The functions audited should be documented so that another auditor can confirm the conclusions reached. A report containing audit scope and conduct and audit results and conclusions should be prepared. The Environmental Auditing Roundtable imposes six articles of professional conduct and five articles of conduct of membership on environmental auditors.

TIPS FROM SUCCESSFUL COMPANIES TO IMPROVE ENVIRONMENTAL AUDITING

Excellent descriptions of environmental auditing at various companies can be found in a technical report entitled *Environmental Auditing*[6] and in the report entitled *Environmental Auditing: A Useful Tool that Can Improve Environmental Performance and Reduce Costs.*[7] The environmental audit should help managers to know the extent of compliance of laws, regulations, and company policies by their companies. It should help to comply with laws at a lower cost and, at the same time, reduce environmental impacts of activities that are not subject to regulations. In addition, environmental auditing should tell managers how to reduce costs and what more they can do to improve environmental results. To examine each functional area in depth, Allied-Signal does functional audits of sites on air pollution, water pollution, solid waste disposal, occupational health, medical programs, loss prevention, and product safety.[8] The British Petroleum Group, on the other hand, conducts various types of environmental audits. It does corporate audits to examine organization structure and understanding of roles and responsibilities of top management, communication among top managers, and so on. A second type of audit, entitled issues audit, focuses on the responses to specific environmental issues of key concern. An activity audit examines how corporate policies are incorporated into the activities that cross business boundaries. Internal divisional audits are conducted to get an objective view about the compliance status of a facility. Compliance audits are done to verify legal compliance. Site audits are done to examine the environmental compliance status of a site with potential problems.

Environmental audits should be well-planned. They should have the full support of top management. Without top management support, an audit program will suffer from lack of resources, trained auditors, and effective follow-up. Formal environmental policy, incorporation of environmental factors in personal evaluations, and punitive actions against employees for environmental violations are some effective methods to show top management support. Environmental auditing results should not be used to compare plant managers' performance. There should not be any elements of surprise in environmental auditing. The frequency of auditing of facilities should be based on their degree of hazards.

The composition of the environmental auditing team is critical for the success of an audit. The audit team should be made up of two to eight people, depending upon the size and complexity of the plant being audited.

The team should consist of environmental experts, industry experts, and, possibly, external consultants.

The site audit should include the examination of policies and principles, systems, procedures, practices, and performance. The British Petroleum Group has identified 11 areas for auditing, consisting of management issues, such as policy, procedures, training, and external relations, and technical issues, such as regulations, emergency planning, air and water pollution reduction, air and water pollution treatment, waste and ground water pollution reduction, waste and ground water pollution treatment, and land management. The audit report should be prepared immediately after the audit and should include action plans to correct any deficiencies. It is essential to maintain high quality of environmental auditing for its continued success. Allied-Signal maintains high audit quality by improving communication among team members, by providing structured protocol for auditing, and by requiring auditors to prepare audit working papers that document data collection and conclusions reached.

Some advantages of environmental auditing include:

independent verification of operations and compliance status,

increased environmental awareness among employees,

reduced risk of criminal prosecution,

safer environment for employees, neighbors, and customers,

identification of potential cost savings,

up-to-date database on environmental results,

evaluation of training program,

lower environmental hazards,

reduced legal scrutiny,

improved environmental performance, and

easier facilities' planning and budgeting.

CONCLUSIONS

A Coopers & Lybrand ad, "An audit is only as useful as the information uncovers," summarizes the critical characteristic of an audit. More and more companies are adopting environmental auditing because it improves the long-run competitive status of a company. It improves compliance, reduces liabilities, lessens costs, improves efficiency, decreases environmental hazards, increases workers' health and safety, and significantly enhances positive perception about a company. Therefore, it is of no surprise that 19 of 20 companies surveyed indicated that they perform environmental compliance audits and that approximately three of four domestic sites have been audited during the past two years.[9]

NOTES

1. U.S. Environmental Protection Agency Environmental Auditing Statement, *Federal Register,* 25004, Vol. 51, No. 131, Wednesday, July 9, 1986, 25004–10.

2. U.S. Environmental Protection Agency, *Incentives for Self-Policing: Discovery, Disclosure, Correction and Prevention of Violations,* (Washington, D.C.: U.S. Environmental Protection Agency, 1995).

3. U.S. Environmental Protection Agency Environmental Auditing Statement, *Federal Register*, pp. 25004–10.

4. International Chamber of Commerce, *Position Paper on Environmental Auditing,* (Paris: International Chamber of Commerce, 1989).

5. William A. Yodis and Gilbert S. Hedstrom, *Environmental Auditing Roundtable Establishes Formal Standards for Environmental, Health and Safety Audits,* in John T. Willing (Ed.) *Auditing for Environmental Quality Leadership.* (New York: John Wiley & Sons, 1995), pp. 263–70.

6. United Nations Environment Programme, *Environmental Auditing,* Technical Report Series No. 2, (Paris: United Nations Environment Programme, 1990).

7. General Accounting Office, *Environmental Auditing: A Useful Tool That Can Improve Environmental Performance and Reduce Costs* (GAO/RCED-95-37). (Washington, D.C.:General Accounting Office, 1995).

8. United Nations Environment Programme, *Environmental Auditing*, p. 8.

9. Investor Responsibility Research Center, *1995 Corporate Environmental Profiles Directory*, (Washington, D.C.: Investor Responsibility Research Center, 1995), p. 86.

III

PRODUCT AND PROCESS
ASSESSMENTS

7

Environmental Product Evaluation Methodologies

Life-cycle assessment is a methodology to evaluate environmental attributes of a product. It helps to ascertain whether cloth diapers are environmentally preferable to disposable diapers or whether paper cups are more environmentally friendly than polystyrene cups. The focus of life-cycle assessment is on the entire life cycle of a product, rather than on just one or two phases. The emergence of life-cycle assessment can be traced to the energy shortage decade of the 1970s, when the goal was to track material and energy flows in industrial systems. Life-cycle assessment examines energy and material flows during the extraction and processing of raw materials, production, transportation, distribution, use, and final disposal. It is a systematic process of collecting and evaluating the potential environmental impacts of a product during its life cycle.

Life-cycle assessment is still in its infancy. There are no well-defined approaches. We know that it involves the development of inventory of all inputs and outputs, mostly in terms of materials and energy during the entire life cycle of a product, and the expression of effects of this inventory on the environment. Life-cycle assessment has been defined as an attitude by which a manufacturer accepts responsibility for the pollution caused by products from design to disposal. This is contrary to conventional belief that the responsibility begins with the raw material acquisition and ends with the dispatch of finished products. Life-cycle assessment is considered a quantitative tool that ensures real pollution reduction.

As a useful tool for developing decisions involving environmental criteria, life-cycle assessment has been used by consumers to compare different production technologies, materials, products, and packaging based on environmental impacts. It provides objective yardsticks for evaluating various products and processes. Therefore, life-cycle assessment has been used by environmental consumer groups to help consumers to decide what to buy, by manufacturers to identify areas for improvement, and by legislators to develop criteria for environmental labeling schemes. Life-cycle assessment is very different from risk assessment. Risk assessment deals with environmental safety, whereas life-cycle assessment deals with environmental quality. The risk assessment identifies risks and evaluates them; life-cycle assessment generates an inventory of inputs and outputs and evaluates their impact on the environment. Risk assessment tries to predict potential harm; life-cycle assessment sums up environmental degradation. Risk assessment deals with potential accidents, inadvertent releases of hazardous chemicals, and fires; life-cycle assessment deals with energy and material inputs and emissions. Risk assessment is typically site and time specific; life-cycle assessment is done over space and time.

LIFE-CYCLE ASSESSMENT PROCESS

Life-cycle assessment is a holistic approach toward examining the environmental effects of a product. Companies use life-cycle assessment to identify waste reduction opportunities. Government regulations typically focus on one aspect of pollution, for example, the Clean Air Act deals with air pollution and the Clean Water Act addresses water pollution. Consequently, pollution reduction activities also address pollution problems of a given medium. Such approaches frequently reduce pollution in one area and increase it in another. However, the life-cycle assessment approach can eliminate such narrowly focused decision making by concentrating instead on the sum total of pollution generated by a product.

One major benefit of life-cycle assessment is that it focuses evaluation on products rather than processes. By widening the evaluation process, evaluations are performed both up and down the supply chain. Because little pollution is generated during the design phase, most analyses are focused on the production, distribution, use, and disposal stages. Environmental tools, such as auditing, total quality environmental management, and so on, rarely examine the greenness of design decisions, even though, during design stages, significant decisions that influence pollution during production and subsequent stages are made. Therefore, the systems approach adopted by the life-cycle assessment begins analysis with the design.

Life-cycle assessments mean different things to different people. The life-cycle assessment performed by Franklin Associates, called the resource and environmental profile analysis, identifies consumption of energy and materials at each physical stage of a product. The Society of Logistics Engineers's life-cycle costing program estimates ownership costs over the complete life span of a product. The Association of the Dutch Chemical Industry's integrated substance chain management shows areas for reducing environmental impact through life-cycle, full-cost systems. Based on a review of more than 6.6 million references on life-cycle assessments, the Danish Packaging and Transportation Research Institute and the Swedish Packaging Research Institute[1] conclude that most models consider consumption of raw materials, energy, and water, but only a few models consider energy recovery, work environment, resource consumption, and environmental emissions. The resource and environmental profile analysis model of the Midwest Research Institute deals with energy balances and pollutants of products from raw material extraction to waste disposal. The detailed personal computer–based life-cycle assessment model developed by Sundstrom begins with the raw material extraction from mines, forests, and wells and ends with the final waste management by incineration and disposal. The Boustead model used by the Industry Council for Packaging and the Environment incorporates raw material consumption and energy during various phases of a product's life cycle and has background data from several European countries. Some life-cycle assessments consist of two stages. In the first stage, an inventory of all inputs and outputs in terms of energy and materials during the life cycle of a product is generated. In the second stage, the environmental effects of this inventory are identified. The data generated during the second stage can be used to develop improvements; this is called life-cycle management. According to the 1990 Society of Environmental Toxicology and Chemistry conference, the complete life-cycle assessment should consist of three separate but interrelated stages: an inventory stage, an impact analysis stage, and an improvement stage.[2] The Canadian Standards Association suggests four phases: the initiation phase (consisting of the problem and objective definition), the inventory phase (defining raw materials and energy inputs and solid, liquid, and gaseous wastes), the impact analysis (connecting inputs and outputs to real world environmental problems), and the improvement phase (focusing on the overall environmental performance). Life-cycle assessment is not carried out in sequential steps; information from any stage can be used in other stages.

Life-Cycle Scoping

The first step in performing a life-cycle assessment is to identify the purpose of analysis. The assessment may be done to compare materials, products, or processes, to compare resource use, to train employees in waste reduction, to develop policy, or to educate the public. The studies could be generic or product specific. The next step is to define the system boundaries. The system definition should include where the cradle begins and where the grave ends. It should begin with material extraction and end with final disposal of the product into landfills or into air or water. The system definition also should take into account depth of analysis, for example, should oil discarded from manufacturing equipment used to drill a hole be included? The system boundaries can affect the outcomes of a life-cycle assessment study. Therefore, when comparisons between two products are made, it is essential to ensure that the same system boundaries are used in both studies. One major difficulty during this step is the lack of a consensus about what should form the system boundaries and what phases should be covered.

Life-Cycle Inventory Analysis

The purpose of life-cycle inventory analysis is to develop a model to account for all inputs and outputs during each stage in the life cycle. Typically, the system is broken down into various stages, such as raw material extraction, raw material processing, manufacture, product fabrication, filling and packaging, assembly, distribution, use, reuse, maintenance, and recycle and waste disposal. The material and energy flows are indicated for each process (Figure 7.1). Raw material acquisition includes extraction of raw materials from the earth, harvesting of trees, and their transportation. The manufacturing stage includes a transformation process consisting of manufacture, fabrication, assembly, filling, and packaging. Use, reuse, and maintenance include energy consumption, storage, and consumption of a finished product. A recycle and waste management stage includes energy consumption and environmental wastes produced during recycling and waste disposal. Energy requirements at each stage include energy consumed during process as well as transportation. Environmental wastes typically are categorized into discharges into air, water,

FIGURE 7.1
Life-Cycle Assessment

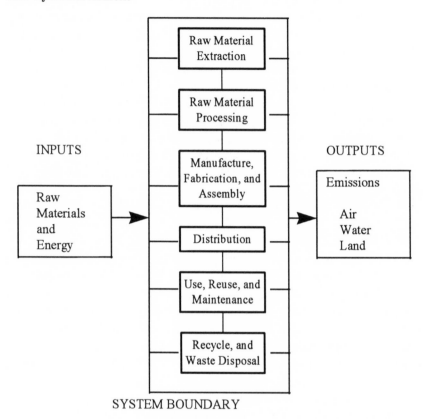

and land. A variety of waste disposal alternatives, including landfilling, incineration, recycling, and composting, are considered.

Even though life-cycle assessment should analyze a production system rather than a product, most current applications focus on specific products. A system that is a collection of operations has a well-defined function. Without knowing what a system is trying to accomplish, it is not possible to adequately define a system. It also is not possible to define a system's boundaries without knowing its function. For example, paper can be used to produce packaging material, to print newspaper, or to produce a reference book to be stored in libraries. Therefore, a life-cycle inventory analysis that does not consider the likely use of the paper will be erroneous.

The focus of inventory analysis is data collection. Precisely measuring material and energy inputs at various stages is tedious and time-consuming. The data can be collected from various sources. Government and industrial databases, government reports, life-cycle analysis reports, and laboratory test data and facilities are some sources for data. Consultants are also a valuable source for data. The amount of materials and energy expended may vary among different geographical regions. Therefore, caution is suggested while using such data. One way to overcome errors is to express results of life-cycle assessment as ranges (maximums and minimums). Life-cycle assessment output suffers from the garbage in, garbage out phenomenon. Accuracy will be affected directly by the data used. Therefore, it is essential to use reliable, comprehensive, and up-to-date data.

Life-Cycle Impact Analysis

Life-cycle impact analysis is to evaluate the effects of resources and emissions identified in life-cycle inventory analysis. One major problem during this step is deciding how to account for recycling and by-products. Once the data are collected and an inventory of inputs and outputs is prepared, the next step is to quantify the effect of the inventory on the environment. Impact analysis is still in the early stages of development. It should take into account environmental and human health impacts, resource depletion, and social welfare. Impact analysis typically consists of classification, characterization, and valuation. The first step in the impact analysis is to assign an item from inventory analysis to categories of environmental stressors. Stressors represent conditions that may lead to an impact. Stressor categories for each impact area have been identified and typically include resource depletion, ecological degradation, and human health. However, quantification of effects involves two serious problems: translating the effects and determining their aggregation. Currently, most impact analysis methods involve some kind of scoring system. The ecological scarcity method uses ratios of actual to maximum accepted environmental loading, the environmental theme method uses affect categories in relation to environmental policy objectives, and environmental priority strategies in a product design method use ecological scores. The Danish Technological Institute uses a panel of experts similar to the one in the Delphi method for technological forecasting to develop impacts.[3] In view of the arbitrary nature of impact analysis, inventory itself often is used to compare two options. In this approach, differences in resources used and emissions generated are used to choose an option, and we do not make any evaluation of environmental harm done by the emissions and resource depletions. This approach has several drawbacks. First, it ignores differences between processes that produce environmental harm and those that do not. Second, there are many uncertainties in evaluation, because we are ignoring environmental harm done by emissions and resource consumption. Third, because output of such an analysis presents results that look precise, the decision makers are likely to misinterpret them.

Life-Cycle Improvement Analysis

The purpose of improvement analysis is to identify opportunities to reduce energy and raw material consumption and emissions. The emphasis of the improvement analysis is on the entire life cycle of a product.

PROBLEMS

As burgeoning literature on life-cycle assessment indicates, there is no one correct approach to employing this method of analysis. Energy requirements typically include the inherent energy of raw materials because life-cycle assessment is based on thermodynamic principles; however, some models include only inherent energy in materials used as fuels. The second problem relates to the allocation of energy and wastes generated in processes producing several products; the common allocation method is based on the mass ratios of products. The third problem relates to the allocation of energy savings from recycling. If energy savings are attributed to the process generating the wastes, such allocations will promote processes with wastes that can be recycled. However, if the energy savings are attributed to the processes that are using the recycled products, then such computations will encourage use of recycled products. When site-specific data are not available, industry average data typically are used. Industry average data may or may not be a proxy for site-specific data. Another fundamental problem of life-cycle assessment relates to definitions of boundaries for analysis. The definition of boundaries, the quality of data, and the assumptions can significantly affect results. In the case of paper production, should analysis include fertilizer used to foster trees to grow? The life-cycle assessment approach has been used to compare such products as disposable and cloth diapers, groundwood and polystyrene hamburger containers, and returnable and reusable glass bottles. It has failed to provide clear-cut answers about the greenness of these products. The major problem with life-cycle assessment relates to comparison of data. Energy consumption can be aggregated in mega-joules. However, combining the energy consumption during transportation with the inherent energy in the inputs can be misleading. Solid wastes can be combined in terms of their volume or weight. Different impacts of emissions make it difficult to aggregate emissions into air, although emissions are expressed in parts per million, for example, the impact of one part of sodium chloride on humans is different from the impact of one part of potassium cyanide. Aside from problems of aggregating data, life-cycle assessment also is problematic in evaluation of environmental impacts. Some environmental impacts are local; others are global. Emissions into air and water typically have significant impact at the local level. The local impacts of emissions depend on time, site, and factors such as concentration of emissions. For example, impacts of emissions in urban areas are much more serious than impacts of emissions in rural areas, because they typically are more concentrated. Often, a combination of chemicals can have a more serious impact on humans than individual chemicals. Therefore, adding pollution may not represent actual impacts. Another problem relating to the impact assessment is the differences in long- and short-term impacts. Life-cycle assessments consider only environmental factors. However, socioeconomic and political factors do affect the interpretation of these environmental factors. For example, durability of a product should be considered in the evaluation. In short, life-cycle assessment suffers from serious aggregation of emissions and energy consumptions and their conversion to environmental impacts.

USES OF LIFE-CYCLE ASSESSMENTS

Life-cycle assessment can be used for a variety of purposes. Anyone who wants to evaluate the greenness of a product can start with life-cycle assessment. Such an analysis can provide valuable information about environmental burdens of a product to its manufacturer and also can provide information about how to improve the greenness of a product. Because life-cycle assessment provides valuable information about wastes generated at different phases, a manufacturer can develop effective design and production changes to reduce waste. Life-cycle assessment can help a product or process designer by directing him or her through appropriate development work. Life-cycle assessments are an objective basis for ecolabeling schemes and informing consumers about environmentally friendly products.

Manufacturers generally advertise their products as ecofriendly based on a single criterion, such as recycling or the amount of wastes generated during one or two stages of a product's life. Life-cycle assessment helps to prevent such claims by a comprehensive analysis of wastes generated. It considers every stage of a product's life and analyzes all inputs and outputs generated at all stages. Traditionally, manufacturers took responsibility for wastes generated from the time the raw material entered the production stage to the time the finished product left the factory. However, life-cycle assessment now includes stages from the extraction of raw materials to final disposal of a product. It considers the entire life cycle of a product. In short, life-cycle assessment represents an integrated approach.

Life-cycle assessment goes beyond factory walls to examine a product's environmental impact. By evaluating both the upstream and the downstream activities of a product, life-cycle assessment provides more data on which informed decisions can be based. Although this method advocates a systems approach, it also can be used to select a process, material, product, or policy. For example, battery-powered electric vehicles are wrongly called zero emission vehicles because they do not generate air emissions during a use stage. Because gasoline vehicles emit hydrocarbons, carbon monoxide, and nitrogen oxides during a use stage, electric vehicles are considered greener than gasoline vehicles. However, power plants that generate the electricity used to charge these batteries do emit sulphur dioxides and particulate matters. Life-cycle assessments can be extremely useful in analyzing these types of situations.

EXTENSIONS OF LIFE-CYCLE ASSESSMENTS

Value-Impact Assessment

We should not evaluate products solely on life-cycle assessments. Although some products may generate more waste than others, at the same time, they may provide better value to the consumer. Products should be judged in terms of both waste generated and their value, which may be measured in terms of performance, condition of the product, and consumer satisfaction.[4]

One reason for a low market share of several green products may be that they are not delivering performance. The goal should be to provide maximum performance with minimization of wastes. The strategy is to incorporate performance measurements while performing life-cycle assessments. The value represents how well a product performs compared with what the consumer wants and is willing to pay — in other words, the value measures fitness for use. The fitness for use of a product may vary from consumer to consumer. It will depend on how well a product satisfies a customer's needs. These needs are identified by asking customers for inputs by means of questionnaires, group discussions, and focus groups. Once needs are identified, products advance to the research and development phase. The product then is tested in laboratories and homes. Based on the responses received from the testing, the product is improved. Other aspects of products that need to be evaluated include the cost and total risk (Figure 7.2).

FIGURE 7.2
Value-Impact Analysis

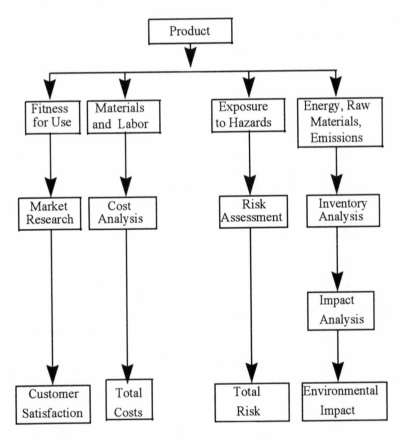

Environmental Option Assessment

One major drawback of life-cycle assessment is the need for technical experts to make environmental trade-offs. In addition, life-cycle assessment fails to provide a comprehensive analysis of environmental effects and economic costs and benefits. The objective of the environmental option assessment is to help decision makers to evaluate options to diminish the environmental impacts of a product during its life cycle.[5] The environmental option assessment begins with the estimation of volume flows and identification of environmental issues involved. This step consists of drawing volume flow diagrams, identifying major environmental issues, defining options, and selecting options for detailed evaluation. Major environmental concerns can be pollution issues (e.g., global warming, ozone depletion, acidification, and disposal of waste), conservation issues (e.g., depletion of mineral and energy resources, soil degradation, and depletion of biological resources), and diversity issues (e.g., decrease of biological diversity). Priorities are set in the next phase, which consists of collecting data, determining the economic profile, and positioning options. Both hard and soft data must be gathered concerning the environmental impacts of each option. Economic data concerning annual, operating, and capital costs of the options also are collected. Once both environmental and economic data are collected, the next step is to estimate the environmental yields and economic impacts of each option. This estimation is calculated by decision makers rather than by environmental experts. Economic impacts and environmental yields then are plotted on an option map. Using option maps, policymakers establish goals, allocate resources, and assign responsibilities.

Impact Analysis Matrix

An impact analysis matrix is a valuable tool with which to make decisions on pollution prevention options.[6] An impact analysis matrix comprises columns of inputs and outputs and rows of environmental impacts. The inputs may be raw materials and energy; outputs may be atmospheric emissions, liquid wastes, and solid wastes. The impact areas may include global warming, ozone depletion, acidification, waste disposal, depletion of energy resources, soil degradation, and decrease in biological diversity. The columns and rows are application dependent. Once inputs, outputs, and impact areas are established, the next step is to assign unweighted scores. A score of +1 or greater typically represents a larger environmental impact than the base option, a −1 or less represents lesser impact, and a 0 represents no significant difference in impact. This matrix can be improved by using weighted scores.

THE BENEFITS OF LIFE-CYCLE ASSESSMENT

By providing comparisons of environmental burdens of similar systems, the life-cycle assessment approach is an objective evaluation method. Life-cycle assessment also can be used to compare different products, but interpretation will require more care. Life-cycle assessment is an integrated approach that includes all components; inputs and emissions from the system; inputs and emissions over the entire life cycle of a product; facilities and raw material acquisition methods; distribution and disposal methods; and issues including recycle and reuse. It expresses environmental degradation in terms of multiple criteria, rather than a single criterion. Life-cycle assessment provides a framework for communication between scientists and engineers, purchasers and suppliers, and regulators and polluters. It helps an industry to understand the global effects of its decisions. It encourages companies to realize the need to initiate pollution prevention activities. Life-cycle assessments improve environmental audits by providing inventory of emissions. By supplying data on the effects of various pollutants, life-cycle impact analysis helps management to rank pollution-reduction activities. Life-cycle assessment highlights the seriousness of various pollutants and can, thus, help policymakers to develop "green taxes," for example, Richard Ottinger describes various ways to incorporate externalities in the pricing of electricity.[7]

EXAMPLES OF ENVIRONMENTAL IMPACTS

When the environmental impacts of a product are considered, the focus typically is on manufacturing operations. However, many environmental impacts occur other than during manufacturing operations, for example, according to the American Fiber Manufacturers Association, an "average" polyester blouse consumes more resources during washing and drying than during its manufacture.[8] Steel is one of the primary materials used in the manufacture of combustion engine vehicles. Using steel as a basis, the following are some examples of environmental impacts during various stages of the life cycle of a combustion engine vehicle.

Steel is made out of iron, which is extracted through surface operations. The ore is concentrated using separation techniques. Extraction degrades landscapes, flora and fauna, and surrounding water systems because of storm water runoffs. The concentration operation produces dusts, liquid wastes, and tailings. Extraction of one ton of iron ore produces five tons of wastes. Steel is produced by purifying iron. This energy-intensive process releases significant quantities of off-gases in addition to producing slags. The scrubbers used to clean off-gases generate wastewaters that need to be disposed of.

Car manufacturing also produces a variety of hazardous wastes. Manufacturing operations generate dirty water that contains metals, dirt, oils, and grease. The assembly steps involve cleaning, sanding, and painting, processes that generate metal scraps and packaging wastes. Painting can release significant quantities of volatile organic compounds to the atmosphere. Shrink-wrap plastic coating used to protect finished surfaces during transportation ends up in a landfill as solid waste.

Vehicles with internal combustion engines generate most of their wastes during use and maintenance. They pollute air by generating carbon monoxides, nitrogen oxides, and particulates. Road building can contaminate surface water and ground water by surface runoff. Steel found in cars typically is recycled, but many other car products, including upholstery, foam, plastics, fiberglass, and rubber, will end up in a landfill. This is increasingly problematic because steel parts now often are replaced with hard-to-recycle plastics.

Process materials inputs and outputs and fabricated metal products manufacturing processes along with inputs and outputs are given in Table 7.1 and Figure 7.3. These could be used as a starting point for life-cycle inventory analysis.

ISO 14000 STANDARD FOR
LIFE-CYCLE ASSESSMENT

Although ISO 14001 does not mention anything about life-cycle assessment, organizations can use life-cycle assessment for labeling programs and environmental performance evaluations. Life-cycle assessment is one of the major tools of implementing concepts such as "life-cycle principles," "cradle-to-grave approaches," and so on. The life-cycle assessment standards currently are categorized into principles and framework, inventory analysis, impact assessment, and interpretation.

The ISO 14040 environmental management addresses principles for performing and reporting life-cycle assessment studies. ISO 14041 deals with inventory analysis. According to ISO 14040, the principles of life-cycle assessment include the following.

The life-cycle assessment should deal with the environmental aspects of a product throughout the life cycle.

TABLE 7.1
Fabricated Metal Products: Process Materials Inputs and Outputs

Process	Material Input	Air Emission	Process Wastewater	Solid Waste
Metal shaping Metal cutting and forming	Cutting oils, degreasing and cleaning solvents, acids, alkalis, heavy metals	Solvent wastes (e.g., 1,1,1-trichloroethane, acetone, xylene, toluene)	Waste oils (e.g., ethylene glycol) and acid (e.g., hydrochloric, sulfuric, nitric), alkaline and solvent wastes	Metal chips (e.g., scrap steel and aluminum), metal-bearing cutting fluid sludges, solvent still-bottom wastes
Surface preparation Solvent degreasing and emulsion, alkaline and acid cleaning	Solvents, emulsifying agents, alkalis, acids	Solvents (associated with solvent degreasing and emulsion cleaning only)	Solvent, alkaline, and acid wastes	Ignitable wastes, solvent wastes, still-bottom wastes
Surface finishing Anodizing	Acids	Metal ion–bearing mists, acid mists	Acid wastes	Spent solutions, waste-water treatment sludges, base metals

Chemical conversion coating	Metals, acids	Metal ion–bearing mists, acid mists	Metal salts, acid and base wastes	Spent solutions, waste-water treatment sludges, base metals
Electroplating	Acid and alkaline solutions, heavy metal–bearing solutions, cyanide-bearing solutions	Metal ion–bearing mists, acid mists	Acid and alkaline, cyanide, and metal wastes	Metal and reactive wastes
Plating	Metals (e.g., salts), complexing agents, alkalis	Metal ion–bearing mists	Cyanide and metal wastes	Cyanide and metal wastes
Painting	Solvents, paints	Solvents	Solvent wastes	Still bottoms, sludges, paint solvents, metals
Other metal finishing techniques (including polishing, hot-dip coating, and etching)	Metals, acids	Metal fumes, acid fumes	Metal and acid wastes	Polishing sludges, hot-dip tank dross, etching sludges

Source: U.S. Environmental Protection Agency, *Profile of the Fabricated Metal Products Industry*, EPA 310-R-95-007. (Washington, D.C.: U.S. Environmental Protection Agency, 1995), p. 22.

FIGURE 7.3
Fabricated Metal Products Manufacturing Processes:
Inputs and Outputs

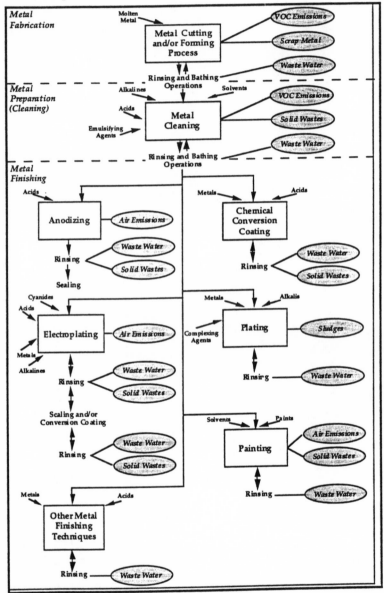

Note: VOC = volatile organic compounds

Source: U.S. Environmental Protection Agency, *Profile of the Fabricated Metal Products Industry*, EPA 310-R-95-007. (Washington, D.C.: U.S. Environmental Protection Agency, 1995), p. 23.

The breadth and intensity of a life-cycle assessment study will depend on the life-cycle assessment goals and scope.

The scope, assumption, data quality parameters, methodologies, and output should be described completely.

There should be flexibility to incorporate confidential and proprietary matters in the life-cycle assessment study.

Life-cycle assessment methodology should be flexible enough to incorporate advances in science and technology.

Life-cycle assessment studies making comparative assertions should be subject to specific requirements.

A single overall score will not completely indicate environmental impact, because trade-offs and complexities are involved in a system analyzed.

The life-cycle assessment methodology should not be rigid.

Life-cycle assessment methodology that follows the model developed by the Society for Environmental Toxicology and Chemistry consists of four phases: goal and scope definition, inventory analysis, impact assessment, and interpretation. The standard describes guidelines for defining goals, determining scope, specifying functional unit and function, defining system boundaries, determining data quality, comparing systems, verifying quality, performing inventory analysis, performing impact assessment, interpreting results, preparing reports, and reviewing studies.

ISO 14041 presents procedures for conducting life-cycle inventory analysis and presenting life-cycle inventory results. This standard consists of sections on scope; definitions; guidance on product systems, unit processes, and data categories; definition of goal and scope; guidance on conducting life-cycle inventory analysis; and report preparation. This standard also contains examples and checklists of data collection sheets, allocation procedures, and life-cycle inventory analysis. The scope section focuses on the definition of scope, establishment of system boundaries, data requirements, and so on. It also describes a procedure to conduct a life-cycle inventory analysis with guidance on data preparation, calculation procedures, allocation procedures, and so on.

ISO 14042 addresses life-cycle impact assessment. The objective is to present procedures to assess the significance of environmental impacts in life-cycle assessment studies. This standard, consisting of four areas, describes how to assign inventory data to impact categories, characterization of impact categories, significance of life-cycle assessment results, and valuation.

ISO 14043 deals with interpretation of life-cycle assessment results. The objective is to draw conclusions within the scope and goal. The four elements that make up this standard are synthesis of results, comparison to scope, conclusions, and recommendations.

IMPLEMENTATION

Life-cycle assessment emphasizes a systems approach to company problem solving and offers a new perspective for company decision makers. Life-cycle assessment is performed best by a team consisting of personnel from manufacturing, design, engineering, marketing, and accounting. The team should formulate objectives of the life-cycle assessments and then define system boundaries and develop assumptions. The team also should decide time frames within which environmental impacts will be studied. While deciding a time frame, the team should take into account the sensitivity of the time frame on the environmental impacts. The team must develop an inventory checklist, which should include decisions about various aspects of life-cycle assessment, such as purpose, system boundaries, geographic scope, data categories, data collection procedures, data quality indicators, model development, and presentation of the results. Because life-cycle assessment involves several subjective decisions, it is essential to have a peer group review the process, and they should examine system boundaries, data collection, key assumptions, and interpretations of the study. Data collection is the next major step. For data collection, the whole system may be broken down into subsystems. For each subsystem, input materials, energy consumed, transportation, outputs of products and by-products, emissions into air, discharges into water, solid wastes generated, and other releases should be identified. Industrial and government electronic databases, government reports, and laboratory test data are some sources of data for life-cycle inventory analysis. The material balance analysis is one approach to develop data. The next step is to construct a model. Computer spreadsheets are extremely useful in calculating inventory. The final step is to present the results of the analysis. The full report should present original data, details of the model (including system boundaries, assumptions, and sources of data), sensitivity analysis of various assumptions, inventory of inputs and outputs, and the basis for impact analysis.

CONCLUSION

Life-cycle assessment is an important tool for environmental management. By measuring greenness from cradle to grave, it provides an objective basis for comparison and improvement. As more life-cycle assessments are performed, systems definition, methodology, and databases will become standardized. Consensuses about converting life-cycle inventories into environmental burdens will emerge. As more life-cycle assessments are published, public debates about a variety of environmental issues will follow. Peer reviews will significantly improve the quality of life-cycle assessments. The next few years should be an exciting period for developments in life-cycle assessments. By providing objective measuring tools, life-cycle assessments are likely to improve the quality of our environment.

NOTES

This chapter is revised from Vasanthakumar N. Bhat, "Life-cycle Assessment: Measuring Greenness," in Vasanthakumar N. Bhat (ed.), *The Green Corporation: The Next Competitive Advantage.* (Westport, Conn.: Quorum, 1996), pp. 52–66. An imprint of Greenwood Publishing Group, Inc., Westport, Conn.

1. Sven-Olof Ryding, *Environmental Management Handbook.* (Amsterdam: IOS Press, 1992), pp. 439–41.
2. Society for Environmental Toxicology and Chemistry, *A Technical Framework for Life-cycle Assessments.* (Washington, D.C.: Society for Environmental Toxicology and Chemistry, 1991).
3. Ryding, *Environmental Management Handbook,* pp. 444–45.
4. Peter Hindle, Peter White, and Kate Minion, "Achieving Real Environmental Improvements Using Value:impact Assessment," *Long Range Planning,* 26 (1993): 36–48.
5. Pieter Winsemius and Walter Hahn, "Environmental Option Assessment," *The Columbia Journal of World Business,* 27 (Fall & Winter 1992): 248–66.
6. Bruce Vigon, "Life-Cycle Assessment," in *Industrial Pollution Prevention Handbook,* edited by Harry M. Freeman. (New York: McGraw-Hill, 1995), pp. 305–07.
7. Richard L. Ottinger, "Incorporating Externalities — The Wave of the Future," in *Proceedings of the Expert Workshop on Life-Cycle Analysis of Energy Systems, Methods and Experience,* Paris, May 21–22, 1992, pp. 54–70.
8. Jennifer Nash and Mark D. Stoughton, "Learning to Live with Life Cycle Assessment," *Environmental Science and Technology,* 28, no.5 (1994): 236A–37A.

8

Environmental Labeling

More than one in four products introduced in 1990 bragged that they were environmentally friendly in some way. There have been several deceptive and false claims. A large segment of the U.S. population believes that environmental claims are "mere gimmickry." Therefore, governments have passed laws regulating green claims. Green labels have been introduced in several countries to help consumers to identify environmentally friendly products. Green labels first were introduced in West Germany in 1978. They are now awarded in most of the European countries, including Austria, Denmark, France, Germany, Norway, Spain, Sweden, and the United Kingdom. Japan and South Korea also award green labels, and Singapore, Brazil, Columbia, India, Poland, and China plan to establish or already have established green labeling programs. The purpose of green labeling is to steer consumers toward green products and encourage manufacturers to develop environmentally friendly products. Green labels make markets more efficient by providing information to consumers and generally improve sales by projecting an image of a safe product.

GREEN LABELS

A green label serves several purposes: it provides independent evaluation of a product, it protects consumers by providing credible information, and it helps to achieve policy goals. There are three categories of green labels: single issue voluntary labels (that focus on one aspect of a product, such as "energy efficient," "chlorofluorocarbon free," "ozone friendly"), single issue mandatory labels (that provide either positive or negative information on one aspect of a product, such as "flammable," "ecotoxic," "biodegradable"), and information labels (that provide information about the overall environmental quality of a product).

According to a 1993 Environmental Protection Agency (EPA) study, *Status Report on the Use of Environmental Labels Worldwide*,[1] there are five types of environmental labeling programs: seal-of-approval, single attribute certification, report card, information disclosure, and hazard warnings. Seal-of-approval and single attribute certification programs inform consumers of the positive aspects of a product. These programs are generally voluntary in nature; manufacturers typically use them to demonstrate that their products have certain positive environmental properties as compared with similar products with the identical functional attributes. Report cards express neutral attributes and are voluntary; report cards contain information about several environmental attributes, and consumers are required to make trade-offs among them. Information disclosure communicates neutral characteristics of a product and often is mandatory. Hazard warnings disclose negative properties of a product and usually are mandatory.

The purpose of green labeling programs is to communicate to consumers that labeled products are relatively environmentally less harmful than others in the same category. However, because most products harm the environment during some phases of their life cycle, only a few products are considered environmentally benign. Therefore, making such relative evaluations requires estimates that take into account a product's overall environmental impact.

Seal of Approval

The seal-of-approval programs involve permission to use a logo on products to inform consumers that these products are less environmentally harmful than comparable products. Programs to award seal-of-approval follow similar procedures:[2]

Criteria to award green labels are based on the environmental impacts during the entire life cycle of a product category.

Programs are voluntary.

Impartial organizations, including governments and not-for-profit organizations, run the programs.

Award criteria and evaluations are done by committees consisting of environmental groups, academics and scientists, business representatives, consumer groups, and government representatives.

The environmental seal or logo is legally protected.

Both domestic and foreign manufacturers can apply for an award.

Award criteria are set to encourage development of less environmentally harmful products.

Seals of approval are awarded for a certain number of years, and award criteria are reviewed periodically.

Most environmental labeling programs follow similar procedures. They identify the product group to be labeled, such as light bulbs or printing papers. The life-cycle analysis is done to identify areas of maximum environmental impacts. Based on the life-cycle analysis, criteria that products must satisfy to qualify for labeling are established. For example, 90 percent of the environmental consequences arising from a washing machine occur during the use stage. Therefore, criteria to award green labels for washing machines generally are based on the use-related environmental impacts. Public comments are considered before final decisions about the awarding criteria are made. Then, the criteria for awarding green labels are publicized, and manufacturers are encouraged to apply for the label. Only about 10 to 20 percent of the market share qualify for green labels. A green labeling contract typically involves charges and is valid for a fixed duration.

The product categories are defined to stimulate the development of green products by manufacturers and their use by consumers. Definition of a product category can significantly affect the criteria for awarding green labels and environmental impacts. Often, product categories are selected to achieve a certain policy goal. For example, low-noise mopeds are selected as a product category by Germany's green labeling program, Blue Angel, to encourage the reduction of noise pollution. Canada's Environmental Choice Program completely depends on published research to establish product categories and set product standards to award green labels. Japan's EcoMark labeling program uses a set of guiding principles to establish product categories and award criteria.[3] The guiding principles include:

Products generate only a small environmental impact during use.

Products have a positive effect on the environment during use.

Products produce a small environmental impact after use when disposed of.

Products encourage environmental preservation.

Environmental pollution is reduced during the production stage.

Product use leads to energy or resource preservation.

Products comply with safety and quality regulations.

Product prices are not high.

Even though product categories often are selected based on one attribute in Japan, life-cycle analysis is tried to help product category selection.

The products either qualify or do not qualify for green labeling. Typically, only a few products qualify for green labeling. When a higher proportion of products satisfy green labeling criteria, the standards usually are raised to ensure that only 10 to 20 percent of the market share is satisfied by products with green labels. Even though green labels should be awarded based on multiple criteria, qualification for awarding involves only one environmental impact. This is done not only to reduce confusion among customers but also to help easy implementation. The European Community (E.C.) has introduced green labeling programs involving mandatory and secondary award criteria. Before a product can qualify for green labeling, it has to meet all mandatory criteria and a certain percentage of secondary criteria. Such an approach is considered to be comprehensive. From the manufacturers' perspective, such an approach offers flexibility to select a variety of manufacturing and operating alternatives to satisfy green labeling requirements.

Public review of the awarding criteria and awarding process is an essential requirement for green labeling. Public reviews improve credibility of a green labeling program among consumers and help to incorporate concerns of stakeholders in the program. Press releases, mailings, public hearings, and announcements in government publications are some ways of encouraging public involvement in the green labeling programs.

Single Attribute Certification Programs

Environmental Choice of Australia and Scientific Certification Systems' Single Claim Certification are two examples of single attribute certification programs. They typically are issued to products that meet a specific criterion. Environmental Choice is a government-approved labeling program for products that meet claims that can be tested or quantified. According to the Environmental Choice program, environmental claims can be classified into quantifiable claims, qualitative claims, meaningless claims, and misleading claims, and only the first two categories of claims are allowed to be used. Compliance is monitored through random testing of products.

The Scientific Certification System has issued single claim certification for more than 500 products in the United States based on recycled content, recycling rate, biodegradability, sustainable forestry, and so on. The single claim certificates vouch for accuracy of the environmental claim, and the manufacturer has to release all information relevant to its claim. Based on the average industry performance indicators and on-site inspections, the Scientific Certification System either approves or disapproves a product for its Environmental Claims Certification.

Report Cards

Unlike single claims certification, report card labels provide quantitative information about multiple environmental impacts of a product. Because a report card informs consumers about the multiple impacts, a consumer can choose a product using multiple criteria. Report cards provide comprehensive information without either praising or criticizing a product. Lack of information and display of information are major sources of difficulties in developing a report card approach to product labeling. The Environmental Report Card issued by the Scientific Certification Systems presents data on resource consumption, energy use, air emissions, water emissions, and solid waste generation during manufacturing, use, reuse, and disposal stages.

Information Disclosure Labels

Information disclosure labels usually are mandatory, because manufacturers may not like to disclose negative information about a product. Information disclosure labels provide neutral information to consumers for making purchasing decisions. The Energy Guide program, indicating energy costs for household appliances, is an excellent example of an information disclosure label. Currently, energy labels can be seen on refrigerators, freezers, water heaters, clothes washers, dishwashers, and room air conditioners.

Hazard and Warning Labels

Hazard and warning labels are mandatory labels conveying negative information about a product. The Federal Insecticide, Fungicide and Rodenticide Act mandates warning labels on pesticides. The Toxic Substances Control Act requires warning labels on products containing specific hazardous substances. The Clean Air Act Amendments 1990 mandate labels for products containing ozone-depleting substances.

ENVIRONMENTAL LABELING
IN VARIOUS COUNTRIES

A comprehensive survey about environmental labeling can be found in *Environmental Labelling in OECD Countries.*[4] Table 8.1 presents major environmental labeling programs in various countries as of mid-1993, and Figure 8.1 presents logos of environmental labels. Germany (formerly West Germany) was the first country to launch environmental labeling by introducing the Blue Angel labeling program in 1978. Germany's Blue Angel labeling program consists of three steps: product category selection, establishment of award criteria, and award process. Three institutions — the Environmental Label Jury, the German Institute of Quality Assurance and Labeling, and the Federal Environmental Agency — take part in the labeling program. Anyone can suggest product categories. The Federal Environmental Agency reviews new proposals, conducts tests, and drafts proposals for labeling criteria. The Environmental Label Jury, consisting of representatives of citizens and environmental, industry, and labor groups, decides product categories and awards criteria. The German Institute of Quality Assurance and Labeling does expert reviews and awards Blue Angel labels to products that meet awarding criteria.

Canada's Environmental Choice program, the Ecologo" uses the following guidelines to rank product categories and products for green labeling: conserve renewable resources for future generations, encourage the efficient use of nonrenewable resources, protect ecosystem and species diversity, and manage chemicals in products appropriately. Any interested party can propose product categories. Guidelines for awarding criteria are developed with the help of a consultant and an advisory board. The Environmental Choice Program, based on the recommendation of the technical agency on the applications for the green labels, decides whether to certify products. Besides publicizing awarding criteria, the Canadian program outlines environmental burdens and environmental benefits of the labeled product.

TABLE 8.1
Major Environmental Labeling Programs (as of mid-1993)

Program Name	Country	Date Founded	Number of Product Categories	Number of Products Awarded
Seal of Approval				
Blue Angel	Germany	1978	64	3,600
Environmental Choice Program	Canada	1988	26	700
EcoMark	Japan	1989	49	2,300
White Swan	Nordic Council	1989	1	Not available
Green Seal	United States	1989	35	5
Good Environmental Choice	Sweden	1990	12	Not available
Environmental Choice	New Zealand	1990	3	Not available
EcoMark	India	1991	16	Not available
EcoMark	Korea	1992	12	96
Green Label	Singapore	1992	5	Not available
Environmental Labeling Program	European Community	1992	0	0

Single Attribute Certification
Science Certification System

Environmental Claims Certification	United States	1989	—	500
Environmental Choice Australia	Australia	1991	—	Not available
Report Card				
Environmental Report Card	United States	1991	—	9
Negative Labeling				
Pesticide Labeling	United States	1976	1	Not available
Toxic Substances Control Act Labeling	United States	1976	4	Not available
Information Disclosure				
Energy Guide	United States	1975	7	Not available
Fuel Economy Information Program	United States	1975	1	Not available

Source: U.S. Environmental Protection Agency, *Status Report on the Use of Environmental Labels Worldwide*, EPA 742-R-9-93-001. (Washington, D.C.: U.S. Environmental Protection Agency, 1993), p. 41.

FIGURE 8.1
Environmental Labels in Different Countries

Canada (Environmental Choice)   Nordic Countries (White Swan)

Germany (Blue Angel)   Japan (EcoMark)

United States (Scientific
Certification Systems)   United States (Green Seal)

Source: U.S. Congress, Office of Technology Assessment, *Green Products by Design: Choices for a Cleaner Environment*, OTA-E-541. (Washington, D.C.: U.S. Government Printing Office, 1992), p. 12.

Product categories for Japan's EcoMark Labeling Program are suggested by the Promotion Committee or members of the public. The Promotion Committee, in consultation with the Expert Committee, establishes standards for awarding EcoMark labels. The Expert Committee approves or disapproves applications for an award. The fees for environmental labels are based on the retail price of the product.

There are no government-sponsored labeling programs in the United States. However, computer manufacturers satisfying the requirements of the EPA's Energy Star Computer program can use the Energy Star logo to label their equipment. In addition, the U.S. Department of Energy governs the energy-efficiency labeling program for household appliances that consume about one-fifth of the electricity consumed in the United States. There are two major private green labeling programs in the United States. The Scientific Certification System, after verifying manufacturers' claims, allows manufacturers to use Green Cross symbols on their products. To reduce the environmental impacts of consumer products, Green Seal, an independent, nonprofit organization, issues its seals to products that meet its criteria. It uses the environmental impact evaluation of products to set standards for awarding a Green Seal. The criteria emphasize reduced toxic chemicals, reduced harmful effects on fish and wildlife and their habitats, reduced destruction of natural areas, and increased energy efficiency. The products must satisfy safety and performance standards in addition to environmental regulatory requirements.

To reduce environmental impacts of products during their life cycle and provide better information to consumers, the E.C. has introduced an eco-label award scheme. The E.C. Commission (consisting of 17 member states), the Consultation Forum (composed of stakeholders), Competent Bodies in each member state, the Regulatory Committee of Member States, and the Council of Ministers are involved in setting the award criteria and awarding process. Competent Bodies in each member state review applications for product categories received from any interested parties and send them to the E.C. Commission for approval. The E.C. Commission then allocates the product category to the Competent Body in a "lead country" to perform life-cycle analysis and come up with the awarding criteria using an indicative assessment matrix (Table 8.2). After draft criteria have been considered by the Consultation Forum and voted on by the Regulatory Committee, the Commission sends the criteria to the Committee of Member States for approval. The Council of Ministers has the final say on the awarding criteria and awarding process. Competent Bodies in each country evaluate the applications and test products. However, Competent Bodies of all countries must approve before Competent

Bodies in one country can award an ecolabel for a product. The public review of the awarding criteria and process is achieved through the Consultation Forum.

EFFECTIVENESS OF LABELING PROGRAMS

A comprehensive study of the effectiveness of environmental labeling programs can be found in *Determinants of Effectiveness for Environmental Certification and Labeling Program*.[5] The paramount goal of an environmental labeling program is to reduce environmental degradation of product consumption and use. Therefore, as a result of environmental labeling, the market share of environmentally harmful products should fall and environmentally benign products should rise. Consumer awareness stimulates change in consumer behavior and can be increased through effective promotions involving accurate definition of target audience, appropriate selection of media, generation of extensive media coverage, and adequate allocation of resources. Studies indicate that public education can significantly encourage a consumer with environmental awareness to use products with environmental labels.[6]

A consumer will be receptive to an environmental labeling program if he or she understands relevant issues. Issues, by themselves, may not cause a consumer to use a particular product unless he or she realizes how buying choices will affect the relevant environmental issues. This is possible only if product characteristics are clearly presented to the consumers. In addition, labeling programs should indicate to consumers what they can do in response to what they have read on the label. Labeling programs will be more effective if they come from credible sources. Different types of environmental labels have different impacts on consumers. The seal of approval presents condensed information that is easy to read and understand. Other formats provide more detailed information. There is a high likelihood of consumers perceiving environmental labels as endorsement of products.

Environmental labels, by themselves, may not change consumer behavior. However, integrated campaigns consisting of promotion, education, and incentives are found to be effective in changing consumer behavior. Consumers in the United States take into account environmental label along with price, quality, and brand while making purchasing decisions. Only a small proportion of environmentally conscious consumers buy products with environmental labels.

According to an often quoted CBS and *New York Times* poll conducted in March and April 1990, about three in four respondents said that the

TABLE 8.2
Indicative Assessment Matrix

Product Life Cycle

Environmental Field	Preproduction	Production	Distribution	Use	Disposal
Waste relevance					
Soil pollution					
Water contamination					
Air contamination					
Noise					
Energy consumption					
Effects on ecosystems					

Source: Environmental Protection Agency, *Status Report on the Use of Environmental Labels Worldwide,* EPA 742-R-9-93-001. (Washington, D.C.: Environmental Protection Agency, 1993), p. 100.

environment must be protected regardless of cost, up significantly from 1981. However, one dilemma facing several product managers is that green product sales are dwindling.[7] According to a *Wall Street Journal* and NBC poll conducted in July 1991, only 46 percent of those surveyed purchased any product during the six months preceding the poll specifically because the product or manufacturer had a good reputation for protecting the environment. In other words, consumers may be depicting themselves in a greener light than their actions indicate.

Green marketing has not been successful for all products. Consumers typically appreciate environmental considerations in those products where the effect on the environment is easy to see. According to a survey by the Roper Organization conducted in 1993, consumers value greenness in declining amounts in lawn and garden products, household products, paper products, gasoline, personal-care products, cars, and fast-food restaurants. The greenness value is less than the average for all personal-care products, cars, and fast-food restaurants. However, this does not mean that companies should give up on green marketing. According to the Roper Green Gauge Study, experience, price, quality, advertisements, environmental factors, and sponsorship are some factors that influence buying decisions. Between 1989 and 1993, environmental record increased by 6 points from 12 to 18 as a factor that influenced the buying behavior of a consumer. Quality and experience with brand fell during the same period.[8]

Manufacturers have launched several products that are environmentally superior. Some environmental labels have been considered worthwhile by several companies. However, environmental certification should not involve cost and effort that are too high. Labels that are likely to impact market share will be more receptive to companies. Improved corporate image is another consideration in the increased use of environmental labeling.

According to a study done for the EPA, the environmental certification program will not be successful if it does not have certain features including consumer education, government or third-party sponsorship, affiliation with other programs, consumer self-interest, and manufacturer self-interest.[9]

LABELING STANDARDS

The purpose of labels is to help consumers make informed buying decisions. Environmental labels also are likely to encourage manufacturers to improve the greenness of their products. A plethora of labels is likely to confuse the consumers. It is, therefore, essential to standardize existing labeling procedures. The International Standardization Organization (ISO) labeling standards try to achieve these goals.

ISO 14020 focuses on labeling standards and deals with product marks and their meanings. Labeling standards are likely to affect sales and advertising functions. ISO 14021 deals with general guidelines about environmental claims. ISO 14022 is intended to standardize environmental labels used in various countries. ISO 14024 deals with labeling programs run by governments or private organizations to communicate the greenness within a given product category, based on the environmental attributes. The environmental labels can convey information about environmental attributes of a product to consumers and can help to improve the environmental characteristics of a product. Nine labeling principles in ISO 14020 include:

Environmental labels must be factual and relevant.

The product must have environmental attributes mentioned on labels.

Claims made must be based on experimentation.

Criteria on which claims are based should be publicly available.

Evaluation should be based on the environmental impacts during the life cycle of a product or service.

Administrative work would be limited to proving conformance with the claims.

Labeling requirements should not create trade barriers.

Labeling should not discourage innovation.

Label criteria should be developed by consensus.

The paramount goal of labeling should be to create a level playing field for domestic as well as foreign manufacturers. Therefore, labeling requirements should specify environmental performance criteria rather than conformance to regulations. The testing should not impose restrictions such as language requirements, use of domestic testing facilities, and different costs for domestic and foreign products.

ISO 14021 presents guidelines for environmental claims. The standard is intended to produce accurate claims, encourage environmentally preferable products, and reduce barriers to trade. Terms such as recycled materials, preconsumer material, recyclable, and so on are likely to be defined in this standard.

ISO 14022 standardizes symbols universally. ISO 14023 deals with guidance for self-declaration of environmental claims. ISO 14024 establishes criteria for environmental labels used by the government and private sector organizations. The goal is to develop procedures and requirements for green labeling. This standard also tries to reduce international trade barriers by harmonizing labeling criteria and inclusion of interests of foreign producers in developing labeling procedures and standards. This standard also demands scientific methods for labeling purposes. The labeling criteria are to be developed by consensus, and environmental performance levels will be set realistically rather than arbitrarily. The labeling procedures will encourage use of life-cycle analysis.

ENVIRONMENTAL MARKETING CLAIMS

Environmental marketing claims can help consumers to choose environmentally benign products and can motivate manufacturers to produce products with fewer adverse effects on the environment. However, spurious and ambiguous marketing terms have disrupted the marketplace by creating consumer confusion. Environmental terms such as ozone-friendly, biodegradable, environmentally friendly, source reduced, and pH-balanced are hard to evaluate and mean different things to different people. As a result, a number of companies have voluntarily removed environmental labels from their products. For example, First Brands stopped publicizing Glad trash bags as degradable. Procter and Gamble removed the label "recyclable where facilities exist" from packaging. Mobil was forced to withdraw its claim that Hefty Steel Sak trash and tall kitchen bags were biodegradable. The Amoco Corporation consumer product division touted the recyclability of its polystyrene cups; however, the only plant, as of early 1990, that could recycle them was located near New York. Consequently, these cups were not recyclable for consumers in the other parts of the United States. Scores of such environmental claims have made consumers extremely skeptical of green products. According to a preliminary study of environmental claims, most claims were judged to be vague.[10] Many environmental terms used in marketing claims are not common words in everyday use. Almost all consumer products have some adverse environmental impacts. Therefore, consumers find environmental claims are hard to understand. According to a survey by Environmental Research Associates conducted in 1990, only 80 percent of adults understand the term "recyclable," 68 percent "biodegradable," 48 percent "environmentally friendly," and 16 percent "source reduction."[11]

Based on a search of a Productscan database containing 2,993 new product introductions from January 1989 to June 1992, the percent distribution of environmental marketing claims, by claim type, are as follows:[12]

Toxicity related	42.9
Recyclable	13.9
Degradable	13.1
Recycled	10.4
General environmental	10.3
Pollution	4.1
Wildlife conservation	1.7
Ozone related	1.4
Source reduced	1.3
Energy	0.9

The percent of products bearing environmental claims in each product category during the same period are as follows:

Foods	6.7
Health and beauty aids	25.9
Beverages	9.1
Pets and miscellaneous	6.3
Laundry and cleaning products	35.7
Paper	41.3
Pesticides and insecticides	24.5
Bags	52.3

The U.S. Federal Trade Commission (FTC) and a task force of attorneys general of 11 states — California, Florida, Massachusetts, Minnesota, Missouri, New York, Tennessee, Texas, Utah, Washington, and Wisconsin — have issued guidelines for environmental marketing.[13] The FTC guidelines comprise administrative interpretations of laws administered by the FTC and, therefore, are not legally enforceable. However, they provide an excellent starting point for marketers trying to comply with legal requirements. The FTC guidelines require marketers to disclose whether environmental claims refer to a product, package, or a component of either. It advises marketers not to overstate environmental claims. When comparative claims are made, FTC guidelines mandate that the marketer should substantiate the claim. Broad environmental claims should be avoided. The environmental claims about degradability, biodegradability, photodegradability, compostability, recyclability, recycled content, source reduction, and refillability should be consistent with FTC guidelines. The FTC guidelines do not preempt state laws, and several states have passed their own regulations relating to green marketing. The Green Report II issued by the attorneys general of 11 states provides guidance for environmental marketing so that companies do not violate state deceptive advertising laws. Like the FTC guidelines, the recommendations of the attorneys general are not laws and have neither the force nor the effect of law.

CONCLUSIONS

Manufacturers communicate environmental attributes of their products through green labeling. If consumers become skeptical about environmental claims mentioned on the labels, the labeling program will fail in its purpose. Therefore, stringent standards are required to regulate environmental labeling and claims. The FTC guidelines and the Green Report II are major regulations that govern environmental advertising and labeling in the United States. Federal, state, and town laws have made environmental advertising a nightmare for marketers in the United States. Therefore, the need for standards is most acute in this area.

APPENDIX

Green Report II Guidelines

Environmental claims should be specific, and not general, vague or broad.

Environmental claims should be precise about the environmental benefit that the product provides.

The promotion of existing or unadvertised green attribute should not create the perception that the product has been recently modified or improved.

The promotion of a product from which few environmentally harmful ingredients are removed should not give impression that the product is good for the environment in all respects.

Environmental attributes should be specific whether they refer to a product or its package.

Recycled content claim should specify whether it is post-consumer or recaptured factory material.

When comparative claims are made, they should be complete and should include basis for comparison.

Product life cycle assessment results should be used to advertise until uniform method for conducting them are developed.

Promotion of green certifications must be done with great care.

Source reduction claims should be specific, clear and complete.

Claims about disposableness should include availability of such option where the product is sold.

Products currently disposed in landfills or through incinerations should not claim to be degradable, biodegradable and so on. .

Compostable claim should not be made unless a significant portion of the product is currently composted.

Recyclability claim should not be made unless a significant portion of the product is currently recycled.

Product should specify what environmentally dangerous material has been eliminated instead of vague claims about disposal.

Claims should be substantive.

Insignificant and irrelevant claims should be avoided.

Single-use products promotion on the basis of environmental attributes should be done carefully.

All environmental claims should be based on reliable scientific evidence.

Federal Trade Commission
Environmental Marketing Guidelines

Guides for the Use of Environmental Marketing Claims
THE APPLICATION OF SECTION 5 OF THE FEDERAL TRADE
COMMISSION ACT TO
ENVIRONMENTAL ADVERTISING AND MARKETING
PRACTICES
Federal Trade Commission
July 1992

Table of Contents

G. Environmental Marketing Claims
    1. General Environmental Benefit Claims
    2. Degradable/Biodegradable/Photodegradable
    3. Compostable
    4. Recyclable
    5. Recycled Content
    6. Source Reduction
    7. Refillable
    8. Ozone Safe and Ozone Friendly

A. Statement of Purpose:

These guides represent administrative interpretations of laws administered by the Federal Trade Commission for the guidance of the public in conducting its affairs in conformity with legal requirements. These guides specifically address the application of Section 5 of the FTC Act to environmental advertising and marketing practices. They provide the basis for voluntary compliance with such laws by members of industry. Conduct inconsistent with the positions articulated in these guides may result in corrective action by the Commission under Section 5 if, after investigation, the Commission has reason to believe that the behavior falls within the scope of conduct declared unlawful by the statute.

B. Scope of Guides:

These guides apply to environmental claims included in labeling, advertising, promotional materials and all other forms of marketing, whether asserted directly or by implication, through words, symbols, emblems, logos, depictions, product brand names, or through any other means. The guides apply to any claim about the environmental attributes of a product or package in connection with the sale, offering for sale, or marketing of such product or package for personal, family or household use, or for commercial, institutional or industrial use.

Because the guides are not legislative rules under Section 18 of the FTC Act, they are not themselves enforceable regulations, nor do they have the force and effect of law. The guides themselves do not preempt regulation of other federal agencies or of state and local bodies governing the use of environmental marketing claims. Compliance with federal, state or local law and regulations concerning such claims, however, will not necessarily preclude Commission law enforcement action under Section 5.

C. Structure of the Guides:

The guides are composed of general principles and specific guidance on the use of environmental claims. These general principles and specific guidance are followed by examples that generally address a single deception concern. A given claim may raise issues that are addressed under more than one example and in more than one section of the guides.

In many of the examples, one or more options are presented for qualifying a claim. These options are intended to provide a "safe harbor" for marketers who want certainty about how to make environmental claims. They do not represent the only permissible approaches to qualifying a claim. The examples do not illustrate all possible acceptable claims or disclosures that would be permissible under Section 5. In addition, some of the illustrative disclosures may be appropriate for use on labels but not in print or broadcast advertisements and vice versa. In some instances, the guides indicate within the example in what context or contexts a particular type of disclosure should be considered.

D. Review Procedures:

Three years after the date of adoption of these guides, the Commission will seek public comment on whether and how the guides need to be modified in light of ensuing developments.

Parties may petition the Commission to alter or amend these guides in light of substantial new evidence regarding consumer interpretation of a claim or regarding substantiation of a claim. Following review of such a petition, the Commission will take such action as it deems appropriate.

E. Interpretation and Substantiation of Environmental Marketing Claims:

Section 5 of the FTC Act makes unlawful deceptive acts and practices in or affecting commerce. The Commission's criteria for determining whether an express or implied claim has been made are enunciated in the Commission's Policy Statement on Deception.[1] In addition, any party making an express or implied claim that presents an objective assertion about the environmental attribute of a product or package must, at the time the claim is made, possess and rely upon a reasonable basis substantiating the claim. A reasonable basis consists of competent and reliable evidence. In the context of environmental marketing claims, such substantiation will often require competent and reliable scientific evidence. For any test, analysis, research, study or other evidence to be "competent and reliable" for purposes of these guides, it must be conducted and evaluated in an objective manner by persons qualified to do so, using procedures generally accepted in the profession to yield accurate and reliable results. Further guidance on the reasonable basis standard is set forth in the Commission's 1983 Policy Statement on the Advertising Substantiation Doctrine. 49 Fed. Reg. 30,999 (1984); appended to Thompson Medical Co., 104 F.T.C. 648 (1984). These guides, therefore, attempt to preview policy in a relatively new context — that of environmental claims.

F. General Principles:

The following general principles apply to all environmental marketing claims, including, but not limited to, those described in Part G below. In addition, Part G contains specific guidance applicable to certain environmental marketing claims. Claims should comport with all relevant provisions of these guides, not simply the provision that seems most directly applicable.

1. Qualifications and Disclosures: The Commission traditionally has held that in order to be effective, any qualifications or disclosures such as those described in these guides should be sufficiently clear and prominent to prevent deception. Clarity of language, relative type size and proximity to the claim being qualified, and an absence of contrary claims that could undercut effectiveness, will maximize the likelihood that the qualifications and disclosures are appropriately clear and prominent.

2. Distinction Between Benefits of Product and Package: An environmental marketing claim should be presented in a way that makes clear whether the environmental attribute or benefit being asserted refers to the product, the product's packaging or to a portion or component of the product or packaging. In general, if the environmental attribute or benefit applies to all but minor, incidental components of a product or package, the claim need not be qualified to identify that fact. There may be exceptions to this general principle. For example, if an unqualified "recyclable" claim is made and the presence of the incidental component significantly limits the ability to recycle the product, then the claim would be deceptive.

Example 1: A box of aluminum foil is labeled with the claim "recyclable," without further elaboration. Unless the type of product, surrounding language, or other context of the phrase establishes whether the claim refers to the foil or the box, the claim is deceptive if any part of either the box or the foil, other than minor, incidental components, cannot be recycled.

Example 2: A soft drink bottle is labeled "recycled." The bottle is made entirely from recycled materials, but the bottle cap is not. Because reasonable consumers are likely to consider the bottle cap to be a minor, incidental component of the package, the claim is not deceptive. Similarly, it would not be deceptive to label a shopping bag "recycled" where the bag is made entirely of recycled material but the easily detachable handle, an incidental component, is not.

3. Overstatement of Environmental Attribute: An environmental marketing claim should not be presented in a manner that overstates the environmental attribute or benefit, expressly or by implication. Marketers should avoid implications of significant environmental benefits if the benefit is in fact negligible.

Example 1: A package is labeled, "50% more recycled content than before." The manufacturer increased the recycled content of its package from 2 percent recycled material to 3 percent recycled material. Although the claim is technically true, it is likely to convey the false impression that the advertiser has increased significantly the use of recycled material.

Example 2: A trash bag is labeled "recyclable" without qualification. Because trash bags will ordinarily not be separated out from other trash at the landfill or incinerator for recycling, they are highly unlikely to be used again for any purpose. Even if the bag is technically capable of being recycled, the claim is deceptive since it asserts an environmental benefit where no significant or meaningful benefit exists.

Example 3: A paper grocery sack is labeled "reusable." The sack can be brought back to the store and reused for carrying groceries but will fall apart after two or three reuses, on average. Because reasonable consumers are unlikely to assume that a paper grocery sack is durable, the unqualified claim does not overstate the environmental benefit conveyed to consumers. The claim is not deceptive and does not need to be qualified to indicate the limited reuse of the sack.

4. Comparative Claims: Environmental marketing claims that include a comparative statement should be presented in a manner that makes the basis for the comparison sufficiently clear to avoid consumer deception. In addition, the advertiser should be able to substantiate the comparison.

Example 1: An advertiser notes that its shampoo bottle contains "20% more recycled content." The claim in its context is ambiguous. Depending on contextual factors, it could be a comparison either to the advertiser's immediately preceding product or to a competitor's product. The advertiser should clarify the claim to make the basis for comparison clear, for example, by saying "20% more recycled content than our previous package." Otherwise, the advertiser should be prepared to substantiate whatever comparison is conveyed to reasonable consumers.

Example 2: An advertiser claims that "our plastic diaper liner has the most recycled content." The advertised diaper does have more recycled content, calculated as a percentage of weight, than any other on the market, although it is still well under 100% recycled. Provided the recycled content and the comparative difference between the product and those of competitors are significant and provided the specific comparison can be substantiated, the claim is not deceptive.

Example 3: An ad claims that the advertiser's packaging creates "less waste than the leading national brand." The advertiser's source reduction was implemented sometime ago and is supported by a calculation comparing the relative solid waste contributions of the two packages. The advertiser should be able to substantiate that the comparison remains accurate.

G. Environmental Marketing Claims:

Guidance about the use of environmental marketing claims is set forth below. Each guide is followed by several examples that illustrate, but do not provide an exhaustive list of, claims that do and do not comport with the guides. In each case, the general principles set forth in Part F above should also be followed.[2]

1. General Environmental Benefit Claims: It is deceptive to misrepresent, directly or by implication, that a product or package offers a general environmental benefit. Unqualified general claims of environmental benefit are difficult to interpret, and depending on their context, may convey a wide range of meanings to consumers. In many cases, such claims may convey that the product or package has specific and far-reaching environmental benefits. As explained in the Commission's Ad Substantiation Statement, every express and material, implied claim that the general assertion conveys to reasonable consumers about an objective quality, feature or attribute of a product must be substantiated. Unless this substantiation duty can be met, broad environmental claims should either be avoided or qualified, as necessary, to prevent deception about the specific nature of the environmental benefit being asserted.

Example 1: A brand name like "Eco-Safe" would be deceptive if, in the context of the product so named, it leads consumers to believe that the product has environmental benefits which cannot be substantiated by the manufacturer. The claim would not be deceptive if "Eco-Safe" were followed by clear and prominent qualifying language limiting the safety representation to a particular product attribute for which it could be substantiated, and provided that no other deceptive implications were created by the context.

Example 2: A product wrapper is printed with the claim "Environmentally Friendly." Textual comments on the wrapper explain that the wrapper is "Environmentally Friendly because it was not chlorine bleached, a process that has been shown to create harmful substances." The wrapper was, in fact, not bleached with chlorine. However, the production of the wrapper now creates and releases to the environment significant quantities of other harmful substances. Since consumers are likely to interpret the "Environmentally Friendly" claim, in combination with the textual explanation, to mean that no significant harmful substances are currently released to the environment, the "Environmentally Friendly" claim would be deceptive.

Example 3: A pump spray product is labeled "environmentally safe." Most of the product's active ingredients consist of volatile organic compounds (VOCs) that may cause smog by contributing to ground-level ozone formation. The claim is deceptive because, absent further qualification, it is likely to convey to consumers that use of the product will not result in air pollution or other harm to the environment.

2. Degradable/Biodegradable/Photodegradable: It is deceptive to misrepresent, directly or by implication, that a product or package is degradable, biodegradable or photodegradable. An unqualified claim that a product or package is degradable, biodegradable or photodegradable should be substantiated by competent and reliable scientific evidence that the entire product or package will completely break down and return to nature, i.e., decompose into elements found in nature within a reasonably short period of time after customary disposal.

Claims of degradability, biodegradability or photodegradability should be qualified to the extent necessary to avoid consumer deception about: (a) the product or package's ability to degrade in the environment where it is customarily disposed; and (b) the rate and extent of degradation.

Example 1: A trash bag is marketed as "degradable," with no qualification or other disclosure. The marketer relies on soil burial tests to show that the product will decompose in the presence of water and oxygen. The trash bags are customarily disposed of in incineration facilities or at sanitary landfills that are managed in a way that inhibits degradation by minimizing moisture and oxygen. Degradation will be irrelevant for those trash bags that are incinerated and, for those disposed of in landfills, the marketer does not possess adequate substantiation that the bags will degrade in a reasonably short period of time in a landfill. The claim is therefore deceptive.

Example 2: A commercial agricultural plastic mulch film is advertised as "Photodegradable" and qualified with the phrase, "Will break down into small pieces if left uncovered in sunlight." The claim is supported by competent and reliable scientific evidence that the product will break down in a reasonably short period of time after being exposed to sunlight and into sufficiently small pieces to become part of the soil. The qualified claim is not deceptive. Because the claim is qualified to indicate the limited extent of breakdown, the advertiser need not meet the elements for an unqualified photodegradable claim, i.e., that the product will not only break down, but also will decompose into elements found in nature.

Example 3: A soap or shampoo product is advertised as "biodegradable," with no qualification or other disclosure. The manufacturer has competent and reliable scientific evidence demonstrating that the product, which is customarily disposed of in sewage systems, will break down and decompose into elements found in nature in a short period of time. The claim is not deceptive.

3. Compostable: It is deceptive to misrepresent, directly or by implication, that a product or package is compostable. An unqualified claim that a product or package is compostable should be substantiated by competent and reliable scientific evidence that all the materials in the product or package will break down into, or otherwise become part of, usable compost (e.g., soil-conditioning material, mulch) in a safe and timely manner in an appropriate composting program or facility, or in a home compost pile or device.

Claims of compostability should be qualified to the extent necessary to avoid consumer deception. An unqualified claim may be deceptive: (1) if municipal composting facilities are not available to a substantial majority of consumers or communities where the package is sold; (2) if the claim misleads consumers about the environmental benefit provided when the product is disposed of in a landfill; or (3) if consumers misunderstand the claim to mean that the package can be safely composted in their home compost pile or device, when in fact it cannot.

Example 1: A manufacturer indicates that its unbleached coffee filter is compostable. The unqualified claim is not deceptive provided the manufacturer can substantiate that the filter can be converted safely to usable compost in a timely manner in a home compost pile or device, as well as in an appropriate composting program or facility.

Example 2: A lawn and leaf bag is labeled as "Compostable in California Municipal Yard Waste Composting Facilities." The bag contains toxic ingredients that are released into the compost material as the bag breaks down. The claim is deceptive if the presence of these toxic ingredients prevents the compost from being usable.

Example 3: A manufacturer indicates that its paper plate is suitable for home composting. If the manufacturer possesses substantiation for claiming that the paper plate can be converted safely to usable compost in a home compost pile or device, this claim is not deceptive even if no municipal composting facilities exist.

Example 4: A manufacturer makes an unqualified claim that its package is compostable. Although municipal composting facilities exist where the product is sold, the package will not break down into usable compost in a home compost pile or device. To avoid deception, the manufacturer should disclose that the package is not suitable for home composting.

Example 5: A nationally marketed lawn and leaf bag is labeled "compostable." Also printed on the bag is a disclosure that the bag is not designed for use in home compost piles. The bags are in fact composted in municipal yard waste composting programs in many communities around the country, but such programs are not available to a substantial majority of consumers where the bag is sold. The claim is deceptive since reasonable consumers living in areas not served by municipal yard waste programs may understand the reference to mean that composting facilities accepting the bags are available in their area. To avoid deception, the claim should be qualified to indicate the limited availability of such programs, for example, by stating, "Appropriate facilities may not exist in your area." Other examples of adequate qualification of the claim include providing the approximate percentage of communities or the population for which such programs are available.

Example 6: A manufacturer sells a disposable diaper that bears the legend, "This diaper can be composted where municipal solid waste composting facilities exist. There are currently [X number of] municipal solid waste composting facilities across the country." The claim is not deceptive, assuming that composting facilities are available as claimed and the manufacturer can substantiate that the diaper can be converted safely to usable compost in municipal solid waste composting facilities.

Example 7: A manufacturer markets yard waste bags only to consumers residing in particular geographic areas served by county yard waste composting programs. The bags meet specifications for these programs and are labeled, "Compostable Yard Waste Bag for County Composting Programs." The claim is not deceptive. Because the bags are compostable where they are sold, no qualification is required to indicate the limited availability of composting facilities.

4. Recyclable: It is deceptive to misrepresent, directly or by implication, that a product or package is recyclable. A product or package should not be marketed as recyclable unless it can be collected, separated or otherwise recovered from the solid waste stream for use in the form of raw materials in the manufacture or assembly of a new package or product. Unqualified claims of recyclability for a product or package may be made if the entire product or package, excluding minor incidental components, is recyclable. For products or packages that are made of both recyclable and non-recyclable components, the recyclable claim should be adequately qualified to avoid consumer deception about which portions or components of the product or package are recyclable.

Claims of recyclability should be qualified to the extent necessary to avoid consumer deception about any limited availability of recycling programs and collection sites. If an incidental component significantly limits the ability to recycle the product, the claim would be deceptive. A product or package that is made from recyclable material, but, because of its shape, size or some other attribute, is not accepted in recycling programs for such material, should not be marketed as recyclable.

Example 1: A packaged product is labeled with an unqualified claim, "recyclable." It is unclear from the type of product and other context whether the claim refers to the product or its package. The unqualified claim is likely to convey to reasonable consumers that all of both the product and its packaging that remain after normal use of the product, except for minor, incidental components, can be recycled. Unless each such message can be substantiated, the claim should be qualified to indicate what portions are recyclable.

Example 2: A plastic package is labeled on the bottom with the Society of the Plastics Industry (SPI) code, consisting of a design of arrows in a triangular shape containing a number and abbreviation identifying the component plastic resin. Without more, the use of the SPI symbol (or similar industry codes) on the bottom of the package, or in a similarly inconspicuous location, does not constitute a claim of recyclability.

Example 3: A container can be burned in incinerator facilities to produce heat and power. It cannot, however, be recycled into new products or packaging. Any claim that the container is recyclable would be deceptive.

Example 4: A nationally marketed bottle bears the unqualified statement that it is "recyclable." Collection sites for recycling the material in question are not available to a substantial majority of consumers or communities, although collection sites are established in a significant percentage of communities or available to a significant percentage of the population. The unqualified claim is deceptive since, unless evidence shows otherwise, reasonable consumers living in communities not served by programs may conclude that recycling programs for the material are available in their area. To avoid deception, the claim should be qualified to indicate the limited availability of programs, for example, by stating, "Check to see if recycling facilities exist in your area." Other examples of adequate qualifications of the claim include providing the approximate percentage of communities or the population to whom programs are available.

Example 5: A soda bottle is marketed nationally and labeled, "Recyclable where facilities exist." Recycling programs for material of this type and size are available in a significant percentage of communities or to a significant percentage of the population, but are not available to a substantial majority of consumers. The claim is deceptive since, unless evidence shows otherwise, reasonable consumers living in communities not served by programs may understand this phrase to mean that programs are available in their area. To avoid deception, the claim should be further qualified to indicate the limited availability of programs, for example, by using any of the approaches set forth in Example 4 above.

Example 6: A plastic detergent bottle is marketed as follows: "Recyclable in the few communities with facilities for colored HDPE bottles." Collection sites for recycling the container have been established in a half-dozen major metropolitan areas. This disclosure illustrates one approach to qualifying a claim adequately to prevent deception about the limited availability of recycling programs where collection facilities are not established in a significant percentage of communities or available to a significant percentage of the population. Other examples of adequate qualification of the claim include providing the number of communities with programs, or the percentage of communities or the population to which programs are available.

Example 7: A label claims that the package "includes some recyclable material." The package is composed of four layers of different materials, bonded together. One of the layers is made from the recyclable material, but the others are not. While programs for recycling this type of material are available to a substantial majority of consumers, only a few of those programs have the capability to separate out the recyclable layer. Even though it is technologically possible to separate the layers, the claim is not adequately qualified to avoid consumer deception. An appropriately qualified claim would be, "includes material recyclable in the few communities that collect multi-layer products." Other examples of adequate qualification of the claim include providing the number of communities with programs, or the percentage of communities or the population to which programs are available.

Example 8: A product is marketed as having a "recyclable" container. The product is distributed and advertised only in Missouri. Collection sites for recycling the container are available to a substantial majority of Missouri residents, but are not yet available nationally. Because programs are generally available where the product is marketed, the unqualified claim does not deceive consumers about the limited availability of recycling programs.

5. Recycled Content: A recycled content claim may be made only for materials that have been recovered or otherwise diverted from the solid waste stream, either during the manufacturing process (pre-consumer), or after consumer use (post-consumer). To the extent the source of recycled content includes pre-consumer material, the manufacturer or advertiser must have substantiation for concluding that the pre-consumer material would otherwise have entered the solid waste stream. In asserting a recycled content claim, distinctions may be made between pre-consumer and post-consumer materials. Where such distinctions are asserted, any express or implied claim about the specific pre-consumer or post-consumer content of a product or package must be substantiated. It is deceptive to misrepresent, directly or by implication, that a product or package is made of recycled material. Unqualified claims of recycled content may be made only if the entire product or package, excluding minor, incidental components, is made from recycled material. For products or packages that are only partially made of recycled material, a recycled claim should be adequately qualified to avoid consumer deception about the amount, by weight, of recycled content in the finished product or package.

Example 1: A manufacturer routinely collects spilled raw material and scraps from trimming finished products. After a minimal amount of reprocessing, the manufacturer combines the spills and scraps with virgin material for use in further production of the same product. A claim that the product contains recycled material is deceptive since the spills and scraps to which the claim refers are normally reused by industry within the original manufacturing process, and would not normally have entered the waste stream.

Example 2: A manufacturer purchases material from a firm that collects discarded material from other manufacturers and resells it. All of the material was diverted from the solid waste stream and is not normally reused by industry within the original manufacturing process. The manufacturer includes the weight of this material in its calculations of the recycled content of its products. A claim of recycled content based on this calculation is not deceptive because, absent the purchase and reuse of this material, it would have entered the waste stream.

Example 3: A greeting card is composed 30% by weight of paper collected from consumers after use of a paper product, and 20% by weight of paper that was generated after completion of the paper-making process, diverted from the solid waste stream, and otherwise would not normally have been reused in the original manufacturing process. The marketer of the card may claim either that the product "contains 50% recycled material," or may identify the specific pre-consumer and/or post-consumer content by stating, for example, that the product "contains 50% total recycled material, 30% of which is post-consumer material."

Example 4: A package with 20% recycled content by weight is labeled as containing "20% recycled paper." Some of the recycled content was composed of material collected from consumers after use of the original product. The rest was composed of overrun newspaper stock never sold to customers. The claim is not deceptive.

Example 5: A product in a multi-component package, such as a paperboard box in a shrink-wrapped plastic cover, indicates that it has recycled packaging. The paperboard box is made entirely of recycled material, but the plastic cover is not. The claim is deceptive since, without qualification, it suggests that both components are recycled. A claim limited to the paperboard box would not be deceptive.

Example 6: A package is made from layers of foil, plastic, and paper laminated together, although the layers are indistinguishable to consumers. The label claims that "one of the three layers of this package is made of recycled plastic." The plastic layer is made entirely of recycled plastic. The claim is not deceptive provided the recycled plastic layer constitutes a significant component of the entire package.

Example 7: A paper product is labeled as containing "100% recycled fiber." The claim is not deceptive if the advertiser can substantiate the conclusion that 100% by weight of the fiber in the finished product is recycled.

Example 8: A frozen dinner is marketed in a package composed of a cardboard box over a plastic tray. The package bears the legend, "package made from 30% recycled material." Each packaging component amounts to one-half the weight of the total package. The box is 20% recycled content by weight, while the plastic tray is 40% recycled content by weight. The claim is not deceptive, since the average amount of recycled material is 30%.

Example 9: A paper greeting card is labeled as containing 50% by weight recycled content. The seller purchases paper stock from several sources and the amount of recycled material in the stock provided by each source varies. Because the 50% figure is based on the annual weighted average of recycled material purchased from the sources after accounting for fiber loss during the production process, the claim is permissible.

6. Source Reduction: It is deceptive to misrepresent, directly or by implication, that a product or package has been reduced or is lower in weight, volume or toxicity. Source reduction claims should be qualified to the extent necessary to avoid consumer deception about the amount of the source reduction and about the basis for any comparison asserted.

Example 1: An ad claims that solid waste created by disposal of the advertiser's packaging is "now 10% less than our previous package." The claim is not deceptive if the advertiser has substantiation that shows that disposal of the current package contributes 10% less waste by weight or volume to the solid waste stream when compared with the immediately preceding version of the package.

Example 2: An advertiser notes that disposal of its product generates "10% less waste." The claim is ambiguous. Depending on contextual factors, it could be a comparison either to the immediately preceding product or to a competitor's product. The "10% less waste" reference is deceptive unless the seller clarifies which comparison is intended and substantiates that comparison, or substantiates both possible interpretations of the claim.

7. Refillable: It is deceptive to misrepresent, directly or by implication, that a package is refillable. An unqualified refillable claim should not be asserted unless a system is provided for: (1) the collection and return of the package for refill; or (2) the later refill of the package by consumers with product subsequently sold in another package. A package should not be marketed with an unqualified refillable claim, if it is up to the consumer to find new ways to refill the package.

Example 1: A container is labeled "refillable x times." The manufacturer has the capability to refill returned containers and can show that the container will withstand being refilled at least x times. The manufacturer, however, has established no collection program. The unqualified claim is deceptive because there is no means for collection and return of the container to the manufacturer for refill.

Example 2: A bottle of fabric softener states that it is in a "handy refillable container." The manufacturer also sells a large-sized container that indicates that the consumer is expected to use it to refill the smaller container. The manufacturer sells the large-sized container in the same market areas where it sells the small container. The claim is not deceptive because there is a means for consumers to refill the smaller container from larger containers of the same product.

8. Ozone Safe and Ozone Friendly: It is deceptive to misrepresent, directly or by implication, that a product is safe for or "friendly" to the ozone layer. A claim that a product does not harm the ozone layer is deceptive if the product contains an ozone-depleting substance.

Example 1: A product is labeled "ozone friendly." The claim is deceptive if the product contains any ozone-depleting substance, including those substances listed as Class I or Class II chemicals in Title VI of the Clean Air Act Amendments of 1990, Pub. L. No. 101-549, or others subsequently designated by EPA as ozone-depleting substances. Class I chemicals currently listed in Title VI are chlorofluorocarbons (CFCs), halons, carbon tetrachloride and 1,1,1-trichloroethane. Class II chemicals currently listed in Title VI are hydrochlorofluorocarbons (HCFCs).

Example 2: The seller of an aerosol product makes an unqualified claim that its product "Contains no CFCs." Although the product does not contain CFCs, it does contain HCFC-22, another ozone depleting ingredient. Because the claim "Contains no CFCs" may imply to reasonable consumers that the product does not harm the ozone layer, the claim is deceptive.

Example 3: A product is labeled "This product is 95% less damaging to the ozone layer than past formulations that contained CFCs." The manufacturer has substituted HCFCs for CFC-12, and can substantiate that this substitution will result in 95% less ozone depletion. The qualified comparative claim is not likely to be deceptive.

Endnotes

1.   Cliffdale Associates, Inc., 103 F.T.C. 110, at 176, 176 n.7, n.8, Appendix, reprinting letter dated Oct. 14, 1983, from the Commission to The Honorable John D. Dingell, Chairman, Committee on Energy and Commerce, U.S.House of Representatives (1984) ("Deception Statement").

2. These guides do not address claims based on a "lifecycle" theory of environmental benefit. Such analyses are still in their infancy and thus the Commission lacks sufficient information on which to base guidance at this time.

NOTES

1. U.S. Environmental Protection Agency, *Status Report on the Use of Environmental Labels Worldwide*, EPA 742-R-9-93-001. (Washington, D.C.: U.S. Environmental Protection Agency, 1993), p. ii.

2. United Nations Environment Programme, Industry and Environment Office, *Global Environmental Labelling: International Expert Seminar, Lesvos, Greece, 24-25 September 1991* (Working Group on Policies, Strategies and Instruments of the UNEP/IEO Cleaner Production Programme). (Paris: United Nations Environmental Programme).

3. U.S. Environmental Protection Agency, *Status Report on the Use of Environmental Labels Worldwide*, p. 16.

4. James Salzman, *Environmental Labeling in OECD Countries*. (Paris: Organization for Economic Cooperation and Development, 1991).

5. U.S. Environmental Protection Agency, *Determinants of Effectiveness for Environmental Certification and Labeling Programs*, EPA 742-R-94-001. (Washington, D.C.: U.S. Environmental Protection Agency, 1994).

6. U.S. Environmental Protection Agency, *Determinants of Effectiveness for Environmental Certification and Labeling Programs*, p. 94.

7. V. Reitman, "Green Product Sales Seem to be Wilting," *The Wall Street Journal,* May 18, 1992, p. B1.

8. Peter Stisser, "A Deeper Shade of Green," *American Demographics,* 16, March 1994, pp. 14–29.

9. U.S. Environmental Protection Agency, *Determinants of Effectiveness for Environmental Certification and Labeling Programs*, pp. 96–98.

10. N. Kangun, L. Carlson, and S. J. Gove, "Environmental Advertising Claims: A Preliminary Investigation," *Journal of Public Policy and Marketing,* 10 (Fall 1991): 47–58.

11. Environmental Research Associates, *The Environmental Report,* 1 (Fall 1990).

12. U.S. Environmental Protection Agency, *Evaluation of Environmental Marketing Terms in the United States*, EPA 741-R-92-003. (Washington, D.C.: U.S. Environmental Protection Agency, 1993), pp. 37, 53.

13. Attorneys General of California, Florida, Massachusetts, Minnesota, Missouri, New York, Tennessee, Texas, Utah, Washington, and Wisconsin, *The Green Report II: Recommendations for Responsible Environmental Advertising.* 1991. (Available from the Office of the Attorney General for the respective state).

IV

PERFORMANCE EVALUATION

9

Environmental Performance Metrics

Environmental performance has a significant impact on the stock market value of a company. The growing number of environmental regulations, public pressures, constantly changing environmental laws, proliferating litigations, and increasing environmental liabilities are of serious concern to investors. As a result, more investors are evaluating the environmental performance of companies. However, unlike financial data, environmental information is both quantitative and qualitative and also is subject to differing interpretations. Typically, large organizations such as Reuters, Telerate, Quotron, Dunn and Bradstreet, and Standard and Poor provide financial information about corporations. However, small organizations are providing the bulk of environmental information. Several internet sites provide environmental information. For example, the Econet site on the internet provides information about companies boycotted because of their poor environmental or social performance. In addition, such organizations as the Council on Economic Priorities; Investor Responsibility Research Center (IRRC); and Kinder, Lyndenberg, Domini & Co. have developed indicators on environmental performance.

PUBLIC SOURCES OF
ENVIRONMENTAL INFORMATION

There are several sources of environmental information about companies. More than 20 regulatory agencies and their contractors collect and disseminate information about the environmental performance of companies. The Environmental Protection Agency (EPA) and the Securities and Exchange Commission (SEC) require companies to submit a variety of environmental data. Information from these databases can be obtained by filing Freedom of Information Act requests. Companies themselves are also valuable sources of environmental information. Environmental reports published by companies contain information about environmental missions, policies, programs, achievements, and performance results. Form 10-K filings by companies with the SEC contain reliable information about the environmental indicators of a company.

The Comprehensive Environmental Response and Compensation, and Liability Act, commonly known as the Superfund law, requires the EPA to identify hazardous waste sites that pose the greatest threat to public health and the environment and designate these sites as National Priorities List (NPL) sites. Many of these sites were formed as a result of deposition of industrial wastes by several companies. The costs of cleanup of these sites are the responsibility of companies identified by the EPA as potentially responsible parties. The Site Enforcement Tracking System maintained by the EPA lists the companies responsible for various sites. As of September 30, 1995, the EPA has designated 1,290 sites on the NPL. According to the EPA, the cost of cleaning up a site is roughly $26 million. However, cleanup costs to a company depend upon a variety of factors, including the type and degree of contamination, the volume of waste a company has disposed of at a site, the number of other companies responsible for the site, and the extent of cooperation between the responsible parties and the EPA.

The Resource Conservation and Recovery Act (RCRA) introduced a permit system to treat, store, or dispose of hazardous wastes. Such a permit system requires cleanup of wastes at active industrial sites. The EPA maintains a database called the Resource Conservation and Recovery Information System National Oversight Database that contains information about sites for which a company is required to conduct a RCRA facility investigation and assess the degree of contamination. Although every site cataloged in this system may not require cleanup, costs of such an investigation are usually significant.

The RCRA authorizes the EPA to close down a facility by denying its permit if a facility does not manage its hazardous waste properly. RCRA permit denial information is stored in the Resource Conservation and Recovery Information System National Oversight Database.

The Outer Continental Shelf Lands Act authorizes the Minerals Management Service (MMS) of the Department of the Interior to close down an offshore rig or production facility if it can cause oil spills or explosions. Data about such shut-ins can be obtained from the MMS's National Potential Incident of Noncompliance list and also from the Production Inspection and Drills Inspection database.

The Toxic Release Inventory (TRI) information to be submitted to the EPA under the Emergency Planning and Community Right-to-Know Act (EPCRA) is a valuable source of data on pollution. The purpose of the EPCRA is to encourage planning for emergency responses to possible accidents and to inform the public about possible hazards in their communities. The EPCRA requires manufacturers with ten or more employees who process more than 25,000 pounds or use more than 10,000 pounds of any reportable chemicals to report the amounts of more than 300 toxic chemicals and 20 chemical categories that manufacturers release to the environment or transfer to off-site facilities. The EPCRA also requires the EPA to make these reports available to the public. The TRI database can provide information by site about listed toxic chemicals released, treated, recycled, or burned for energy recovery. In addition, various source reduction techniques employed by companies to reduce pollution also are available from the TRI Public Data Release.

The National Response Center maintains an Emergency Notification System database that contains information about accidental oil and chemical spills. This database contains data about carrier fluid and active chemical compounds. The Aerometric Information Retrieval System database contains information about air permit compliance. The Occupation Safety and Health Administration of the U.S. Department of Labor collects and analyzes data about worker safety and health-related violations.

Broader and stronger enforcement of environmental laws makes compliance with environmental laws and regulations a significant indicator of environmental performance. The documents submitted to the SEC contain valuable information about a company's environmental performance. Form 10-K can provide information about environmental capital expenditures and litigation. U.S. securities laws mandate companies to disclose expenditures or liabilities that may have a "material" impact on the financial or competitive position of a company. Individual enforcement proceedings with costs over $100,000 and environmental litigation that may have a significant financial impact must be disclosed in Form 10-K. In addition, recent changes to accounting regulations require corporate financial officers to designate environmental remediation and compliance costs as annual expenses.

Newspapers, journals, and trade publications contain information about environmental events. Computer-based literature searches can provide extensive information about a company's environmental results. Statistical reports published by various industry associations also provide valuable environmental information about a company. Various EPA publications, the TRI Public Data Release, the Corporate Environmental Profiles Directory published by the IRRC, and other environmental publications are some public sources of environmental information.

MEASURING ENVIRONMENTAL PERFORMANCE

ISO 14001 requires documented procedures for measuring improvements made to achieve targets and goals. Environmental performance indicators are required to measure progress toward achieving goals and targets on a consistent basis. Environmental performance indicators should be developed when a company establishes its goals and targets. A baseline needs to be defined to estimate the progress made. Companies have developed various environmental indicators to gauge the performance of divisions and company facilities. However, no single measure can adequately measure environmental performance, which involves multiple measures. Establishment of environmental measures encourages management and employees to identify areas for improvement. Emissions, compliance, and environmental improvements are some categories of environmental performance measures. Environmental indicators could be qualitative or quantitative.

According to Marcus Peacock, three environmental principles need to be considered when developing environmental performance measures.[1] First, environmental measures should measure changes so that companies will be encouraged to improve environmental performance. Second, employees should consider environmental measures to be fair. Fairness for many employees means consistent application across functions and facilities and regular reevaluation. If measures are not fair, there is a tendency for cheating. Finally, companies should identify offsetting measures. For example, if employee performance is measured in terms of fines and legal violations, there is a tendency to withhold noncompliance. However, if a goal is set in terms of timely reporting of violations, chances of reporting noncompliance are higher. Also, legal violation may be measuring the regulator's efforts. Several issues also impact performance measures. Simpler measures are easy to understand, and complex measures generally are comprehensive. Because quantitative measures are considered objective and fair, quantitative measures should be preferred over qualitative measures. However, community perception about a firm and other indicators are hard to express in quantitative measures. Another moot point is whether to measure means or ends. Result-oriented firms typically like to measure ends or outcomes, but industry association codes and ISO 14000 focus on process. Therefore, it is a good idea to develop measures of both means and ends. Similarly, should measures focus on conservation or compliance? Most industry standards want companies to go beyond compliance. Therefore, conservation measures should be preferred over compliance measures.

Regulators and most environmental groups use TRI reports to gauge the environmental performance of a facility. However, TRI data ignore the risk associated with wastes. Therefore, although waste indicators mandated by laws and regulations may show the environmental performance of a company, they are not suitable to be used for internal decision making to improve environmental performance. Therefore, 3M has established indicators that are accurate and reproducible, adjusted to production volume, and related to waste that can be reduced through source reduction and reuse and recycling.[2] Performance measures relate to total waste generated, including that which is treated and disposed of. In addition, measures could be used as a goal for a division or facility. Measures developed also should motivate employees to improve environmental degradation. One indicator used to measure divisional performance is the waste ratio calculated by dividing waste by total output, that is, waste/(waste + by-product + product).

Marc Epstein suggests ten dimensions for measuring corporate environmental performance: corporate strategy, consideration of environmental factors in product design, procedures to identify environmental impacts, management information systems for internal reporting, an internal environmental auditing system, an external reporting and auditing system, a costing system, a capital budgeting system, integration of environmental measures for performance evaluation, and implementation of environmental strategy.[3] According to Epstein, environmental leaders use life-cycle assessments; are sensitive to environmental impacts; consider environmental impacts of investments, processes, and products; and move toward sustainable development. On the other hand, laggards do not consider environmental impacts, comply with regulations weakly, and cause continuous environmental violations.

Epstein makes several observations about the environmental practices of organizations.[4] Many companies do not use financial tools for environmental decision making even though such tools are used in other parts of the company. The environmental departments typically work in isolation. Environmental know-how rarely is transferred between departments or facilities. The environmental impacts of products, processes, and decisions rarely are considered. Environmental liabilities are defined very narrowly. Most organizations emphasize compliance rather than pollution prevention. Environmental costs rarely are ascertained, and there is very little motivation to improve environmental results. Some highly polluting companies have the best environmental management systems. Many companies are trying to use existing analytical tools to make environmental decisions. Many are using superior environmental performance as their core value. More companies are using life-cycle analysis to identify the cradle-to-grave environmental impacts of their products. Environmental disclosures have improved significantly in recent years. Environmental auditing is becoming a common practice among organizations.

Northern Telecom in cooperation with Arthur D. Little has developed an Environmental Performance Index that measures the overall environmental performance of the corporation.[5] The purpose of this index is to help track environmental improvements against goals and report them to stakeholders. The index is designed to summarize the large volume of data into a single yardstick that will represent the overall environmental performance. This index considers the environmental impacts of operations and also the progress made toward environmental goals. The index uses performance parameters relating to the compliance, environmental releases, resource consumption, and environmental remediation. Each of these parameters is weighted based on importance, added, and normalized appropriately. This index can be used to measure the performance of a company and its individual units.

The IRRC compiles and disseminates a variety of environmental performance indicators.[6] Some indicators include national priority list sites, RCRA corrective actions, number of RCRA permit denials, number of MMS facility shut-ins, toxic chemical releases and transfers, oil spills, and penalties for violations of various environmental laws and regulations. NPL sites for which a company or its subsidiary has been identified as a potentially responsible party by the EPA represent the possibility of future environmental liability. Even though NPL sites are not, by themselves, indicators of poor environmental performance of a company, these sites may mean millions of dollars of cleanup and legal costs. RCRA corrective actions required represent the facilities that need to be investigated for contamination in order to retain an RCRA permit. Even though corrective actions alone may not represent the ultimate cleanup of a facility, the number of RCRA corrective actions means millions of dollars of investigative costs for environmental contaminations and probable cleanups. The number of RCRA permit denials indicates the number of facilities of a company that were not permitted to operate because the EPA determined that a facility was not equipped to properly manage hazardous wastes. The number of MMS facility shut-ins represents the number of times an offshore oil drilling or production facility was shut down because of a determination by the MMS of a high likelihood of oil spills or explosions. Quantities of toxic chemicals released and transferred are another indicator of a company's environmental performance. Number of spills and penalties paid for violation of environmental laws and regulations are other measures of environmental performance. In order to facilitate comparison between companies, all indicators are normalized by sales.

Because various indicators published by the IRRC have very little relevance from an ecological sustainability standpoint, the IRRC plans to add five new generic sustainability indicators: energy consumption in gigajoules per unit of production, water consumption in cubic feet per unit of production, units of raw material per unit of output, total waste generated per unit of production, and country of origin for major production.[7] However, this is not a new initiative. DuPont already reports an index to represent energy use per unit of production. Dow Chemical reports its emission of global warming gases in terms of carbon dioxide equivalents. IBM reports its global generation of wastes and the percentage of these that it recycles.

The report prepared by the President's Commission on Environmental Quality, based on various demonstration projects at different companies, used the following environmental metrics:[8]

AT&T	SARA 313 TCA (pounds/year)
Chevron	Environmental operating costs
Dow Chemical	Waste in effluent (pounds/year)
DuPont	Ammonium sulphate (pounds/year)
Ford	Trichloroethylene (pounds/part cleaned)
GE	Chemicals used (pounds/year) and water consumption (gallons/week)
International Paper	Raw material usage
Merck	SARA 313 releases and off-site transfers for disposal (pounds/year)
MMM	Waste/total output

| Procter & Gamble | Total waste management (raw materials lost, production losses, treatment costs, etc.) |
| US Generating | Federal and state regulatory standards, local zoning requirements. |

The Chemical Manufacturers Association's Responsible Care program requires its members to self-evaluate on community awareness and emergency response, pollution prevention, process safety, product stewardship, employee health and safety, and distribution codes.

Some major metrics used to evaluate implementation of the community awareness and emergency response code include evaluation of employee concerns; training; employee awareness about environmental programs; effectiveness of the employee communication program; outreach programs; dialogue with the local community; ease with which one can learn about the company's products, processes, and facilities; effect of accidents and other emergencies on employees and community members; emergency response plan; training to respond to emergencies; emergency exercises; and sharing of information about emergency response plans.

The pollution prevention code encourages waste reduction and better waste management practices. Some measures used to evaluate progress in implementing this code include management commitment; emissions to the environment; impacts of emissions on employees and the general public; training about the potential risks of products, operations, and so on; establishment of waste reduction goals; communication with employees and the public; encouragement of waste reduction by others; continuous improvement of waste management practices; evaluation of waste management practices of suppliers and contractors; and prompt corrective actions.

The process safety code is intended to eliminate fires, explosions, and accidents. Its purpose is to enhance safety through improved operations and maintenance. Some metrics used to evaluate implementation of the process safety code include senior management involvement through establishment of policy and adequate resource allocation; review of results against targets; performance monitoring and prompt corrective actions; dissemination of safety information; documentation of process technology; documentation of safety hazards; actions to reduce process risk; actions to improve plant safety; evaluation of impacts of new and expanded facilities on employees, community, and the environment; conformance of design, construction, and maintenance to industry codes; safety reviews of new and modified facilities; documentation of maintenance programs; evaluation of employee safety skills; and employee training.

The product stewardship code considers health, safety, and environmental impacts of products from cradle to grave and ensures their incorporation in design, manufacture, distribution, use, recycling, and disposal of products. Some environmental performance measures for this code include senior management commitment, goal setting, allocation of resources, dissemination of information about product safety, risk evaluation of existing and new products, consideration of environmental impacts in product and process design, employee training, supplier evaluation, and dissemination of risk management information to customers.

The employee health and safety code encourages steps to improve the health and safety of employees. Some metrics used to evaluate this code include management commitment, employee involvement, employee health and safety programs at contractors' sites, written safety procedures, conformance to safety procedures, review of safety performance, assessment of potential risks, health surveillance appropriate to the facility, facility improvement to enhance the health and safety of employees, maintenance programs, injury investigations and corrective actions, health training, and availability of medical emergency assistance at the facility.

The distribution code is intended to reduce environmental mishaps during distribution of products. This code focuses on improved transportation and storage of goods. Some indicators used to evaluate adherence to the distribution code include assessment of distribution risks, investigation of accidents and prompt corrective actions, conformance against standards, training of employees, dissemination of safety information to contractors and carriers, evaluation of carriers, documentation of transportation procedures, dissemination of information about proper storage and transportation of products, emphasis on safety and regulatory compliance, communication about emergency response procedures, and communication with the public on safety and emergency preparedness.

The Malcolm Baldrige National Quality Award Examination Categories and Items provides a comprehensive list of factors for evaluating a company for its quality management system.[9] Using 1991 criteria as a basis, we can use the following factors to evaluate the environmental management system of a company:

Leadership
    Senior executive leadership
    Green values

Management of environmental, health, and safety functions
Public responsibility

Information and analysis
Environmental management information system
Competitive comparisons and benchmarks
Analysis of environmental data and information

Strategic environmental planning
Planning process
Goals and plans

Human resources utilization
Human resources management
Employee participation
Environmental education and training
Environmental performance measurement and recognition system
Employee safety and well-being

Environmental impacts of products and services
Design and introduction of green products.
Environmental process analysis
Continuous improvement
Life-cycle analysis
Documentation
Supplier evaluation

Environmental results
Environmental performance of products and services
Environmental results of processes, facilities, and other services
Supplier environmental performance

Stakeholder satisfaction
Evaluating stakeholder needs and expectations
Stakeholder relationship management
Environmental standards for plants, facilities, products, and services
Commitment to stakeholders
Dispute resolution for environmental excellence
Evaluating stakeholder satisfaction
Stakeholder satisfaction results
Stakeholder satisfaction comparison

The European Green Table has developed various indicators for specific industries, such as petrochemicals, oil refining, paper, and aluminum smelting.[10] Some indicators for a petrochemical facility include:

Materials use   Raw material weight
Energy   Gigajoules, carbon dioxide, sulfur dioxide
Emissions
  Air   Process sulfur dioxide, nitrous oxides, volatile organic
                compounds, process carbon dioxide, hydrocarbons, and
                so on
  Water   Pollutants in effluent water
  Soil   Percent land investigated, contaminated, contaminated
                and restored
Waste   Solid waste, hazardous solid waste, waste classified by
                method of disposal
Incident   Noncompliance fines, noncompliance incidents, number
                of complaints

All data except those relating to incident are normalized using output weight.

Another important area relating to performance metrics is ratings of companies based on environmental risk. A number of financial institutions have developed systematic procedures to evaluate environmental risks of companies for the purpose of lending and investing. Ken Beecham and Chris Burgess suggest that environmental risk ratings should be intuitively obvious, easy to understand, comparable across and within industries, useful to likely users, easy to prepare and update, and capable of improvement by a company.[11] They suggest factors such as the risk of legal violations, the risk of site contamination, the risk of environmental impacts on markets, and the management capability to rate companies. Eco-Rating International uses such factors as environmental impact, logistics, infrastructure, greenness of products, compliance, research and development environmental risks, management, and soft issues to rate companies on environmental risk.[12]

STANDARDS OF THE INTERNATIONAL STANDARDIZATION ORGANIZATION

Performance evaluation involves comparison of achievements against goals and objectives. Performance evaluation is an element of a management system that involves establishing mission, planning, setting goals, reviewing performance against goals, and taking corrective action. The ISO 14031 Environmental Performance Evaluation (EPE) describes indicators to evaluate environmental performance. If something cannot be measured, it cannot be improved. Section 4.4 of ISO 14001 requires companies to establish procedures to examine and measure performance on a regular basis. The measurement and monitoring should focus on compliance. These measures should be objective and should be able to measure performances consistent with environmental policy and objectives. ISO 14004 presents a list of performance criteria: management systems, employee responsibilities, property management, suppliers, contractors, product stewardship, environmental communication, regulatory relationships, environmental accidents, environmental training, process risk reduction, pollution prevention, capital projects, process changes, hazardous materials management, waste management, air quality, energy, and transportation.

Environmental performance measures should be consistent with policies and objectives and also with government regulations and permits. They should be objective and easy to measure. Because management performance is measured in terms of progress made in these indicators, they should represent environmental performance.

The EPE standard only presents indicators; it does not specify what the performance levels should be. The purpose of these indicators is not to present a comparison of one company's performance against another company's performance. These indicators should be applicable to all types of organizations and should stimulate improvements in the environmental results. They should highlight opportunities for pollution reduction and should reflect some measure of efficiency.

The goal of the EPE standard is to provide objective and valid indicators of environmental performance. The performance measurement process should include procedures for data collection, data analysis, data conversion to performance indicators, comparison of performance against goals, and methods to communicate environmental performance.

There are several differences between EPE and auditing. Environmental auditing typically is done by a third party, whereas EPE is a line function. Environmental auditing typically is done on a periodic basis, whereas EPE is done on a continuous basis. Environmental auditing verifies conformance of environmental management systems to criteria set by the organization; EPE is about environmental performance.

ISO 14031 deals with the process of EPE. The EPE will focus on planning; management factors; the relationship of environmental aspects to EPE; indicators for planning, management, and environmental aspects; associations among planning, management, and environmental aspects; and evaluation of environmental performance. Management plays a significant role in environmental results. However, management evaluation often involves subjective factors. Operational performance measures include emissions and waste generation. Typically, operational indicators need to be normalized to account for changing production rates. Measuring the environmental performance is hard because several factors affect environmental degradation. Some environmental performance indicators include tons of emissions generated, pounds of hazardous waste generated, percentage reductions in spills, and number of employees trained.

Implementation of EPE begins with management commitment. A task force or an outside consultant needs to be hired to study the current system and identify what changes need to be made to develop indicators. Companies in industries may be studied to develop indicators. Management should decide what to measure. Data gathering and analysis procedures need to be decided. Environmental aspects need to be studied in terms of their impacts. The help of environmental groups also may be sought in developing indicators.

BALANCED SCORECARD

Environmental metrics have strong effects on the behavior of managers and employers. Therefore, metrics should be linked to performance measures. A balanced scorecard is a suitable approach to linking environmental metrics to performance measures.[13] Because each organization is unique, it needs to develop its own tailor-made approach to building a balanced scorecard (Figure 9.1). The first step is preparation to develop a balanced scorecard. The goal is to identify the business unit or site for which a scorecard needs to be developed. Typically, a business unit should have its own customers, production facilities, and financial performance measures. The next step is to interview top managers. During this step, a company executive or an outside consultant discusses with top management the environmental policy, environmental aspects, compliance requirements, objectives, and environmental programs. The top management also will be asked about environmental measures. During this step, interviews will be conducted with stakeholders, such as major shareholders, suppliers, union leaders, and customers, to learn about their expectations about environmental performance. The next step is a workshop. During this step, environmental policy, environmental aspects, compliance requirements, objectives, and programs will be debated and a consensus reached. The group then will deliberate changes that will be felt by stakeholders — employees, shareholders, financial institutions, customers and consumers, local communities, environmental groups, media, and regulators — if the company succeeds in meeting goals and objectives. The critical success factors then will be identified. The group then will formulate a tentative balanced scorecard containing indicators that will measure accomplishments in environmental policy and objectives. Once tentative scorecards are made, a second round of interviews with top executives will be conducted to elicit their opinions about indicators and also to discuss issues involved in implementing the scorecard. A second round of workshops attended by top management and their subordinates and many middle management personnel will be held to debate environmental policy and objectives and the tentative scorecard. During this workshop, participants will be asked to come up with stretch objectives for each environmental performance measure and targeted rates of improvements. Top management again will deliberate environmental policy, objectives, and measures to stretch measures on the scorecard and develop action programs. The top management will develop an implementation program, which will involve connecting the measures to databases and information systems, communication of scorecard to employees, and development of metrics for lower level management. Reviews should be done annually as a part of environmental strategic planning, policy revision, objective setting, and resource allocation processes.

Environmental programs can be evaluated in terms of their effectiveness. For example, program effectiveness can be measured in terms of appropriateness of the program to the stakeholders, such as shareholders, employees, customers and suppliers, and regulators. Operational effectiveness can be measured in terms of structural and process measures. Costs can be used to gauge the cost-effectiveness of the program. Optimal use of technology to reduce pollution gives an indication about the technological effectiveness of the program. A decrease in the environmental degradations and an increase in the environmental improvements measure the impact of the program on the stakeholders. Communication effectiveness can be measured in terms of interaction between the company, regulators, community, employees, and customers.

CONCLUSIONS

What you measure is what you get. Environmental metrics are, therefore, important elements of an effective environmental program. Without appropriate environmental metrics, an organization cannot focus its efforts to improve environmental results. Even though there are not many companies with an effective environmental metrics program, more companies are recognizing the value of such a program in delegating environmental efforts and increasing employee involvement.

FIGURE 9.1
Linking Environmental Metrics to Environmental Policy and Objectives

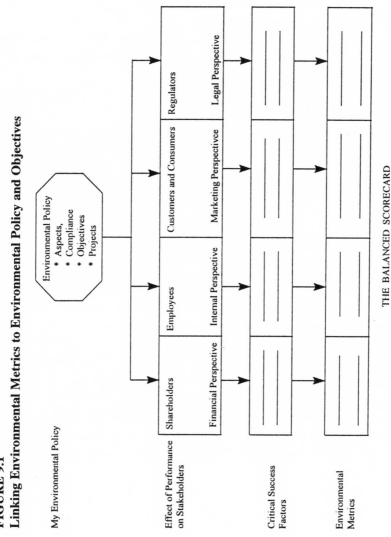

NOTES

1. Marcus Peacock, "Developing Environmental Performance Measures," *Industrial Engineering*, 25 (September 1993): 20–23.

2. Thomas W. Zosel, "3M's Methods for Measuring Actual Results." In *GEMI'95 Conference Proceedings, Environment and Sustainable Development: Making It Happen.* (Washington, D.C.: Global Environmental Management Initiative, 1995), pp. 43–48.

3. Marc J. Epstein, *Corporate Environmental Performance: Best Practices for Costing and Managing an Effective Environmental Strategy.* (Chicago, Ill.: Irwin Professional Publishing, 1996), p. 235.

4. Epstein, *Corporate Environmental Performance*, p. 239.

5. *HTTP://WWW.NT.COM/COOL/ENVIRON/EPI/SUMMARY.HTML*, Internet.

6. Investor Responsibility Research Center, *Corporate Environmental Profiles Directory.* (Washington, D.C.: Investor Responsibility Research Center, 1993).

7. Scott A. Fenn, "Sustainable Development — Beyond the Buzzword to Measurement." In *GEMI'95 Conference Proceedings, Environment and Sustainable Development: Making It Happen.* (Washington, D.C.: Global Environmental Management Initiative, 1995), pp. 82–87.

8. Quality Environmental Management Subcommittee, *Total Quality Management: A Framework for Pollution Prevention.* (Washington, D.C.: President's Commission on Environmental Quality, 1993), p. 94.

9. *1991 Application Guidelines: National Quality Award.* (Gaithersburg, Md.: National Institute of Standards and Technology, 1990), p. 5.

10. European Green Table, *Environmental Performance Indicators in Industry.* (Oslo: European Green Table, 1993).

11. Ken Beecham and Chris Burgess, "Environmental Risk Ratings," *Capital Market Strategies,* 2 (1994): 1–7.

12. E. Bruce Harrison, *Going Green: How to Communicate Your Company's Environmental Commitment.* (Homewood, Ill.: Business One Irwin, 1993), p. 109.

13. R. S. Kaplan and D. P. Norton, "Putting the Balanced Scorecard to Work," *Harvard Business Review*, 71 (September–October 1993): 134–47.

10

Environmental Accounting and Capital Budgeting

Environmental costs typically do not add any value. They represent wasted raw materials, labor, and overhead. Because effective management decisions can either reduce or eliminate environmental costs, their accurate recording is essential. Even though companies complain about rising environmental costs, the conventional management accounting system hides them in overhead accounts. In the words of Frank P. Popoff, chief executive officer and chairman of the Dow Chemical Company, "they build mountains of waste that they never account for."[1] Companies are discovering that an environmental accounting system can guide managers to improve their environmental performance and reduce their costs. Accurate environmental costs can help companies to develop cost-effective environmental strategies. Strategic management decisions such as product design, process design, facility location, procurement of materials, capital investments, cost reduction, waste management, product mix, and product pricing require accurate environmental costs. Environmentally effective decisions can provide competitive advantage. Better accounting of environmental costs can help management to realize potential benefits of pollution prevention.

TYPES OF ENVIRONMENTAL ACCOUNTING

There are three types of environmental accounting. The environmental accounting at the national level deals with accounting of consumption of natural resources. Financial accounting at the firm level focuses on reporting of environmental liabilities and environmental costs. Management accounting that helps management to identify, collect, and analyze costs typically is used for internal purposes. Unlike financial accounting that has to satisfy the requirements of the Financial Accounting Standards Boards (FASB) and generally accepted accounting principles, management accounting does not have to meet any external guidelines; it is designed to support management decisions.

National Accounting

According to Maureen Cropper and Wallace Oates, costs of environmental regulations are "the change in consumer and producer surpluses associated with regulations and with any and/or income changes that may result."[2] Costs of environmental regulations include monitoring and enforcement costs; capital and operating costs of compliance; other environmental regulatory costs, such as legal, managerial and disrupted production costs; benefits (negative costs) of worker health, innovation, and natural resource inputs; general equilibrium effects, such as product substitution, impediments to investment, and innovation; and transactional costs such as unemployment, capital underutilization, and social costs (job losses and economic security impacts).[3]

Direct compliance costs have been rising steadily in the United States in absolute terms and as a percentage of gross national product (GNP). Total costs of pollution control rose from $33,094 million in 1972 to $141,375 million in 1992. As a percentage of GNP, pollution control costs rose from 0.88 percent in 1972 to 2.32 percent in 1992. This cost is expected to reach 2.61 percent of GNP in the year 2000.[4]

Financial Accounting

Specific guidelines regarding reporting of environmental liabilities have been formulated, and an interested reader should refer to them to understand their full implications. The Statement of Financial Accounting Standards (SFAS) No. 5: Accounting for Contingencies was issued in 1975. SFAS 5 was intended to address contingencies in general. Based on SFAS 5, environmental liabilities should be accrued for in the financial statements if the loss is likely to occur and can be reasonably estimated. The event must be indicated in the notes to the financial statements if the loss is possible. If estimating the potential liability is hard, it must be so indicated. If loss probability is low, no disclosure is required.

FASB Interpretation No.14: Reasonable Estimation of the Amount of a Loss: FIN 14, a FASB interpretation of SFAS 5, states that a most likely estimate of loss within a range of losses should be accrued. If there is no better estimate of loss than any others, the minimum of the range of amounts should be accrued.

Emerging Issues Task Force (EITF) 89-13: Accounting for the Costs of Asbestos Removal recommends that costs of asbestos removal may be treated as capitalized costs if such costs will be recovered eventually though the use or sale of property.

EITF 90-8: Capitalization of Costs to Treat Environmental Contamination provides guidance on whether environmental contamination costs should be capitalized and indicated as an asset on a company's balance sheet or should be shown as an expense in the period. According to EITF 90-8, costs to treat environmental contamination should be charged as an expense unless costs improve safety, efficiency, or capacity or prevent future contamination costs or are incurred to prepare a property for sale.

EITF Issue No. 93-5: Accounting for Environmental Liabilities requires evaluation of an environmental liability independent of any potential claim for recovery. Loss from environmental liabilities can be reduced only when a claim for recovery has a probability of realization. Environmental liabilities can be discounted at a specific cleanup site only if time and payments for the site are fixed or reliably determinable.

The Securities and Exchange Commission mandates several disclosure requirements. Instruction 5 to Item 103 (Legal Proceedings) requires disclosure of pending or threatened legal proceedings by the government. Item 303 of Securities and Exchange Commission Regulation S-K: Management's Discussion and Analysis requires disclosure of events or trends that are likely to have a material impact on earnings and liquidity. A company is required to disclose if it is designated as a potentially responsible party under Superfund. A company also is required to disclose significant exposure to asbestos treatment costs.

Management Accounting

Environmental management accounting deals with the identification, compilation, and analysis of environmental costs. The goal is to account for total environmental effects of a facility or a company. The focus is on the environmental consequences of a product from cradle to grave. The design of the management accounting system is to help incorporate environmental issues in every aspect of corporate decision making. This chapter presents essential elements of a management accounting system that will help management to consider environmental costs in decision making.

ENVIRONMENTAL COSTS

Environmental costs include all costs incurred to maintain the environmental soundness of a company. Environmental costs include not only costs associated with environmental, legal, public relations, and design departments but also those associated with finance, personnel, engineering, and other departments. Management decisions are based on costs and benefits. Therefore, whether a particular cost is an environmental cost or not is not really important. What is important is whether a cost relevant to and environmental decision has been used in management decision making.

Classification of Environmental Costs

Following quality costs, environmental costs are classified into four types: internal failure costs, external failure costs, appraisal costs, and prevention costs. Internal failure costs represent costs associated with environmental degradation before a product is received by a customer. Internal failure costs may be caused by a product, material, or process and include costs related to testing, analyzing, reworking, repairing, and scrapping a product. External failure costs relate to environmental degradation costs after a product is sold to a customer; examples include product repair and recall, environmental accidents, penalties, cleanup costs, liability costs, and goodwill costs. Appraisal costs are associated with inspection and testing of products and measurements of emissions. The purpose of appraisal activities is to ensure the environmental soundness of products, processes, and disposal. Some examples of appraisal costs include costs of environmental auditing programs, equipment monitoring, and government reporting. Prevention involves the use of conscious strategies to reduce pollution. The entire life cycle of a product should be redesigned to reduce pollution. These strategies include product redesign, process redesign, recycling, and disposal. Costs associated with waste minimization, pollution prevention, and product redesign fall under prevention costs.

Management accounting systems classify costs as direct costs (materials, labor, and overhead) and indirect costs (factory overhead, general and administrative overhead, selling and distribution overhead). Environmental costs also are classified as conventional costs, potentially hidden costs, contingent costs, and image and relationship costs. Table 10.1 presents examples of environmental costs.

Costs of materials, labor, supplies, utilities, and capital equipment typically are recorded as direct costs and are not considered as environmental costs. However, a process that produces less waste is preferred to a process that generates a significant amount of waste. One way to account for lower yield and higher generation of wastes is to record costs of materials, labor, and overhead that go into the production of wastes as environmental costs.

Potentially hidden costs can be classified into regulatory, up-front, back-end, and voluntary costs. These costs typically are recorded as overheads and are, therefore, hidden from the potential decision makers.

Contingent costs are incurred only if some uncertain events occur in the future. Costs of accidents and cleanups, penalties, and fines are some examples of contingent costs.

Image and relationship costs involve costs incurred because of bad publicity.

Accurate accounting systems are essential to make cost-effective pollution prevention decisions. One major drawback of current accounting systems is their lack of inclusion of all environmental costs. The traditional system typically ignores engineering and environmental costs required to choose the right pollution prevention alternatives. Aggregation of environmental costs under overhead costs hides environmental costs. The traditional overhead absorption costing system fails to identify significant environmental costs that can be eliminated. A full cost accounting system, by accounting for conventional, potentially hidden, contingent, and image and relationship costs, captures all environmental costs.

Several software tools are available to incorporate environmental costs into decision making.[5] Arthur Andersen & Company's EcoAccounting software helps to identify, accumulate, and estimate environmental costs. The EcoAccounting program consists of three steps — identification of environmental costs, establishment of a set of environmental performance measures, and analysis of strategic alternatives. The identification of environmental costs involves examination of accounting documents and interviews with employees. Performance indices are based on process and output measures that include penalties and emissions. The final step of analysis of alternatives focuses on compliance, reduction of liability,

TABLE 10.1
Examples of Environmental Costs

Potentially Hidden Costs		
Regulatory	**Upfront**	**Voluntary (Beyond Compliance)**
• Notification • Reporting • Monitoring/testing • Studies/modeling • Remediation • Recordkeeping • Plans • Training • Inspections • Manifesting • Labeling • Preparedness • Protective equipment • Medical surveillance • Environmental insurance • Financial assurance • Pollution control • Spill response • Stormwater management • Waste management • Taxes/fees	• Site studies • Site preparation • Permitting • R&D • Engineering and procurement • Installation ┌ **Conventional Costs** ┐ │ Capital equipment │ │ Materials │ │ Labor │ │ Supplies │ │ Utilities │ │ Structures │ │ Salvage value │ └──────────────┘ **Back-End** • Closure/ decommissioning • Disposal of inventory • Post-closure care • Site survey	• Community relations/ outreach • Monitoring/testing • Training • Audits • Qualifying suppliers • Reports (e.g., annual environmental reports) • Insurance • Planning • Feasibility studies • Remediation • Recycling • Environmental studies • R & D • Habitat and wetland protection • Landscaping • Other environmental projects • Financial support to environmental groups and/or researchers
Contingent Costs		
• Future compliance costs • Penalties/fines • Response to future releases	• Remediation • Property damage • Personal injury damage	• Legal expenses • Natural resource damages • Economic loss damages
Image and Relationship Costs		
• Corporate image • Relationship with customers • Relationships with investors • Relationship with insurers	• Relationship with professional staff • Relationship with workers • Relationship with suppliers	• Relationship with lenders • Relationship with host communities • Relationship with regulators

Source: U.S. Environmental Protection Agency, *An Introduction to Environmental Accounting as a Business Management Tool: Key Concepts and Terms*, EPA 742-R-95-001. (Washington, D.C.: U.S. Environmental Protection Agency, 1995), p. 9.

pollution elimination, remediation, and positioning. Product and process changes can be analyzed. This Windows-based program, consisting of a series of Excel spreadsheets, has an activity dictionary of more than 100 environmental activities. Environmental costs can be categorized under compliance, liability reduction, pollution reduction, remediation, and positioning.

Allocation of Overhead Costs

Misallocation of environmental costs to products is a major drawback of traditional accounting. The product costs are estimated by aggregating costs of direct materials, direct labor, direct overhead, and allocated indirect overhead. Direct material and direct labor costs are easy to estimate for each product. However, overhead costs such as salaries to managers, material handling costs, and waste management costs need to be allocated based on some criteria. These allocation methods have several drawbacks. First, waste management costs are hidden in the aggregation. Second, the wrong allocation method will result in miscalculation of product profits. Third, because waste management costs are hidden within overhead costs, no manager has an incentive to reduce them. One way to overcome this problem is to identify wastes generated for each product and allocate them to individual products (Figures 10.1 and 10.2).

An activity-based costing system is another method to overcome some drawbacks of the traditional absorption costing system. In the traditional management accounting system, costs are assumed to be caused by products and services. The activity-based costing system assumes that activities cause costs. Therefore, costs are first allocated to the activities. Activity costs are then allocated to products and services that benefit from activities. Therefore, environmental costs are first accumulated and assigned to activities, and activity costs then are allocated to products.

CAPITAL BUDGETING

The purpose of capital budgeting is to analyze projects and determine whether they should be included in the capital budget. The product of a capital budgeting exercise is a list of approved expenditures of fixed assets. Capital budgeting decisions are strategic in nature because they have long-term impact on a company and are hard to reverse. The changing regulations and contingent nature of costs make an environmental capital budgeting exercise extremely complex. In addition, involvement of personnel from legal, financial, production, health and safety, engineering,

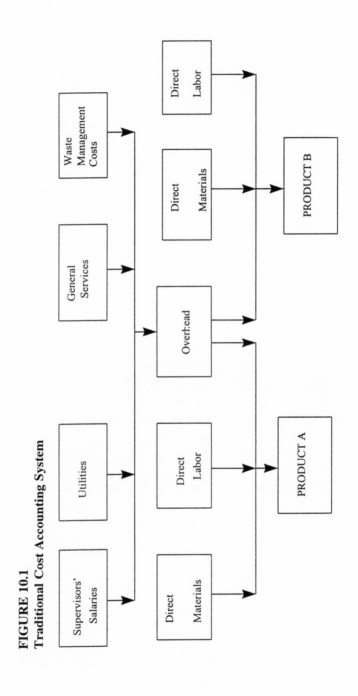

FIGURE 10.1
Traditional Cost Accounting System

FIGURE 10.2
Environmental Cost Accounting System

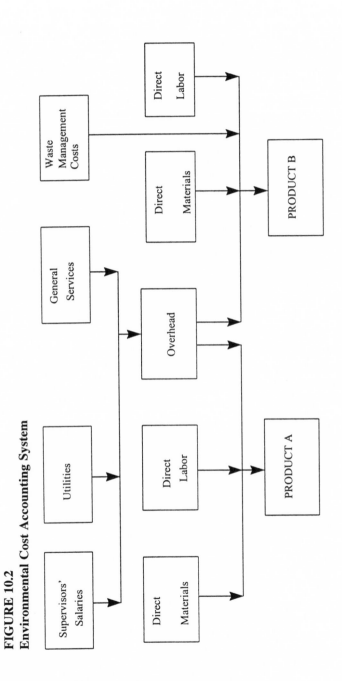

and environmental departments makes environmental decision making long and tedious. The costs of a bad decision and savings from a good decision are extremely high in environmental function. As a result, environmental problems are hard to resolve. The risks involved in environmental decision making make conventional financial analysis tools inappropriate to analyze environmental problems. Environmental project evaluation, in addition to conventional costs, should consider potentially hidden costs, contingent costs, and image and relationship costs. Conventional costs, such as capital costs of buildings, equipment, and project management, and operating costs, of raw materials, labor, and waste disposal, are easy to estimate. However, liability costs that involve penalties and fines, legal claims, and compensation for personal injury are hard to calculate. There are several ways to factor them in the financial analysis. One way is to qualitatively indicate the risk reduction potential of a project. Another is to use the dollar value of risk reduction based on penalties or settlements in previous similar cases. The third approach is to reduce the internal rate of return requirements or increase payback periods. Hidden costs, which include compliance, insurance, and site studies (if these can be directly identified with the project), are included in the analysis. Image and relationship costs are incorporated in the analysis by increased revenues, reduced health costs, increased productivity gains, and so on.

The focus of the appropriate capital budgeting technique is total cost assessment. Total cost assessment, unlike traditional capital budgeting techniques, takes into account a broader range of costs and contingent costs and savings. The total cost assessment methodology suggested by the Environmental Protection Agency consists of a four-step process.[6] At each step, pollution prevention alternatives are compared with current practices. First, only usual costs are considered, and financial indicators are calculated. If the project satisfies investment criteria, the project is selected for implementation; otherwise, the financial indicators are again calculated after including hidden costs. The process is repeated until liability costs and less-tangible costs are considered.

The details of the total cost assessment methodology are as follows (Figure 10.3): Tier 0: usual costs identify pollution-prevention alternatives, estimate usual costs of various alternatives, and complete Tier 0 worksheet. The Tier 0: usual costs include depreciable capital expenditures (equipment, materials, utility connections, site preparation, installation, and engineering and procurement) and expenses (start-up, permitting, salvage value, training, catalysts, working capital, disposal costs, utilities, raw materials, labor, supplies, insurance and others).

FIGURE 10.3
Total Cost Assessment Methodology

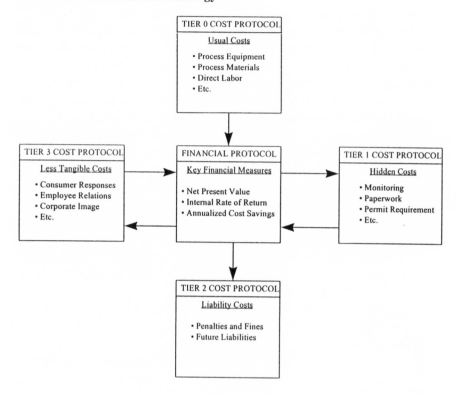

Source: U.S. Environmental Protection Agency. *Pollution Prevention Benefits Manual*, EPA/230/R-89/100. (Washington, D.C.: U.S. Environmental Protection Agency, 1989), pp. 1–4.

Tier 1: hidden regulatory costs identify regulations applicable to the company, estimate hidden capital expenditures, estimate hidden expenses, and complete Tier 1 worksheet. Hidden capital expenditures include depreciation of monitoring equipment, protective equipment, and additional technology. Hidden expenses include costs of notification, reporting, monitoring, record keeping, planning, training, inspections, labeling, medical surveillance, insurance, and so on.

Tier 2: liability costs identify regulations for which a facility could be subjected to penalties and fines for noncompliance, estimate annual penalties and fines, identify wastes and materials management activities for which there could be future liabilities, estimate expected future liabilities for each activity, estimate the year in which these liabilities will be incurred, and estimate the company's share of total expected liabilities. The liability costs include penalties and fines, future liabilities of treatment, transportation, disposal, and others.

Tier 3: less tangible costs identify less tangible benefits of pollution prevention and quantify these benefits. Consumer acceptance, employee relations, and corporate image are some benefits of pollution prevention. The financial protocol calculates financial indicators, such as net present value (NPV), internal rate of return (IRR), and so on, and evaluates whether a pollution prevention alternative is financially feasible.

NPV, IRR, profitability index (PI), and payback period are some financial indicators used to compare investments. The NPV represents the sum of the present values of cash flows discounted at the cost of capital. The returns from projects with positive NPVs are higher than the cost of capital and, therefore, are worthwhile to pursue. Similarly, negative NPV indicates returns lower than the cost of capital. If the capital is scarce, projects with the highest positive NPVs are chosen.

The IRR represents the rate of return from a project for which the net present value of the project is zero. If IRR is greater than the cost of capital, it is worthwhile to pursue the project.

The PI represents the ratio of the present values of cash inflows to the present values of cash outflows. Projects with a PI greater than 1.0 are worthwhile to pursue.

The payback period represents the number of years required to recover the investments made. The shorter the payback period, the more superior is the project in terms of financial returns. Although the payback method is the simplest of all methods, it has several drawbacks. It does not take into account the time value of money or the cost of capital. The payback period ignores cash flows beyond the payback period.

Several capital budgeting approaches consisting of both paper workbooks and software are available. The most significant approaches include Financial Analysis of Waste Management Alternatives, developed by the General Electric Corporation, and PRECOSIS, developed by the George Beetle Company.

Financial analysis of waste management alternatives developed by General Electric consists of workbook, worksheets, and financial calculation software that uses Lotus 1-2-3, version 2.01. This software calculates after-tax incremental cash flow streams of the investment, the NPVs for the current and alternative projects, break-even points, return on investments, and IRRs. Input data requirements include capital costs and operating costs for current and alternative waste generation, management, and disposal activities. It estimates future liability from the data provided by the user about the type of treatment, storage, and disposal facilities; population density in the surrounding community; nearness to a water supply; history of leaks; quantity of waste managed; and hazardous constituents of the waste. Users also should indicate inflation rates, discount rates, investment tax credit rates, federal tax rates, and depreciation schedule.

PRECOSIS, developed by the George Beetle Company, calculates payback periods and IRRs using data on resource effects (labor, material, and facility costs), revenue effects (changes in output quantity, quality, and secondary products), and waste management effects (waste handling, insurance, litigation, and so on).

It is hard to make an environmental decision based on only financial considerations. Every project should be evaluated for technical feasibility, financial soundness, and other qualitative factors. For example, 3M evaluated alternatives in terms of current and potential waste reductions, resources conserved, technological improvements, and savings.[7] The purpose of technical analysis is to ascertain whether the proposed projects are technically feasible for a specific application. During this process, a review needs to be made to determine whether necessary technologies currently are available and, if not, whether development efforts will be successful. In addition, time required to implement the project, effects of the process on the quality control, capacity, and other factors need to be considered. If the project does not involve capital expenditure, the feasibility can be verified by experimenting with the alternative. Technical feasibility can be evaluated for safety, output quality, productivity, installation costs, and new pollution created by the project.

Environmental projects involve multiple dimensions. Improved compliance, lower treatment and disposal costs, improved safety, lower quantity of wastes generated, lower risk, lower insurance costs, better working environment for employees, increased production, and recovery of valuable by-products are some benefits gained from environmental projects. It is, therefore, incorrect to use a single criterion, such as NPV or payback period, to rate a project. Union Carbide Corporation, for example, uses a detailed health, safety, and environmental checklist for screening project proposals.[8] Criteria for screening project proposals are categorized under environmental, safety and health, and product safety. Environmental factors are further subdivided into general, air emissions, surface and ground water protection, waste management, compliance and permits, and site conditions. Safety and health factors are subclassified into general, compliance, public impact, facility design, and compliance with risk management systems. Product safety issues are further subcategorized into general, product design, distribution, and product image.

WASTE MINIMIZATION ASSESSMENT

The waste minimization assessment program suggested by the Environmental Protection Agency consists of:

planning and organization (obtaining management commitment, setting goals, and organizing task for assessment program),

assessment (compiling process and facility data, prioritizing and selecting assessment targets, selecting team members, reviewing data and inspecting the site, generating options, and screening and selecting options for further study),

feasibility analysis (technical evaluation, economic evaluation, and selecting options for implementation),

implementation (justifying projects and obtaining funding, installing equipment, implementing procedures, and evaluating performance), and

operating waste minimization projects.

The assessment team should consist of representatives from operations, engineering, maintenance, scheduling, materials, procurement, shipping, facilities, quality control, environmental, personnel, accounting, research and development, legal, management, contractor, and safety. Data regarding the site (including equipment age), personnel (including their age, years of formal education, and hours of training), process information (including flow diagrams, process description, operating manuals, permits and permit applications, audit report, and production schedules), input materials (including annual consumption rate, purchase price, delivery mode, shelf life, transfer mode, and storage mode), product summary (including annual production rate, revenues, shipping mode, shelf life, and possibility of rework), and characteristics of the waste stream (including density, viscosity, flash point, and disposal method) should be collected. The waste streams for minimization should be selected based on compliance, disposal cost, potential liability, quantity generated, waste hazard, safety hazard, minimization potential, potential to remove bottleneck, and potential by-product recovery. Options to minimize wastes can be source reduction such as equipment changes, procedure changes, or material changes. Recycling and reuse are other waste minimization alternatives. Each option should be evaluated in terms of reduction in waste hazard, reduction of disposal costs, reduction of safety hazards, reduction of material costs, effect on product quality, capital cost, operating cost, implementation period, and ease of implementation. Technical feasibility is evaluated in terms of commercial availability of equipment, use of equipment in similar applications elsewhere, effectiveness in waste reduction, problems relating to scale up, availability of utilities, and so on. Economic evaluation should involve capital costs, including those of equipment, materials, utility connection, site preparation, and training, and savings from utilities, operations, waste disposal, material consumption, liability and insurance, and increased revenues. Payback, NPVs, and IRR are some evaluation methods.

OBSTACLES TO WASTE ELIMINATION

There are several obstacles to waste prevention. Fixed costs and small savings are two major factors that prevent waste reduction. Research and development costs are another barrier. Pollution reduction activities can increase costs that consumers may be unwilling to pay. Sometimes the product produced using less-polluting processes may be of an inferior quality, also discouraging consumers. Liability costs of waste handling and disposal are difficult to estimate. A company's short-term vision may prevent investments in equipment that take a long time to pay off. Some companies can save money by not investing in pollution reduction technologies. This creates an uneven playing field in the short run. Low profitability also may discourage companies from investing in pollution prevention. The option of process changes is inefficient in many older plants.

Pollution reduction projects need to be tailored for each organization. It is not generally possible to copy a project from another plant and expect spectacular success. Unavailability of technology for specific applications inhibits the implementation of pollution reduction projects, especially in small plants. Though substitution of a toxic material with a less-toxic one can reduce pollution, it often is difficult to come up with such projects.

Initiation and implementation of waste reduction projects require good managers and employees. The lack of well-trained personnel is a major hurdle in initiating pollution prevention projects. Downsizing and restructuring have resulted in the reduction of the number of competent people employed in waste management. In a time of technical personnel shortages, companies are less inclined to use engineers for pollution reduction projects than for production projects. Waste reduction projects typically involve changes. However, waste treatments using end-of-pipe projects do not involve changes because they typically focus on treating what comes out of the pipe or smokestack. This prevents companies from supporting pollution reduction projects.

The risks involved in introducing new projects often discourage companies from venturing into waste prevention projects. Management attitude poses another problem. Resistance to change prevents management from trying new approaches. Lack of reliable information about waste reduction is another obstacle to waste prevention. Emphasis on compliance has forced management to think in terms of only regulated wastes rather than all wastes.

Operational problems also can hinder pollution reduction projects. Pollution reduction projects can slow production, creating a bottleneck in the operation. With subsequent process changes, equipment may need more intensive maintenance, requiring a more highly skilled labor force. Reworking defective products and lowering quality can increase the work load. Work stoppage during project implementation is a major disincentive for carrying out pollution prevention projects. Inadequate utilities such as electricity also could be an obstacle to pollution reduction projects.

ANALYTIC HIERARCHY PROCESS

Environmental projects need to be evaluated based on multiple criteria. A checklist like the following will help to identify various benefits:

Sales and marketing
 Improves product quality
 Reduces costs
 Improves market share

Production
 Reduces energy consumption
 Reduces waste generated
 Improves efficiency

Financial
 Reduces input costs
 Improves profits
 Reduces financing costs
 Improves accessibility to finance
 Lowers employee wages
 Lowers employee health care costs
 Lowers liability

Distribution
 Reduces packaging costs
 Reduces transportation costs

Public relations
 Better investor relations
 Improved community relations

Personnel
    More motivated employees
Legal
    Improved compliance

Multiple criteria should be used to prioritize projects. There are several mathematical methods to rate projects using multiple criteria. Goal programming and analytic hierarchy process (AHP) are some mathematical methods that can be used to make decisions involving multicriteria problems. We will demonstrate the application of AHP through an example.

The AHP can provide solutions to problems involving multiple criteria. The AHP provides prioritized ranking of alternatives using a decision maker's relative importance of each criteria and preference for each alternative on each criterion.

Step 1: Identify Projects and Criteria

The first step in the application of the AHP is to come up with projects and develop criteria that need to be considered in choosing projects. Typical criteria include investment requirements, operating costs, risk reduction, cost effectiveness, NPV, payback period, increased revenue, increased safety, better resource utilization, lower insurance costs, improved public relations, timeliness, use of technology in other plants, and improved yields. For the purpose of this example, we will call the projects P1, P2, and P3 and the criteria C1, C2, C3, and C4.

Step 2: Develop the Hierarchy

In this step, a decision maker will indicate the overall goal, the criteria, and the projects. He or she will indicate the relative importance of each criterion in terms of its value in achieving the goal. The decision maker will express priority for each project in terms of each criterion.

Step 3: Prioritize Projects in Terms of Each Criterion

The decision maker will be asked to provide a pairwise comparison of projects in terms of each criterion. The relative importance of each project with respect to another project will be expressed using a numerical scale from 1 to 9, 1 being equally preferred and 9 extremely preferred. We present the priorities for three projects in terms of the criterion C1 using a matrix of the pairwise comparison ratings. The pairwise comparison matrix for three projects, based on a decision maker's preferences, is given below:

	P1	P2	P3
P1	1	9	6
P2		1	3
P3			1

The relative importance of project P2 in relation to P1 is 9. This means that project P2 is extremely preferred over project P1. The relative importance of project P3 in relation to P1 is 6 and in relation to P2 is 3. The relative importance of P1 in relation to P2 and so on can be written easily by taking reciprocals of the relative importance of P2 in relation to P1 and so on. Therefore, a pairwise comparison matrix will be as follows:

	P1	P2	P3
P1	1	9	6
P2	1/9	1	3
P3	1/6	1/3	1

Synthesization involves computation of the priority of each project in terms of criteria. The approximate synthesization procedure is as follows:
    Sum the values of each column:

	P1	P2	P3
P1	1	9	6
P2	1/9	1	3
P3	1/6	1/3	1
	23/18	31/3	10

Divide each element by its column totals:

	P1	P2	P3
P1	18/23	27/31	6/10
P2	2/23	3/31	3/10
P3	3/23	1/31	1/10

Calculate the average of elements in each row:

	P1	P2	P3	Average
P1	0.7826	0.8701	0.6	0.7512
P2	0.0870	0.0968	0.3	0.1613
P3	0.1304	0.0323	0.1	0.0875

The average provides the priorities of each project based on the criteria 1. Pairwise comparison of projects in terms of criteria is a key step in the AHP. However, if projects are not prioritized consistently, the priority calculated using the synthesized process may not be accurate. Consistency of the pairwise comparison matrix can be evaluated as follows:

Multiply each column of the pairwise comparison matrix by the respective average priorities and add, resulting in the weighted sum vector:

1	9	6
0.7512	1/9	+0.1612
1	+0.0875	3
1/6	1/3	1

Weighted Sum Vector

$$0.7512 \times 1 + 0.1612 \times 9 + .0875 \times 6 = 2.727$$
$$0.7512 \times 1/9 + 0.1612 \times 1 + .0875 \times 3 = 0.5072$$
$$0.7512 \times 1/6 + 0.1612 \times 1/3 + .0875 \times 1 = 0.2664$$

Divide weighted sums by corresponding priority values:

$$2.727 / 0.7512 = 3.63$$
$$0.5072 / 0.1612 = 3.15$$
$$0.2664 / 0.0875 = 3.044$$

Compute λ_{max} the average of the values calculated:

$$\lambda_{max} = (3.63 + 3.15 + 3.044) / 3 = 3.27$$

The consistency index is defined as:

$CI = (\lambda_{max} - n) / (n-1)$, where n is the number of projects

$$CI = (3.27-3) / (3-1) = 0.135$$

The consistency ratio, defined as $CR = CI / RI$, where RI is given by the table below:

n	RI
3	0.58
4	0.90
5	1.12
6	1.24
7	1.32
8	1.41

$$CR = 0.135 / 0.58 = 0.023$$

The consistency ratio of around 0.1 or less is considered to be acceptable to assume consistency; whenever the ratio is more than 0.1, the pairwise comparison should be reconsidered.

Priority vectors for other criteria can be calculated similarly and are given below:

	$C1$	$C2$	$C3$	$C4$
P1	0.7512	0.1	0.3	0.6
P2	0.1613	0.2	0.2	0.2
P3	0.0875	0.7	0.5	0.2

In addition to the pairwise comparison for the projects, the same pairwise comparison procedure to set priorities for all four criteria in terms of their importance toward the overall goal of selecting projects should be done. A pairwise comparison matrix for the four criteria is as follows:

	$C1$	$C2$	$C3$	$C4$
C1	1	1/4	1/4	1/3
C2	4	1	2	2
C3	4	1/2	1	1/2
C4	3	2	2	1

A pairwise comparison matrix using the synthesization process can be converted into priorities for the four criteria:

C1	0.085
C2	0.299
C3	0.218
C4	0.398

The overall priority of different projects can be calculated by multiplying the priorities for the four criteria by priority vectors of various criteria as follows:

Overall priority for project P1 =
0.085 x 0.7512 + 0.299 x 0.1 + 0.218 x 0.3 + 0.398 x 0.6 = 0.3980

Overall priority for project P2 =
0.085 x 0.1613 + 0.299 x 0.2 + 0.218 x 0.2 + 0.398 x 0.2 = 0.1967

Overall priority for project P3
0.085 x 0.0875 + 0.299 x 0.7 + 0.218 x 0.5 + 0.398 x 0.2 = 0.4053

Based on the AHP, we can say P3 and P1 have almost equal priorities and P2 has the lowest priority. The AHP can be implemented easily using a personal computer and software packages such as Expert Choice (marketed by Decision Support Software).

DECISIONS INVOLVING RISKS

Decisions involving risks often are solved using decision trees. Decision making using decision trees involves identification of alternatives and states of nature that will occur, drawing decision trees, and solving them. We present a decision tree (Figure 10.4) in which a decision maker has to decide whether to go for existing technology at $1 million or wait a year until new technology is developed. However, there is only a 0.5 probability that new technology will be developed within a year, and the cost of new technology and liability cost during which no technology is implemented is about $600,000. If no new technology is developed within a year, the company will have to implement existing technology and pay liability costs for a year, which is $1.2 million. All dollar values are in present values. In this case, decisions are made based on the expected values. Because the expected value of waiting for new technology is $900,000, it is better to wait.

GREEN ACCOUNTING AT AT&T

The green accounting at AT&T involves using costs of environmental materials and activities in environmental management decisions.[9] The purposes of green accounting include meeting informational needs for design for the environment, supporting development of cost-effective solutions

FIGURE 10.4
Decision Tree

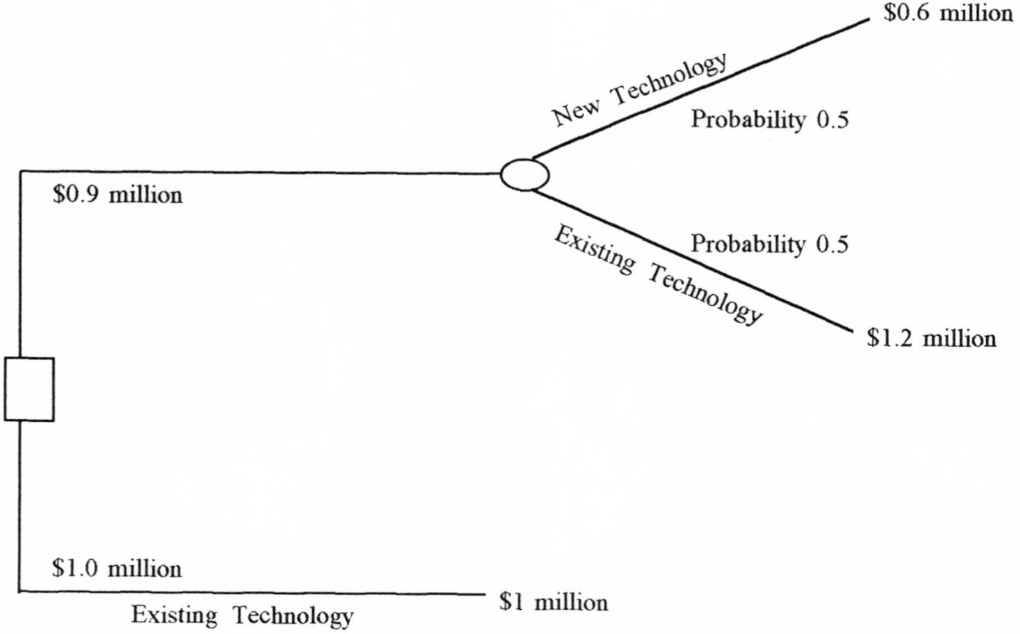

for pollution prevention and environmental compliance, and providing evidence of compliance. Advantages of green accounting include reduction of process costs, identification of environmental costs, improved investment decisions, better evaluation of designs, improved compliance, improved response to stakeholders, and stronger profitability growth. The green accounting was implemented at AT&T through the following steps:

top management commitment,

establishment of multifunctional teams with representatives from various departments,

definition of green accounting,

literature review and appointment of experts in different subject matters,

preparation of green accounting glossary,

development of self-assessment tools, which include a protocol, status survey, activities dictionary, and data matrix,

test of self-assessment tools at three facilities and improvment of the tool,

implementation of complementary initiatives, such as total quality management, design for environment, pollution prevention, activity based accounting, supply-line management, and product takeback programs.

THE STATUS OF ENVIRONMENTAL ACCOUNTING FOR CAPITAL BUDGETING IN THE UNITED STATES

Several studies have been conducted to evaluate the status of environmental accounting in the United States. One of the detailed studies of environmental accounting was done by Price Waterhouse in 1992.[10] According to this study, based on responses from 523 companies, 23 percent of companies have environmental oversight function at the board of directors level. Only one in five companies currently has environmental affairs in the legal departments. Most companies think they are proactive in environmental affairs. However, only one in three has written guidelines on accounting for environmental costs. Six in ten companies have significant environmental exposures that have not accrued because the SFAS 5 criteria are yet to be satisfied. Outside contractors' costs for remediation, regulatory agencies' costs of site cleanup, costs of remedial investigation and feasibility study, maintenance costs of closed sites, property write-off costs, and internal payroll costs for performing remediation are costs included as environmental costs. Internal audits conduct audits of compliance with environmental policies and procedures in six of ten companies.

A more recent study of environmental cost accounting for capital budgeting was done by Tellus Institute for the EPA.[11] According to this study, production and operations, environmental, and finance and accounting departments routinely are involved in cost estimates for environmental projects. More than 70 percent of companies include on-site monitoring, energy, on-site wastewater treatment, licensing, water, production efficiency, on-site hazardous waste treatment, and on-site hazardous waste handling costs in financial analysis. Revenue from sales of by-products, natural resource damage, legal staff labor time, and revenue from environmentally friendly products are items less likely to be considered in financial analysis. Costs are calculated typically for water, energy, production yield, marketable by-products, plant shutdown, licensing, insurance, and on-site hazardous waste management. Few companies calculate specific values of costs for future regulatory costs, natural resource damage, reporting to government agencies, and corporate image effects. More than one in two companies always assign most of the environmental costs to overhead. Very few companies always assign environmental costs to product and process. Among all environmental costs, energy costs are more likely to be assigned always to product and process costs. Overhead costs are allocated to products on the basis of labor hours, production volume, material use, square footage of facility space, and so on. Financial accounting data, purchasing data, production logs, engineering estimates, and materials tracking system are the major sources of cost information when assigning costs to products and processes. Return on investment, payback, IRR, and NPV are the financial indicators used for screening projects. Among companies who use the payback period to screen projects, six in ten companies use a payback period of less than three years to approve a project for financing. About 42 percent of companies using IRR for project screening look for an IRR of more than 20 percent to approve a project for financing. About half the companies who use NPV and IRR go for a time horizon of one to five years and other half, six to ten years.

NOTES

1. Joseph A. Avila and Bradley W. Whitehead, "What is Environmental Strategy," *The McKinsey Quarterly*, No. 4 (1993): 53–68.

2. Maureen L. Cropper and Wallace E. Oates, "Environmental Economics: A Survey," *Journal of Economic Literature*, 30(2) (1992): 721.

3. Adam B. Jaffe, Steven R. Peterson, Paul R. Portney, and Robert N. Stavins, "Environmental Regulations and the Competitiveness of U.S. Manufacturing: What Does the Evidence Tell Us?" *Journal of Economic Literature*, 33 (March 1995): 132–63.

4. U.S. Environmental Protection Agency, *Environmental Investments: The Costs of a Clean Environment.* (Washington, D.C.: U.S. Environmental Protection Agency, 1990), pp. 8-20–8-21.

5. U.S. Environmental Protection Agency, *Incorporating Environmental Costs and Considerations into Decision Making: Review of Available Tools and Software*, EPA 742-R-95-006. (Washington, D.C.: U.S. Environmental Protection Agency, 1996).

6. U.S. Environmental Protection Agency, *Pollution Prevention Benefits Manual*, EPA/230/R-89/100. (Washington, D.C.: U.S. Environmental Protection Agency, 1989).

7. Joseph Ling, "3M Company: Creating Incentives within the Individual Firm," in *Corporations and the Environment: How Should Decisions Be Made*, ed. David L. Brunner, Will Miller, Nan Stockholm. (Stanford, Calif.: Stanford University, Graduate School of Business, Committee on Corporate Responsibility, 1980), p. 99.

8. Marc J. Epstein, *Measuring Corporate Environmental Performance.* (Chicago, Ill.: Irwin Professional Publishing, 1996), pp. 199–211.

9. U.S. Environmental Protection Agency, *Environmental Accounting Case Studies: Green Accounting at AT&T*, EPA 742-R-95-003. (Washington, D.C.: U.S. Environmental Protection Agency, 1995).

10. Price Waterhouse, *Accounting for Environmental Compliance: Crossroad of GAAP, Engineering, and Government, A Survey of Corporate America's Accounting for Environmental Costs.* (Pittsburgh, Pa.: Price Waterhouse, 1992).

11. Tellus Institute, *Environmental Cost Accounting for Capital Budgeting: A Benchmark Survey of Management Accountants*, EPA 742-R-95-005. (Washington, D.C.: U.S. Environmental Protection Agency, 1995).

11

Environmental Reporting: Total Quality Environmental Management Framework

Coherent communication is essential to convey to stakeholders that a company is doing its best to improve its environmental performance. The exponential growth in environmental regulations has made environment a priority concern in the corporate boardrooms. The Toxic Release Inventory requires facilities to report emissions of more than 300 chemicals. The Emergency Planning and Community Right-to-Know Act (EPCRA) mandates companies to disclose to local planning committees information about substances that the companies store and emit. Although companies have improved their environmental performance significantly, very few have received credit for it. Therefore, companies feel a need to publicize their environmental performance. However, any mistake in communication strategy is likely to backfire. Therefore, a company should treat its environmental communication with the same care that it handles other business functions. According to an international survey, about two-thirds of companies published materials and safety data sheets indicating risks associated with their products.[1] A majority of companies include safety information and product contents on their product labels. Emergency planning was a significant public relations activity for more than one-half of the companies surveyed. One in two companies donated to environmental organizations, held annual meetings with environmental officials, issued separate environmental annual reports, and established a formal environmental policy. However, fewer than one-third of these companies disclosed product or process risk information or provided the public with access to environmental research and development results.

Principle 10 of the Rio Declaration on Environment and Development states that

Environmental issues are best handled with the participation of all concerned citizens, at the relevant level. At the national level, each individual shall have appropriate access to information concerning the environment that is held by public authorities, including information on hazardous materials and activities in their communities, and the opportunity to participate in decision-making process. State shall facilitate and encourage public awareness and participation by making information widely available. Effective access to judicial and administrative proceedings, including redress and remedy, shall be provided. (Appendix, Chap. 1, this volume)

Environmental reporting is fundamental to an effective environmental management system (EMS). Most business codes, standards, and regulations require voluntary and mandatory environmental reporting. The purpose of this chapter is to present environmental reporting within the framework of total quality environmental management.

MANDATORY DISCLOSURES

The Securities and Exchange Commission and Environmental Protection Agency (EPA) are two key agencies of the U.S. government that collect and disseminate environmental information. Securities and Exchange Commission regulations establish requirements for disclosing information periodically and also when securities are issued. Many of these disclosures should be consistent with the standards issued by the Financial Accounting Standards Board. Environmental liabilities, pending legal actions, environmental events that may affect future operations of the business, the effect of designation by the EPA as potentially responsible parties, and future cleanup costs are some items required to be disclosed to the public. Of 500 Standard & Poor companies, 96 disclosed their current and 86 their projected environmental capital expenditures on their 10-K forms; 118 reported government environmental legal proceedings; and 46 their private environmental legal proceedings on their 10-K forms.[2]

The EPCRA is a major legislation that regulates the disclosure of environmental information. The four major provisions of this act deal with planning for emergencies, emergency notification of accidents and releases, reporting of hazardous inventories, and reporting of toxic chemical releases. Facilities that have "extremely hazardous substances" in quantities above a certain level should report to state emergency response commissions (SERC) and local emergency planning committees (LEPC) for the purpose of planning to respond to chemical emergencies. Facilities are required to report accidental releases of hazardous substances over a certain level to SERC and LEPC and submit written reports about actions taken and medical effects. Facilities must submit material safety data sheets and lists of hazardous chemicals on site to SERC, LEPC, and local fire departments. In addition, manufacturing facilities covered by EPCRA should submit quantities of toxic chemical releases to states and the EPA. All this information will be made available to the public.

VOLUNTARY DISCLOSURES

More than 1,000 companies worldwide have endorsed the Business Charter for Sustainable Development: Principles for Environmental Management, published by the International Chamber of Commerce (Chap. 4). This charter requires companies "to foster openness and dialogue with employees and the public, anticipating and responding to their concerns about potential hazards and impacts of operations, products, wastes or services, including those of transboundary or global significance." It also mandates companies "to measure environmental performance; to conduct regular environmental audits and assessments of compliance with company requirements, legal requirements and these principles; and periodically to provide appropriate information to the board of directors, shareholders, employees, the authorities and the public." The progress toward fulfilling the charter can be an excellent basis for environmental reporting. The elements of this charter include corporate priority, integrated management, process of improvement, employee education, prior assessment, products and services, customer advice, facilities and operations, research, precautionary approach, contractors and suppliers, emergency preparedness, transfer of technology, contributing to common effort, openness to concerns, and compliance and reporting. Bristol-Myers Squibb reports progress in implementing these principles in pledge and policies, manuals and guidelines, and programs and initiatives.[3]

The Coalition for Environmentally Responsible Economies (CERES) has established a formal reporting procedure for companies that endorse its principles. The element "audits and reports" states, "We will conduct an annual self-evaluation of our progress in implementing these Principles. We will support the timely creation of generally accepted environmental audit procedures. We annually complete the CERES Report, which will be made available to the public." All companies endorsing CERES principles have to submit a standardized report. The standardized format helps stakeholders to evaluate the performance of a company easily.

The Public Environmental Reporting Initiative has established reporting guidelines based on the principles of "continuous improvement" and "what gets measured, gets done." This initiative is supported by companies such as Amoco, British Petroleum, Dow, DuPont, IBM, Northern Telecom, Phillips Petroleum, Polaroid, Rockwell, and United Technologies. Public Environmental Reporting Initiative guidelines suggest inclusion of organizational structure, environmental policy, environmental management, emissions, resource conservation activities, risk management activities (including audit programs), compliance information, product stewardship activities, employee reward programs, and involvement of stakeholders in the environmental reports.[4]

Communication is a major element of the Responsible Care initiative of the Chemical Manufacturers Association. The guiding principles require members to take a pledge to report chemical-related health or environmental hazards promptly to all concerned. All codes demand members to have dialog with stakeholders and respond to their concerns. Self-evaluations involving identification of strengths and weaknesses in the implementation of various requirements are a critical aspect of the Responsible Care initiative. The progress in implementing various codes is indicated by no action, evaluating company practices, developing an implementation plan, implementing an action plan, management practice in place, and reassessing implementation.

Environmental reporting is a critical element of an effective EMS. ISO 14001 Section 4.3.3 stresses the need for the development of procedures for communication and reporting with external interested parties on environmental aspects and EMSs. Communication can be used to broadcast management commitment to the environment. It can answer questions about environmental aspects of activities, products, and services. Communication can motivate employees through environmental policies, objectives, and programs. It also can report progress being made in improving environmental performance. Management review results should be communicated to those who are responsible for environmental performance. To enhance communication between a company and stakeholders, procedures must be developed for responding to the concerns of stakeholders, communicating policies and performance, reporting audit results, making environmental policy available to the public, and communicating with employees to improve performance. The reports should include the organization's profile; environmental policy, objectives, and targets; management structure; environmental results; opportunities for environmental improvements; and third-party verification of the report.

FRAMEWORKS FOR ENVIRONMENTAL COMMUNICATIONS

Quality communication involves the right communication at the right time to the right audience. Communication should be an essential component of an EMS. The planning and implementation of an EMS should begin with communication, so that it will be easier to get the cooperation of all those affected. To sustain momentum, it is necessary to communicate regularly. Every environmental communication model stresses the need for stakeholder approval. It is, therefore, essential to identify stakeholders, understand their needs, and take actions to satisfy their needs.

Every organization ascribes its existence to its customers. Therefore, every environmental communication should involve customers. However, unlike other stakeholders, customers are neither homogenous nor well-informed about environmental matters. Thus, education is the key element of environmental communication with customers. Customers want information to select, use, repair, and dispose of products in an environmentally sound manner. Product stewardship is a significant component of environmental communication with customers. The goal of product stewardship is to reduce product risks from cradle to grave. Product stewardship programs involve:

determination of customer's health, safety, and environmental needs;

design of products to satisfy customer needs and expectations;

avoidance of toxic materials;

reduction of wastes, conservation of energy, and reduction of environmental impacts;

improvement of packaging and observance of transportation guidelines;

selection of right transporters, distributors, and sellers of products;

communication with customers with material safety data sheets and technical literature;

getting rid of wastes through recycling, reuse, and environmental waste management; and

continuously improving the health, safety, and environmental impacts of products.

The local community can break or make a company. Unlike other stakeholders, they do not share a company's interests. They stand for the concerns of the population living in the neighborhood of a company's plants and facilities. Even though their concerns will be primarily emissions and accidents of business operations and their impact, community groups also are concerned about the overall welfare of the people they represent. Community right-to-know regulations have significantly improved the availability of environmental information to local communities.

Employees are a crucial link in a successful environmental communication program. Employees can be staunch allies or enemies of a company, depending on how they are treated. Employees are concerned about workplace safety. Thus, they are interested in environmental hazards and risks. Protecting employees from diseases and injuries in the workplace should be one of the major responsibilities of management. Several environmental laws require companies to communicate with their employees. The Occupational Safety and Health Administration (OSHA) has a hazard communication policy for workers handling chemicals that requires employers to inform workers about hazardous chemicals in the workplace and how to handle them.

Communication with employees is essential for effective implementation of an EMS. With a view to encouraging employee involvement, it is essential to begin communication with employees early in planning and implementation. In addition, management should set precise objectives of communication to develop the right message for employees. The EMS communication should focus on the major elements, people responsible, schedule, benefits, and impacts.

Annual reports are the primary documents through which companies communicate with their investors. Typically, companies spend a paragraph or a page showing the company's commitment to the environment. Some companies also distribute publications highlighting what they are doing to reduce pollution. Many companies publicly affirm their commitment to the environment by adopting the Business Charter of Sustainable Development (Chap. 4), Responsible Care guiding principles, and CERES principles that include:

protection of the biosphere — we will reduce and make continual progress toward eliminating the release of any substance that causes environmental damage to the air, water, or earth or its inhabitants; we will safeguard all habitats affected by our operations and will protect open spaces and wilderness while preserving biodiversity.

sustainable use of natural resources — we will make suitable use of renewable natural resources, such as water, soils, and forests; we will conserve nonrenewable natural resources through efficient use and careful planning;

reduction and disposal of wastes — we will reduce and, where possible, eliminate waste through source reduction and recycling; all waste will be handled and disposed of through safe and responsible methods;

energy conservation — we will conserve energy and improve the energy efficiency of our internal operations and of the goods and services we sell; we will make every effort to use environmentally safe and sustainable energy sources;

risk reduction — we will strive to minimize the environmental, health, and safety risks to our employees and the communities in which we operate through safe technologies, facilities, and operating procedures and by being prepared for emergencies;

safe products and services — we will reduce and, where possible, eliminate the use, manufacture, or sale of products and services that cause environmental damage or health or safety hazards; we will inform our customers of the environmental impacts of our products or services and try to correct unsafe use;

environmental restoration — we will promptly and responsibly correct conditions we have caused that endanger health, safety, or the environment; to the extent feasible, we will redress injuries we have caused to persons or damage we have caused to the environment and will restore the environment;

informing the public — we will inform in a timely manner everyone who may be affected by conditions caused by our company that might endanger health, safety, or the environment; we will regularly seek advice and counsel through dialog with persons in communities near facilities; we will not take any action against employees for reporting dangerous incidents or conditions to management or to appropriate authorities;

management commitment — we will implement these principles and sustain a process that ensures that the board of directors and chief executive officer are fully informed about pertinent environmental issues and are fully responsible for environmental policy; in selecting our of board of directors, we will consider demonstrated environmental commitment as a factor;

audits and reports — we will conduct an annual self-evaluation of our progress in implementing these principles; we will support the timely creation of generally accepted environmental audit procedures; we annually will complete the CERES report, which will be made available to the public;

disclaimer — these principles establish an environmental ethic with criteria by which investors and others can assess the environmental performance of companies; companies that sign these principles pledge to go voluntarily beyond the requirements of the law; these principles are not intended to create new legal liabilities, expand existing rights and obligations, waive legal defenses, or otherwise affect the legal position of any signatory company and are not intended to be used against a signatory in any legal proceeding, for any purpose.

Although environmental groups were perceived as radical groups of the 1960s, they have won popular support in several countries. Support for them among consumers has risen from 15 percent in 1987 to 42 percent in 1992 in the United States.[5] Their influence has risen along with their membership. A recent story in *The Wall Street Journal* describes how Greenpeace outsmarted one of the world's largest oil companies, Royal Dutch/Shell, by forcing it to dispose of its Brent Spar oil-storage rig on land rather than in the sea.[6] Alar's manufacturer was forced to withdraw the pesticide as a result of a campaign by the Natural Resources Defense Council. More than 10 million dolphins have died in tuna nets since 1960. The environmental group Earth Island Institute has forced tuna manufacturers to use only "dolphin safe" tuna. Although the objectives of the environmental groups and those of the companies can be in conflict, companies can form strategic alliances with environmental groups for green marketing, public relations, and image improvement. The first step in forming such a partnership involves establishment of objectives for partnership. Educational programs, donations for products sold, employee matching gifts, plant-a-tree promotions, and vehicle-owner education are some examples of alliances between environmental groups and companies. Such alliances help companies to extend the reach of their product marketers. In addition, such alliances help companies to access expertise, access marketing information, and increase influence. Based on the objectives, the next step is to choose an environmental group. There are several worldwide environmental groups with local chapters. The technique is to choose an environmental group that is noncontroversial and compatible. The environmental group should strengthen a company's ability to achieve its objective. When selecting a partner, a company should think about a long-term relationship. Once a partner is selected, the next step is to make a long-term working relationship. When selecting partners, a company should ensure that there is no conflict of interest. A company should evaluate the partnership from the financial perspective. Every time there is a partnership between an environmental group and a company, there will be in-depth scrutiny; therefore, all deals should be open.

Like any public policy issue, environmental issues go through a series of stages, such as developmental, legislative, executive, and, finally, judicial.[7] The life cycle of an environmental issue typically begins with a gap between corporate environmental performance and the public's expectation about the performance. Dramatic events like accidents or widening expectation gaps can cause people to form opinions about the issue. Entry of environmental groups and politicians soon can take this issue in the developmental stage to a legislative stage. During this stage, the issue will be discussed widely in the media, and a politician may introduce new legislation and regulations establishing new agencies to oversee the performance. Once the law is passed, the issue moves into an executive stage. If the corporation is not happy with the legislation, it may challenge it in the courts. Typical communication strategies during the developmental stage are annual reports, television and radio talk shows, advertising, and direct meetings. Once the issue moves into a legislative stage, the strategies to thwart legislation include building alliances with like-minded groups, lobbying, making political action committee contributions, and using trade associations. Cooperating with agencies, litigation, and compliance are strategies once the regulations are passed.

Several models can help to develop green communications. The total quality management framework of Global Environmental Management Initiative,[8] the QUALITY model of Harrison,[9] the R.A.C.E. process,[10] and effective public accountability guidelines by CERES and the Interfaith Center on Corporate Responsibility are some frameworks for developing green communications programs.

The total quality management framework of the Global Environmental Management Initiative begins with an internal management system consisting of plan, do, check, and act. Plan will identify consumers and their aspirations, do will implement measurement and reporting plans, check will identify gaps between achievements and performance goals, and act will choose options to make up shortfalls. The consumers could be employees, shareholders, customers, or the general public. Each of these consumers has different aspirations. Employees, for example, may prefer a safe workplace free from accidents and health risks. Employees will welcome strong management commitment toward the environment. The shareholders, bondholders, and insurers will like efficient operations and lower future liabilities. Customers will favor green products with very little packaging. The public, especially those living close to company plants, will demand compliance with the laws and regulations and safe operations. Often, all of these objectives may not be consistent. Therefore, one goal of management should be to make trade-offs among objectives. The next step is self-evaluation. Self-evaluation could be done against the

Business Charter for Sustainable Development or various codes of management practices developed by the Chemical Manufacturers Association as a part of their Responsible Care program or CERES principles (Chap. 4). The third step is to generate reports, one focusing on results and another on activities. For example, a report of the number of spills focuses on results, whereas the number of employees trained in inspecting for leakages, preventive maintenance activities, number of inspections conducted, and so on deal with activities. These reports can form the basis for step four of management actions — to make needed changes and achieve goals set in step one.

Corporations have to divulge enormous amounts of information to their stakeholders. The external reports should be generated using the same procedures as for internal reports. The steps to be followed are the same: identify stakeholders' needs, develop management systems, identify shortfalls between goals and achievements, and take actions to close the shortfalls.

The seven-step QUALITY model stands for quantification of audiences, understanding of audiences' needs, asking the right questions and getting responses from audiences, listening to their aspirations, interpreting their responses and taking appropriate actions, taking charge of the public relations process, and you playing the key role in the communication process. According to Bruce E. Harrison, a company can achieve sustainable communication by following a five-step process that begins with the development of environmental mentality. The next step is to observe what winning companies are doing; typically, they ensure compliance and establish a written policy. The written policy will clearly state environmental protection as the paramount goal, source reduction as the primary means of pollution reduction, and open dialog as the means to achieve understanding with employees and the public and cooperation with regulatory agencies. The next step is to empower employees. Because the community plays a vital part in a company's success, bringing it to the company's side is the next step for sustainable communication. The fifth step toward sustainable communication is to actively participate in the public policymaking.

The R.A.C.E. process for community relations consists of four steps. Research collects data about community needs. Analysis identifies audiences, determines key message points, and develops long- and short-term strategies. Communication involves initiation of dialog with the public through community meetings, plant tours, and so on. Evaluation involves measuring the effectiveness of the program through questionnaires, media monitoring, and so on.

CERES and the Interfaith Center on Corporate Responsibility have adopted 12 guidelines to evaluate public accountability of environmental responsibility.[11] They are:

1. Accountability. Are there mutually agreed-upon guidelines for the evaluation of environmental performance and progress with a group outside of the industry and representing the broader public interest?

2. Measurement. Is there an agreed-upon method of measuring progress against stated goals?

3. Disclosure. Is information on environmental performance available in a public report?

4. Dialog. Is the company conducting regular dialog with national and local groups, including those critical of its performance?

5. Participation. Are representatives of local and national groups and issues involved in the advisory processes of the company in a mutually agreeable way? Are those representatives accountable to any groups outside the company?

6. Accessibility. Is information about environmental performance easily available? Are persons in the company easily accessible to interpret data and systems?

7. Simplicity of understanding. Is available information easily understood and useful for comparison on an annual basis and with similar companies?

8. Consistency of policy and practice. Are the practices of the company consistent with corporate policy?

9. Veracity of advertising image. Is public advertising based on company practice or primarily intended to enhance image?

10. Trust. Is a spirit of trust and cooperation exhibited between corporate and public representatives?

11. Credibility. Is provided information reliable, and are persons believable?

12. Independent assessment. Is information provided by the company confirmed by independent, third-party assessement?

These 12 guidelines are an excellent basis for evaluating environmental reports.

SCOPE OF ENVIRONMENTAL REPORTS

More and more companies are voluntarily reporting their environmental performance. Several companies publish an environmental report on an annual basis. According to focus group analysis, government, corporate environmental reports, environmental groups, print media, annual reports, brokerage reports, and television, in order of importance, are the major sources of environmental information. However, in terms of credibility, government and brokerage reports are given higher ratings.[12] A checklist for types of information that can be included in the environmental reports follows:

Management System
> Company profile, chief executive officer statement, environmental organization (including responsibilities of key personnel), corporate goals and targets, corporate policy, environmental strategy, environmental auditing, programs and initiatives, worldwide corporate standards, community relations program, environmental awards, employee training, monitoring and control activities, reporting policy, charitable contributions, compliance programs, environment, health and safety system, emergency response plans, personnel, research and development, senior management involvement

Environmental Performance Measures
> Air emissions including toxic release inventory, greenhouse, ozone-depleting, global warming gases, noise and odor, energy consumption, risk management, habitat management, hazardous waste generated, materials conservation, energy conservation, efficiency programs, packaging, solid waste generated, water conservation, water effluents, and trends of major performance measures

Compliance Measures
> Enforcement actions, permit restrictions, fines and penalties, consent agreement, spills and incidents, workplace hazards, OSHA violations, litigation

Finance
> Senior management compensation, environmental budget, environmental expenditures, environmental cost accounting, superfund liabilities, remediation, litigation, reserves for environmental contingencies

Product Issues
> Product impacts, product stewardship, packaging, labeling, product recalls, solid waste, life-cycle design, technology development

Stakeholder Issues
> Industry association, lobbying activities, supplier education, third-party verification, ISO 14000 certification, environmental partnership, public policy initiatives, legislative positions, community relations

External stakeholders preferred balanced environmental reports with information on compliance, audit results, environmental trends, use of toxics, environmental strategy, spill trends, emissions reduction, OSHA, and adoption of standards. More than 100 U.S. corporations issue environmental annual reports. Many of them can be accessed over the Worldwide Web.

CONCLUSIONS

Businesses have made significant improvements in environmental performance. Still, the public perceives businesses as the villains of the environment. One reason for such perceptions is the lack of effective communication. Companies can do several things to improve their image. Green communication essentially boils down to identifying the stakeholders, finding their needs, evaluating a company's performance, determining the gap between needs and performance, taking action to fill this gap, and reporting the performance to the stakeholders.

NOTES

1. United Nations Center on Transnational Corporations, *Environmental Management in Transnational Corporations*, (New York: United Nations Center on Transnational Corporations, 1993), pp. 75–77.

2. Investor Responsibility Research Center, *1995 Corporate Environmental Profiles Directory*, (Washington, D.C.: Investor Responsibility Research Center, 1995), p. 79.

3. Marc J. Epstein, *Measuring Corporate Environmental Performance: Best Practices for Costing and Managing an Effective Environmental Strategy*, (Chicago, Ill.: Irwin Professional Publishing, 1996), pp. 122–23.

4. Public Environmental Reporting Initiative, *Guidelines*, (Washington, D.C.: Global Environmental Management Initiative, 1994).

5. Jacquelyn A. Ottman, *Green Marketing* (Lincolnwood, Ill.: NTC Business Books, 1994), p. 87.

6. "How Greenpeace Sank Shell's Plan to Dump Big Oil Rig in Atlantic," *The Wall Street Journal*, July 7, 1995, pp. A1, A4.

7. Mike H. Ryan, Carl L. Swanson, and Rogene A. Buchholz, *Corporate Strategy, Public Policy and the Fortune 500: How America's Major Corporations Influence Government.* (New York: Basil Blackwell, 1987), pp. 40–45.

8. Global Environmental Management Initiative, *Environmental Reporting in a Total Quality Management Framework : A Primer,* (Washington, D.C.: Global Environmental Management Initiative, 1994).

9. E. Bruce Harrison, *Going Green: How to Communicate Your Company's Environmental Commitment.* (Homewood, Ill.: Business One Irwin, 1993).

10. Cynthia Leslie-Bole and Stephen J. Nelson, "Environmental Communicty Relations: A Vital Component in TQEM," in *Environmental TQM*, ed. John T. Willig. (New York: Executive Enterprises Publications, 1994), pp. 111–18.

11.   J. Andy Smith, III, "The CERES Principles and Corporate Environmental Accountability: A New Model of Partnership," in *GEMI '94 Conference Proceedings*. (Washington, D.C.: Global Environmental Management Initiative, 1994), pp. 200–201

12.   Global Environmental Management Initiative, *Environmental Reporting and Third Party Statements*. (Washington, D.C.: Global Environmental Management Initiative, 1996), pp. 6–7.

V

IMPLEMENTATION

12

Training

Training is an essential ingredient for successful implementation of total quality environmental management (TQEM). Well-trained employees can identify environmental hazards and take actions to avoid them. Training can help employees to be effective communicators to customers and the public. Without training of employees, improving compliance with environmental regulations and company policies will be hard. It is, therefore, not surprising that every industry standard, every code, and the International Standardization Organization (ISO) mandate training. ISO 14001, 4.3.2. Training, awareness, and competence requires organizations to identify training needs and develop procedures for training employees. Implementation of TQEM obviously requires training in elements of TQEM, including tools and techniques. Unlike training for quality, environmental training should emphasize the importance of complying with the environmental policy and procedures and the internal requirements of the environmental management system. Training should make employees aware of significant impacts of their work on the environment and benefits that can be reaped by improved personal performance.

ISO 14001 requires organizations to make employees aware of their roles and responsibilities in achieving compliance with environmental requirements, including emergency preparedness and response requirements. Training should be focused on conformance with environmental policy and the requirements of the environmental management system. Training also should identify environmental impacts so employees can improve environmental results. Training should motivate employees to stick to operating procedures by informing them of the potential consequences of deviations. Training should not be confined to a plant or facility alone. Organizations should demand that contractors working for them show that their employees have the adequate training. All personnel performing tasks involving significant environmental impacts should be examined to ensure that they are competent, based on education, training, and experience. In addition, the knowledge and skills necessary to carry out significant environmental functions should be identified and should be considered in personnel selection, recruitment, training, skills development, and continuing education.

The Community Awareness and Emergency Response Code of Management Practices established under the Responsible Care program requires communications training for key personnel to enhance community awareness and outreach. The distribution code requires training of all affected employees in the implementation of regulations and company requirements. The process safety code requires organizations to identify the skills and knowledge needed to carry out tasks. The training goal is to help employees reach and maintain proficiency in safe work practices and the skills and knowledge required to carry out their jobs. Before any task is assigned to any personnel, finding out whether the person has the necessary proficiency is essential. In addition, the organization should ensure that employees in safety critical jobs are fit for duty and are not under external influences such as alcohol and drug abuse. This code also requires training for employees working for contractors. The product stewardship code requires training of employees on proper handling, recycling, use, and disposal of products and known product uses. The employee health and safety code requires organizations to document training programs and their methods of evaluation.

The International Chamber of Commerce's Business Charter for Sustainable Development Principle 4: Employee Education requires that organizations educate, train, and motivate employees to conduct their activities in an environmentally responsible manner.

To sum up, training is a critical element of a successful TQEM program. This chapter deals with essential elements of training within the framework of TQEM.

TRAINING MANAGEMENT

Consistent with the process of TQEM, the plan-do-check-act cycle could be used to develop an effective training program. The plan evaluates the deficiencies in the existing training programs, sets priorities, and develops an action plan to correct deficiencies identified. The do involves actual training, including selection of participants, scheduling of training programs, and delivery of training. The purpose of the check is to evaluate training programs with a view to identifying any problems. Finally, the act will evaluate results and take corrective actions to redesign and improve training programs.

Top management often consider training programs to be a waste of time and money. Supervisors feel that training takes employees away from their jobs for which they are paid. Impacts of training on performance are uncertain. Payoffs from training are obtained after long periods. The tasks of identifying training requirements are vague and complex. Often, it is difficult to identify causes for poor performance.

The planning phase should start with top management commitment, which will force employees to take training seriously. Top management can demonstrate their commitment for training by allocating adequate funds. It takes time to identify training needs and develop appropriate training programs.

A training program should consider potential employees that need to be trained. Efforts should be made to ensure that employees selected for a particular training program are as homogeneous as possible. In addition, training programs should be developed for employees at various levels in the organization. Training programs should take into account requirements, experience, and background of employees.

A training program should have clear objectives. Objectives should specify measurable results. Such objectives will help participants to know what benefits they can obtain from the training program. In addition, measurable objectives will help a trainer to rank what needs to be taught. Instead of developing training programs from scratch, it is a good idea to expand the existing training program. For example, if a company is planning to train employees about ISO 14000, then broadening ISO 9000 training programs may reduce training development time considerably.

A training program should advance organization objectives. A training program should be evaluated in terms of concepts, philosophy, content, skill requirements, and so on from the organizational perspective. In addition, training programs developed should reinforce the policies and procedures of an organization.

A training program should be expandable. For example, a training program on ISO 14000 should begin with awareness and continue with elements, implementation, documentation, internal auditing, gap analysis, cost reduction, TQEM tools, and so on.

Training programs typically are considered as waste because management believes that training programs do not add value. It is, therefore, important that training should involve elements that will reduce costs and improve compliance. A trainer should have experience in implementing environmental programs and should have background in environmental regulations. In addition, the training program should have a strong business focus.

A planning phase also should develop criteria to identify potential participants for the training. Federal regulations, industry codes, standards, and past experience can be used to develop the criteria, which should be reviewed from time to time and updated. Clear documentation should be maintained about day-to-day activities of the training department, planning and implementation of training programs, and course outlines, attendance, and progress in learning by participants.

Training should go beyond compliance to meet the requirements of ISO 14000. Awareness training should be offered to all employees to emphasize the importance of environmental issues. Competency-based environmental training should be provided to employees whose actions can have significant environmental impacts. Awareness training programs should focus on company goals and objectives, the importance of environmental issues to the company and employee, the right things to do to improve environmental performance, and a broad outline of ISO 14000 and TQEM.

Once a training plan is prepared, the next step is to implement a training program. Awareness programs typically are offered to most employees. However, competency-based training is provided to all employees involved in activities with significant environmental impacts. Several vendors supply excellent training materials. Training materials also can be assembled from contractors and vendors. Installation and equipment manuals can form excellent competency-based training materials. Training can be outsourced from a training organization. When an outside trainer is hired to provide training, his or her qualifications and experience should be evaluated carefully. In addition, he or she should have knowledge of environmental regulations. The trainer should know implementation issues. If a company has several divisions and plants, the training program should be designed for each site. There are a variety of training methodologies. Live instruction in a classroom, videotape, computer-aided training, interactive video, and workbooks are some methods of delivering training.

With a view to continuously improving a training program, it is necessary to collect data about training programs and identify problems. Every participant in a training program should be tested to ensure that he or she has mastered the required technical skills. In addition, the trainer should suggest to the participants methods of keeping up to date on the required skills. Course evaluations, employee performance reviews, review of materials, and posttraining evaluations are some methods of collecting data about training.

Money spent on a training program will be useless unless the results of the training program are evaluated. Every training program should be evaluated concerning objectives and employee needs and should be redesigned based on the deficiencies identified.

PERFORMANCE TECHNOLOGY

Sometimes, training alone may not improve environmental performance. Skills and job knowledge may not be enough to perform effectively on the job. In those cases, performance technology (PT) may be used to understand employees' needs and improve performance.[1] PT helps to identify what prevents people from doing what they are expected to do. PT, by focusing on actual problems, avoids the mistakes of treating symptoms. It begins with identification of unacceptable behavior, and the goal is to ferret out causes for such behavior by asking questions relating to job performance levels, feedback provided to employees about performance levels, consequences of not meeting target performance, and knowledge and skills required for the job. If the causes of unacceptable performance are related to the employee's knowledge and skills, training is the appropriate intervention. However, if it is not the skill or knowledge that is the cause of poor performance, the corrective action required could be process changes, design changes, better recruitment, incentives, new technologies, and so on. Once appropriate interventions to improve performance are identified, the next step is to carry them out. Monitoring performance, identifying deficiencies, providing feedback to employees, and reviewing results are integral parts of PT.

POTENTIAL TOPICS FOR TRAINING

The chapters of this book can provide potential topics for training. TQEM tools and techniques, industry environmental standards, ISO

14000, environmental auditing, life-cycle analysis, environmental metrics, environmental accounting, environmental reporting, and environmental laws are some such topics.

CONCLUSIONS

Effective management of training is challenging. Training costs money, and payoffs usually are a long time away. Benefits from training programs are intangible. Therefore, it is hard for a manager to maintain the momentum of training programs. However, training programs are critical ingredients of an effective environmental program in an organization.

APPENDIX: CHECKLIST FOR AN
EFFECTIVE TRAINING PROGRAM

Planning

Written plan for training has been prepared.

Top management has committed to the training program.

Top management has appointed a champion for the training program.

Top management has allocated adequate resources for the training program.

Every training program has clear, measurable objectives.

Criteria to identify potential participants for each training program have been established.

Training program takes into account the culture of the company, division, plant, and department.

Training requirements for each job have been identified and updated annually.

Regulatory and personnel changes are monitored to develop need for training program.

All new employees are evaluated for training needs.

A team to make training decisions has been assembled by top management.

Every divisional, departmental, or plant training program must have the support of the respective managers.

Every training program should have a certification test to ensure mastery of skills by participants.

Training objectives should be consistent with corporate policies and procedures.

Implementation

Trainers should be qualified.

A team of dedicated trainers should be developed.

Training should use several training approaches.

Standards of training should be high.

Training should satisfy organizational needs.

Training should focus on added value.

Trainer should be competent in laws, regulations, and environmental standards.

Training should have a strong business focus.

Trainer should be well-versed in new trends and developments.

Trainer should know implementation problems.

Documentation

Criteria for participation

Course outline, attendance record, instructor qualifications and experience

Curriculum

Day-to-day training management

Training guidelines

Administration

Every employee should know what he or she needs to know to perform work effectively.

Every employee should do what he or she needs to do.

Every employee's performance on the job should be evaluated.

Every employee should be evaluated periodically on what he or she needs to know to perform work effectively.

NOTE

1. H. D. Stolovitch and E. J. Keeps, *Handbook of Human Performance Technology: A Comprehensive Guide for Analyzing and Solving Performance Problems in Organizations.* (San Francisco, Calif.: Jossey-Bass, 1992).

13

Total Quality Environmental Management Implementation

Implementation of total quality environmental management (TQEM) takes a long time. The implementation process represents an inculcation of the TQEM mindset in the culture of the organization. Therefore, TQEM needs to be implemented in small phases rather than in one quantum step. There are as many approaches to implement TQEM as there are companies. The primer on TQEM published by the Global Environmental Management Initiative suggests the plan-do-check-act cycle to implement TQEM.[1] The quality environmental management subcommittee of the President's Commission on Environmental Quality suggests an eight-step process to implement TQEM.[2] Other methods suggested in the literature to implement TQEM include correcting deficiencies in the current system with respect to the planned system, performing environmental audits and fixing any shortfalls, and identifying the environmental impacts of products and services and taking actions to reduce them.

PLAN-DO-CHECK-ACT CYCLE

The plan-do-check-act cycle is a methodical process for evaluating the current status and taking actions to accomplish the goals. It can help an organization to achieve continual improvement of environmental performance. Planning begins with data collection about the current situation. The focus is on compliance records, major violations, opportunies for environmental improvements that will satisfy stakeholders, environmental vulnerabilities, and so on. The major stakeholders and their concerns and expectations are identified during the planning phase. Based on the current situation and stakeholder expectations and concerns, an action plan to accomplish stakeholder requirements is prepared. Employees are trained in TQEM tools, such as cause and effect diagram, Pareto chart, control chart, flow chart, and histogram. The do phase is to implement the action plan. The data during this step are collected continually to ensure that implementation is proceeding as planned. The check phase is to evaluate the implementation.

The eight-step process to implement TQEM recommended by the quality environmental subcommittee of the President's Commission on Environmental Quality includes management commitment, a quality action team, training, an environmental impact determination, selection of improvement projects, implementation of improvement projects, measurement of performance, and standardization of the improvements (Figure 13.1).

Management Commitment

TQEM implementation begins with management commitment. Without top management realizing the value of TQEM, implementation will be slow and sometimes nearly impossible. Management commitment represents a promise not only to radically change environmental programs but also to take specific actions to maintain momentum. Three specific attributes of management commitment are stakeholder involvement, allocation of adequate resources, and employee empowerment.

Public pressures, the rising influence of environmental groups, consumer demands, and investor reactions have forced managements to go for processes like TQEM to reduce environmental impacts. It is, therefore, natural to involve these groups in the implementation of TQEM. The stakeholder involvement begins with gathering information about stakeholders. Potential stakeholders include environmental groups, local community organizations, employees, suppliers, customers, investors, regulators, and media. It is essential to collect information about the priorities and concerns of these stakeholders. Some stakeholders typically work in an adversarial manner. Still, it is a good idea to contact them and talk about environmental programs. The next step is communication. Every stakeholder program should be evaluated and corrective action taken to improve it.

FIGURE 13.1
Total Quality Environmental Management Framework for Pollution Reduction

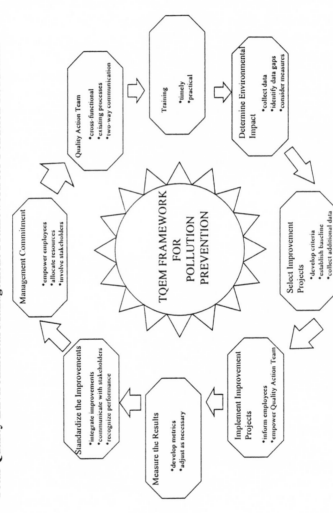

Source: Quality Environmental Management Subcommittee. *Total Quality Management: A Framework for Pollution Prevention.* (Washington, D.C.: President's Commission on Environmental Quality, 1993).

Allocation of resources is essential not only to signal top management commitment to TQEM but also to ensure its implementation as planned. Resource allocation decisions will be affected by factors such as competition for resources from other activities, legal requirements, stakeholder pressures, public relations, and budgetary constraints.

Employee empowerment represents allocation to employees of the authority and resources needed to do their jobs. Empowerment will encourage employees to identify environmental problems, come up with possible solutions, and implement them.

Quality Action Team

The real benefits of TQEM come from its process perspective rather than its functional perspective; therefore, the focus of TQEM is cross-functional rather than functional, and this axiom is translated into reality by quality action teams consisting of employees from different departments. They formulate environmental programs, taking into account the goals and needs of the company.

The specific attributes of the quality action team include cross-functional teams, use of existing resources, and communication with management. Cross-functional teams are essential to create accountability and involvement. Therefore, cross-functional teams should consist of representatives from several departments. Representatives from departments that are critical for the project, including engineering, environment, accounting, purchasing, maintenance, and operations, should be chosen to be members of the quality action team. Carefully picked team members can generate pressures to improve environmental performance by removing implementation obstacles and resolving thorny operational issues that can stall improvement projects. With a view to reducing adversarial reactions to TQEM, it is a good idea to use existing resources to implement TQEM. Use of existing resources also reduces roadblocks for initiating new TQEM projects. Two-way communication is essential to motivate and empower employees. Communication also is necessary to sustain the momentum of TQEM.

Training

Training is one of the most important elements of effective TQEM. Lasting environmental improvements are not possible without improving environmental knowledge and skills of employees. Unless employees realize how TQEM can make a difference in their work performance, only marginal improvements will occur. Therefore, all employees, including line managers, should be taught how to identify environmental problems, opportunities, and decisions. Curriculum for training should include TQEM tools, pollution prevention strategies, statistical quality control, and negotiation and problem-solving skills.

Environmental Impact Determination

Identification of potential environmental projects begins with stakeholder concerns and needs. Environmental projects should be consistent and supportive of corporate goals. In addition, project costs should be within available resources and technology. Three major concerns during this step include use of appropriate quality tools, gathering of information, and metrics to evaluate improvements.

Selection of Improvement Projects

No company has unlimited resources to do every possible project. Therefore, it is essential to prioritize projects. Every project should satisfy explicit, high-priority stakeholder needs. This emphasis on stakeholder needs will help a company understand the origin, nature, and priority of demands on its resources. The success of an environmental improvement project should not be judged based only on timely and within-budget implementation but also on its benefits and stakeholder satisfaction. Without stakeholder focus, a company risks ignoring stakeholder concerns and needs. Some criteria used in selecting projects include waste volume, raw material cost, regulations, disposal methods, potential liability, feasibility, treatment costs, and health and safety. One of the major activities during this step is to collect data needed to prioritize projects. In order to evaluate progress in implementing improvement projects, it is essential to develop waste-related metrics. Metrics could be production related or time related. Production-related metrics are expressed in waste per unit of output. Such measures are extremely useful to express continuous improvements made by the improvement projects, but production-related metrics fail to provide the extent of waste generated by a facility. Most communities are interested in knowing quantities of waste emitted over time. For them, emissions per unit of time is a major concern.

Implementation of Improvement Projects

Implementation of improvement projects begins with communication with employees. Management should communicate environmental problems to the employees and convey the business case for the project. Management should benchmark themselves aggressively against other leading organizations with a view to challenging conventional habits and establishing appropriate goals for change. Management also should identify potential obstacles and take actions to remove them. Sometimes, it may be necessary to train employees.

Measurement of Performance

Once a company decides to go for TQEM, it is essential to establish a result-oriented management process. Companies that focus their efforts on stakeholder needs, make serious efforts to measure performance, and concentrate on environmental improvements are likely to achieve substantially higher levels of performance. Successful companies rely on performance measures to ensure implementation of TQEM. Peformance measures also convey whether TQEM is doing what it is intended to do. Good performance metrics help organizations to learn the progress of TQEM over time.

Standardize the Improvements

It is essential to institutionalize TQEM to bring about continuous improvement in an organization. In order to sustain momentum, top management should identify new issues and provide resources for additional TQEM efforts. Companies should extend TQEM to all divisions, facilities, and departments. The results of TQEM should be communicated to stakeholder groups. Such communication will help not only to increase credibility but also to receive suggestions for further improvements. Teams and individuals who contribute to the success of TQEM should be recognized and rewarded.

INFORM, based on studies of 29 chemical plants, reports the effects of the first eight TQEM programs on the number of source reduction activities initiated by each plant.[3] Cost accounting, employee participation, a formal environmental program, leadership, and material accounting are put in place by a majority of companies. However, fewer than half of these companies have materials balance, environmental goals, and a written source reduction policy as a part of their TQEM programs. Based on statistical analysis, INFORM reports that cost accounting, employee participation, and leadership from environmental as well as other departments can significantly increase source reduction activities initiated by plants. Full-cost accounting increases the number of source reduction activities by as much as three times as compared with plants without full-cost accounting. Plants with employee participation on an average had two times as many source reduction activities as those without it. It is found to be better to have environmental leadership from both line and environmental departments for increased source reduction activities.

The Environmental Protection Agency's *1992 Toxics Release Inventory Public Data Release* reports methods used to come up with a variety of source reduction activities.[4] Percentages of source reduction activities initiated by various methods are:

Internal pollution prevention opportunity audit	21.6
External pollution prevention opportunity audit	2.2
Materials balance audit	7.1
Participative team management	25.3
Informal employee recommendations	10.3
Formal employee recommendations	5.9
Vendor assistance	12.9
Trade and industry program	3.1
Federal and state program	0.7
Others	10.9

Participative team management generated more than one-fourth of all source reduction activities initiated by 23,630 facilities in 1992, followed by the pollution prevention opportunity audit.

CONCLUSIONS

An MCI ad embodies the philosophy behind TQEM:"If a problem is taken care of before it becomes a problem . . . did it ever exist?" The goal of TQEM is to eliminate pollution even before it is generated. In this chapter, we have briefly discussed some systematic approaches to implement TQEM.

APPENDIX: EXAMPLES OF ELEMENTS TO BE REVIEWED TO ASSESS IMPLEMENTATION OF TOTAL QUALITY ENVIRONMENTAL MANAGEMENT IN AN ORGANIZATION

The following examples are based on the Malcolm Baldrige National Quality Award.[1]

LEADERSHIP

Top Management Commitment

    Goal setting

    Planning

    Review of environmental performance

    Communication with employees, customers, suppliers, community members, etc.

    Recognition of environmental performance

    Team building

    Competitor evaluation

    Environmental values and ethics

    Interactions with environmental stakeholders

Environmental Values

    Contents of policy and mission statements and guidelines

    Frequency and manner of communicating environmental issues

    Evaluation of environmental actions and reinforcement of environmental excellence

Management of Environmental Quality

    Organizational structure to encourage environmental excellence

    Team-building strategies and cross-functional interactions to improve environmental results

    Procedures to monitor performance and to take corrective actions

    Environmental performance metrics

Public Responsibility

    Promotion of environmental awareness and communication with external stakeholders

    Methods of increasing employee involvement in environmental activities

    Incorporation of business ethics, public health and safety, environmental protection, and waste management in day-to-day decision making

    Goal setting, evaluation, and reward system

INFORMATION AND ANALYSIS

Data Collection Procedures

    Criteria for selecting environmental quality related data

    Scope and types of data

Methods to ensure validity of data

Procedures put in place to improve data acquisition and storage

Benchmarking

Procedures used to compare company's environmental performance

Scope of benchmarking data — product and service quality, stakeholder satisfaction, supplier performance, employee, internal processes

Method of evaluation of data

Analysis of Data

Use of data for company planning and priorities

Review of environmental performance

Improvements of products, processes, and services

Identification of attributes that improve stakeholder satisfaction

Projection of environmental performance for different strategies and technologies

Lead time reduction in collection and analysis of data

STRATEGIC ENVIRONMENTAL PLANNING

Strategic Environmental Planning Process

Goal setting

Data used to set goals — stakeholder requirements, process capabilities, benchmark data, supplier capabilities

Methods of goal setting, resource allocation, and performance evaluation

Evaluation of strategic planning process

Environmental Goals and Plans

Goals and strategies to achieve them

Short-term plans that include performance indicators and resource requirements

Long-term plans and strategies to meet them

Future projections of environmental quality levels and comparison with those of competitors

HUMAN RESOURCE UTILIZATION

Human Resources Management

Derivation of human resource plans from environmental goals, strategies, and plans

Plans for training, development, hiring, involvement, empowerment, and recognition

Goals for hiring and career development

Analysis and use of employee-related data

Employee Involvement

Management practices including suggestion systems and incentives to increase employee involvement

Company actions for empowerment, responsibility, and innovation

Performance metrics for employee involvement

Indicators for involvement of various levels of employees

Environmental Quality Education and Training

Types and amounts of environmental training of various levels of
employees, training methods, and reinforcement of environmental
knowledge

Summary of and trends in training received by employees

Procedures put in place to improve training

Employee Recognition and Performance Measurement

Procedures in place to recognize, reward, and measure performance of
individuals and groups, including managers

Trends in recognition and reward of individuals and groups

Metrics companies use to evaluate and improve recognition and performance process

Employee Well-Being and Morale

Inclusion of health, safety, satisfaction, and ergonomic factors in environmental improvement activities

Support of employees through mobility, flexibility, and retraining in job
assignments and accommodation of changes in technology, improved
productivity, or work processes

Special services such as counseling, assistance, recreation, cultural, and
non–work-related education

Trends and levels in key indicators of well being and morale such as safety and absenteeism

ENVIRONMENTAL QUALITY ASSURANCE OF
PRODUCTS AND SERVICES

Design and Introduction of Environmental Quality Products and Services

Design procedures that incorporate stakeholder requirements into design,
parts, products, processes, and services

Evaluation of designs using product and service performance, process
capability requirements, supplier capability requirements, and so on

Design strategies to reduce product design to introduction time

Process Environmental Quality Control

Process, product, and service characteristics measurements and types and
frequencies of measurement

Root cause analysis and procedure to make corrections

Evaluation of environmental quality measurement and assurance

Continuous Improvement of Process

Type of data used for continuous improvement

Evaluation of alternatives to make changes

Integration of process improvement in the day-to-day decision making

Environmental Quality Assessment
> Approaches to evaluate greenness of a system, process, practice, product, or service
>
> Use of assessments to improve greenness

Documentation
> Documentation procedures for compliance purposes and tracking of non-conformance of products, processes, and services
>
> Procedures to improve documentation systems

Business Process and Support Service Quality
> Pollution elimination for key business processes and support services
>
> Establishment of environmental goals, process evaluation and improvement activities, metrics to measure environmental performance, and review of progress

Supplier Performance
> Approaches used to communicate environmental requirements to suppliers
>
> Measures used to evaluate environmental performance
>
> Strategy used to improve environmental performance of suppliers

ENVIRONMENTAL RESULTS

Product and Service Quality Results
> Trends and current levels of environmental performance
>
> Methods of benchmarking environmental results

Business Process, Operational, Support Service Environmental Results
> Trends and current levels of environmental measures and effectiveness of business processes, operations, and support services
>
> Comparison of environmental results with those of industry, industry leaders, and world leaders

Supplier Environmental Performance
> Trends and current levels of supplier environmental performance
>
> Comparison of environmental performance with that of competitors

STAKEHOLDER SATISFACTION

Determining Stakeholder Requirements and Expectations
> Method of determining current and future stakeholder requirements, the segmentation of stakeholder groups, the process of collecting information, and so on
>
> Processes of determining environmental attributes of products and services and importance of these attributes to stakeholders
>
> Improvement of process of determining stakeholder requirements

Stakeholder Relationship Management
> Methods by which stakeholders can seek assistance and comment about the products, processes, and services

Methods of contacting stakeholders and asking for suggestions for improvement

Career development stakeholder-contact personnel

Technology and logistic support to stakeholder-contact personnel to provide reliable and responsive services

Analysis of stakeholder-related data and information to assess costs and market consequences for policy development, planning, and resource allocation

Metrics to evaluate stakeholder-relationship management

Stakeholder Service Standards

Stakeholder service standards

Methods to ensure stakeholder service to be effective and timely

Tracking, evaluation, and improvement of stakeholder service standards

Commitment to Stakeholders

Types of commitments company makes to encourage trust and confidence in its products, services, and relationships

Impact of environmental results on commitment to stakeholders

Complaint Resolution for Environmental Quality Improvement

Overall evaluations of aggregated complaints

Methods to ensure prompt and effective resolution of complaints

Analysis of complaints and corrective actions

Metrics to evaluate complaint-related processes

Determining Stakeholder Satisfaction

Determination of satisfaction of various stakeholder groups

Stakeholder satisfaction relative to competitors

Analysis of stakeholder satisfaction data against complaint rates, market share data, and so on

Improvement of process to measure customer satisfaction

Stakeholder Satisfaction Results

Trends and current levels of stakeholder satisfaction with products and services

Trends and current levels of adverse indicators, such as complaints, spills, emissions, litigation, repairs, and breakdowns

Stakeholder Satisfaction Comparison

Comparison of stakeholder satisfaction results with those of the competitors

Evaluations by independent organizations

Market share trends

---

1. The Malcolm Baldrige National Quality Award, *1991 Application Guidelines*. (Gaithersburg, Md.: National Institute of Standards and Technology, 1991).

NOTES

1.   Global Environmental Management Initiative, *Total Quality Environmental Management: The Primer*, (Washington, D.C.: Global Environmental Management Initiative, 1993).

2.   Quality Environmental Management Subcommittee, *Total Quality Management: A Framework for Pollution Prevention,* (Washington, D.C.: President's Commission on Environmental Quality, 1993).

3.   Mark K. Dorfman, Warren J. Muir, and Catherine G. Miller, *Environmental Dividends: Cutting More Chemical Wastes*. (New York: INFORM, 1992).

4.   U.S. Environmental Protection Agency, *1992 Toxics Release Inventory: Public Data Release*, EPA 745-R-94-001. (Washington, D.C.: U.S. Environmental Protection Agency, 1994), pp. 138–39.

14

Implementation Tips from Environmental Leaders

STAGES OF IMPLEMENTATION

Companies have adopted a variety of strategies and tactics to demonstrate their commitment to environmental issues to stakeholders. Companies have developed new approaches to environmental management. Some companies go through a variety of stages of environmental management. Most companies begin with compliance-oriented management. They solve their environmental problems in a "fire-fighting" mode. Their planning horizon is short. Top management involvement is minimal or nonexistent. Environmental planning is done at the departmental level, and pollution reduction strategies are piecemeal. Compliance is achieved by either waste treatment or incineration. Company environmental responsibilities are handled by legal departments. Command-and-control regulations drive their environmental programs. These companies try to lobby legislatures to reduce the stringency of environmental regulations. Public relations strategies are reactive, responding to emergencies or accidents. Supplier selection is based solely on prices. Training of employees is minimal. Management style is paternal, and rarely is any research and development done to improve environmental performance. These companies waste resources flagrantly. Communications in these companies are top down, and employees are evaluated in terms of permit denials, legal violations, discharges, and spills. Reward and recognition is nonexistent for superior environmental results.

Typically, companies move from a compliance-oriented management stage to a proactive stage. Negative experiences such as permit violations, accidental releases, waste disposal liabilities, and explosions in the plant force companies to end the "business as usual" posture and support improved compliance with laws and regulations. Proactive companies start with internal audits to ensure that the company is in compliance with laws and regulations. Companies also begin to undertake projects involving pollution elimination. The management approach shifts from problem solving to problem prevention. The time horizon for decision making is medium term in such companies. Top management involvement is not wholehearted. Planning is done at the plant level. Company policies about environmental issues are not well-written. Costs of compliance are the major factor that drives environmental programs in these proactive companies. Recycling and housekeeping are some approaches to minimize waste. Public relations respond to accidents, and training programs are not well-organized. Management is somewhat paternal. Research and development focuses on compliance. Communication is top down, and environmental performance is measured in disposal costs. Increased liabilities, waste treatment mandates, community right-to-know laws, energy conservation, and taxation are some of the issues that force companies to be proactive.

Public pressures, rising environmental costs, stable environmental regulations, and declining competitiveness force management to use the environment as an opportunity rather than a threat. The goal is to harmonize environmental objectives with corporate goals. This orientation dramatically shifts corporate planning, research and development, and investments to increase returns from environmental activities. The planning horizon becomes long-term. The top management goal is to integrate environmental issues into day-to-day decision making. The focus is on the life cycle of a product. Public relations are used to increase stakeholder satisfaction. Environmental labeling programs, green investors, voluntary regulations, and tax breaks are some factors that drive companies to this strategic mindset.

The ultimate goal of a company is to become a total quality environmental management (TQEM) company. Unlike companies that consider the environment as a cost, TQEM companies believe that improved environmental performance is a source of enormous profits. They consider pollution elimination through source reduction as the key to improved environmental performance. Top management commitment is a hallmark of such companies. The whole company is committed to pollution elimination, and continuous improvement is their canon. "Whatever the process, it always can be improved" is their axiom. There are no performance quotas for employees. Communication is two-way. The chief executive officer leads the environmental program. Environmental programs are companywide, and the focus is from cradle to grave. Suppliers are selected based on their commitment to environmental improvement. Profits are generated by satisfied stakeholders. Environmental programs are driven by new opportunities. A reward system recognizes environmental performance.

MANAGEMENT STRUCTURE

Most companies are in the first three stages, and many of them are striving to become TQEM companies. According to the UN Center on Transnational Corporation's benchmark survey conducted in 1990–91, in three of four companies, top management is involved in launching environmental programs. Strategic planning, research and development, public relations, production, market research, marketing, human resources, and accounting are other departments, in order of frequencies, that are primary initiators of environmental programs.[1] In the United States, 61 percent of manufacturing companies have a committee of directors to oversee environmental responsibilities. The entire board is responsible for environmental affairs in 19 percent of these companies. Public policy committees, audit committees, and environmental health and safety committees are some committees overseeing environmental affairs. The number of reporting levels between the senior environmental officer and the chief executive officer is one in most manufacturing companies. Responsible Care and Business Charter for Sustainable Development are popular environmental codes subscribed to by U.S. companies. About 89 companies apply total quality management (TQM) principles and practices in the management of environmental affairs; however, only half of these companies apply TQM principles on a corporatewide basis.[2]

INDUSTRY PRACTICES

Companies think that the challenges they face in implementing the environmental programs are similar to those of quality programs. However, unlike in quality programs, stakeholders involved in environmental programs include (in addition to suppliers and customers) community groups, investors, neighbors, and regulators. Also, environmental regulations are far more complex than regulations relating to quality. There is no provision for a citizen lawsuit in the quality area. A defective product typically affects a customer; however, environmental issues involve everyone, and there are acrimonious debates and political exploitation. Deterioration in environmental performance typically results in criminal and civil sanctions.

Demonstration project profiles contained in *Total Quality Management: A Framework for Pollution Prevention* prepared by the quality environmental management subcommittee of the President's Commission on Environmental Quality are excellent models for learning about TQEM implementation. However, these implementation demonstrations were typically in a division or a plant, not companywide. The goal of TQEM at AT&T Network Systems was to reduce Toxics Release Inventory emissions. TQEM was implemented using a seven-step problem-solving process. A Pareto chart, process flow diagram, countermeasure chart, and implementation timetable were the key TQEM tools. Lack of resources, potential regulatory barrier, downtime because of implementation, and short life of product line were some obstacles during implementation.

Reduction of environmental operating costs was the objective of Chevron USA Product Company's TQEM program. Employees were trained in TQM techniques. Lack of time was the major obstacle. Continuous improvement was the tool. The process of TQEM was implemented following a seven-step quality improvement process.

The Dow Chemical Company's goal was to identify strategies to reduce fugitive emissions and laboratory waste streams. Benchmarking and various quality tools were used. Lack of technology and resources were the major obstacles to TQEM.

The TQEM program at the DuPont Company plant was to reduce ammonium sulfate in the process sector. It used techniques such as brainstorming, technical evaluations, and process experiment design to develop ideas to achieve goals. Resistance to change, expanded workload, and increased costs were the major obstacles.

The purpose of the TQEM program at the Ford Motor Company was to incorporate environmental quality into the manufacturing decision making. The implementation of TQEM involved quality action teams, collection and review of data, formulation of criteria, prioritizing actions, brainstorming for needs, evaluating options, doing the obvious, performing economic evaluations, recommending options, implementing options, measuring results, and providing feedback on performance. Some TQEM tools included brainstorming, failure mode effects analysis, Pareto charts, histograms, process flow charts, and rainbow charts. Employee awareness, quantifying external benefits, accounting for intangible costs, and absence of pollution credits were the major obstacles.

To make environmental quality an integral part of employee activities was the objective of GE's TQEM program. GE created TQEM awareness through training and partnership with customers, suppliers, and employees. Solid and hazardous waste was the focus of the TQEM program. Inaccurate estimation of employee awareness, making trade-offs between product quality and environmental quality, and inadequacy of human resources were the major obstacles to implementation. Process mapping, brainstorming, and six-step problem solving were some TQEM tools used.

Cause and effect diagrams, brainstorming, Pareto methods, control charts, process flow charts, and benchmarking are some TQEM tools employed at International Paper. The major objective of the TQEM process was to apply TQM to improve environmental compliance. Difficulty in working with regulators was the major obstacle to implementation.

Good manufacturing practices are the foundation of the TQEM program at Merck & Company. The objective of the TQEM program was to reduce SARA Toxics Release Inventory releases by 90 percent worldwide by 1995. Management sets the overall goals. Task teams are formed to implement projects. Technical and engineering expertise is the basis for TQEM implementation. Product quality constraints, limited technology, scarcity of time, and approval from regulators are some major obstacles.

TQM is an integral part of the operating philosophy at 3M. Reduction of environmental waste is a part of every employee's job responsibility. Teams implement TQEM programs based on needs, functions, and experience. An environmental performance measurement system reports contributions made by every employee or team toward waste reduction. Sustaining momentum to a 17-year program is the major challenge.

To implement TQEM companywide at Procter and Gamble, the company focused on vision, design, action, and communication.[3] Vision involves insight that superior environmental performance leads to sustained business success, design should connect business needs to environmental performance, action should institutionalize continuous improvement systems, and communication should disseminate knowledge and leverage accomplishments internally as well as externally.

Vision focuses on product development, product manufacturing, and product stewardship. Product development ensures safe products, product manufacturing means safe facilities, and product stewardship results in sound business. To implement vision, each program area has its own objectives, goals, strategies, and measures. Objectives represent expected outcomes, goals express objectives in quantitative terms, strategies define means, and measures represent specific results that can be used to measure progress. For example, the objective may be to become an environmental leader, the goal may be compliance, the strategy can be an environmental management system, and measures could be penalties or fines and violations.

A continuous improvements plan in product development, product manufacturing, product stewardship, and communication was developed. Life-cycle assessment and evaluation of product ingredients were done to ensure safety. Product manufacturing was improved through audits, site environmental leader certification programs, and systematic pollution prevention programs.

Market surveys, source reduction techniques, and product development consistent with the waste management goals were the elements of the plan to implement product stewardship. Internal communication was improved by sharing performance expectations, goals, and future plans and by networking. External communication improved through open dialog, talking about products to consumers, and publicizing TQEM initiatives.

According to Sandra Woods of Coors Brewing Company, environmental principles, a mission statement, communication, training, experimentation, information sharing, rewards, coalition building, continuing the momentum, and the scrap approach are the major elements of a successful TQEM program.[4]

The TQEM program at Colgate Palmolive is based on the canon of "preserving value and creating value."[5] The TQEM program involves development of a program consistent with its business objectives, understanding of stakeholder needs, defining mission, introduction of the program (called ENVIROPRIDE), and education. ENVIROPRIDE involves "7Rs," namely "reduce, reuse, recycle, reformulate, redesign, reward, and renew."[6]

The strategy of L'oreal was to use research and development to incorporate environmental improvements and quality into the product.[7] L'oreal's process of incorporating environmental performance in products begins with the identification of environmental trends relating to products, processes, packaging, buying habits, and so on. The next step is developing alternatives to respond to these trends and an estimation of costs. Competitor analysis is done at this stage. The next step is research and development to increase competitive advantage. Required regulatory changes are achieved through industry and other partnerships. Communication of accomplishments to stakeholders is one of the key elements of this process.

Anheuser-Busch's packaging reduction strategy is based on two critical principles — "Do the little things right" and "Do not go it alone."[8]

Doing the little things right includes making sure that the packaging provides the highest level of product protection, is competitive with other materials in cost, and has the lowest impact on the environment. Partnerships with suppliers and supplier conferences are ways to involve suppliers in packaging decision making.

CONCLUSIONS

There is no "fits all" approach to implementing TQEM in an organization. TQEM has to be custom-made for each organization. Top management commitment is essential for TQEM, and teamwork is the hallmark. The process of continuous improvement is the driving force. This process can never stop, because, in today's world, as an advertisement of the Electronic Data System points out, "standing still is a sure way to get run over."

NOTES

1. United Nations Center on Transnational Corporations, *Environmental Management in Transnational Corporations: Report on the Benchmark Corporate Environmental Survey.* (New York: United Nations Center on Transnational Corporations, 1993), p. 47.

2. Investor Responsibility Research Center, *1995 Corporate Environmental Profiles Directory.* (Washington, D.C.: Investor Responsibility Research Center, 1995), pp. 82–85.

3. Michael T. Fisher, "Total Quality Environmental Management: The Procter & Gamble Approach," in *Corporate Quality Environmental Management III: Leadership — Vision to Reality*, ed. Global Environmental Management Initiative. (Washington, D.C.: Global Environmental Management Initiative, 1993), p. 33.

4. Sandra Woods, "Making Pollution Prevention Second Nature to Your Employees," in *Corporate Quality Environmental Management III: Leadership — Vision to Reality*, ed. Global Environmental Management Initiative. (Washington, D.C.: Global Environmental Management Initiative, 1993), pp. 51–55.

5. Douglas R. Wright, "Designing a Corporate Environmental Program: The Colgate Palmolive Approach," in *Corporate Quality Environmental Management III: Leadership — Vision to Reality*, ed. Global Environmental Management Initiative. (Washington, D.C.: Global Environmental Management Initiative, 1993), pp. 57–60.

6. Ibid.

7. Kay Breenden and Michael Fontaine, "Eco-Quality: Integrating Product Quality and Environmental Performance through Innovation, L'oreal — A Case

Study," in *Corporate Quality Environmental Management III: Leadership — Vision to Reality*, ed. Global Environmental Management Initiative. (Washington, D.C.: Global Environmental Management Initiative, 1993), pp. 79–85.

8.   Norman F. Nieder, "Anheuser-Busch Packaging and the Environment," in *Environmental Management in a Global Economy, GEMI '94 Conference Proceedings*, ed. Global Environmental Management Initiative. (Washington D.C.: Global Environmental Management Initiative, 1994), pp. 33–36.

Selected Bibliography

Avila, Joseph A., and Bradley W. Whitehead. "What is Environmental Strategy?" *The McKinsey Quarterly* 4 (1993):53–68.

Bhat, Vasanthakumar N. *The Green Corporation, The Next Competitive Advantage.* Westport, Conn.: Quorum Books, 1996.

Casio, Joseph, ed. *The ISO 14000 Handbook.* Milwaukee, Wisc.: ASQC Quality Press, 1996.

Coddington, Walter. *Environmental Marketing.* New York: McGraw-Hill, 1993.

Ditz, Daryl, Janet Ranganathan, and R. Darryl Banks. *Green Ledgers: Case Studies in Corporate Environmental Accounting.* Washington, D.C.: World Resources Institute, 1995.

Epstein, Marc J. *Corporate Environmental Performance: Best Practices for Costing and Managing an Effective Environmental Strategy.* Chicago, Ill.: Irwin Professional Publishing, 1996.

Global Environmental Management Initiative. *Environmental Health & Safety Training: A Primer.* Washington, D.C.: Global Environmental Management Initiative, 1995.

Global Environmental Management Initiative. *Environment and Sustainable Development: Making It Happen.* Washington, D.C.: Global Environmental Management Initiative, 1995.

Global Environmental Management Initiative. *Finding Cost-Effective Pollution Prevention Initiatives: Incorporating Environmental Costs into Business Decision Making, A Primer.* Washington, D.C.: Global Environmental Management Initiative, 1994.

Global Environmental Management Initiative. *Benchmarking: The Primer.* Washington, D.C.: Global Environmental Management Initiative, 1994.

Global Environmental Management Initiative. *Total Quality Environmental Management: The Primer.* Washington, D.C.: Global Environmental Management Initiative, 1993.

Global Environmental Management Initiative. *Corporate Quality Environmental Management III: Leadership — Vision to Reality.* Washington, D.C.: Global Environmental Management Initiative, 1993.

Harrison, Bruce, E. *Going Green: How to communicate your company's environmental commitment.* Homewood, Ill.: Business One Irwin, 1993.

Kolluru, Rao V. *Environmental Strategies Handbook.* New York: McGraw-Hill, 1994.

Levy, Geoffrey M., ed. *Packaging in the Environment.* London: Blacki Academic and Professional, 1993.

North, Klaus. *Environmental Business Management.* Geneva: International Labor Office, 1992.

Porter, Michael, E., and Claas van der Linde. "Green and Competitive: Ending the Stalemate." *Harvard Business Review* 73 (September–October 1995):120–34.

Quality Environmental Management Subcommittee. *Total Quality Management:A Framework For Pollution Prevention.* Washington, D.C.: President's Commission on Environmental Quality, 1993.

Repretto, Robert. *Jobs, Competitiveness, and Environmental Regulation:What Are the Real Issues?* Washington, D.C.: World Resources Institute, 1995.

Ryding, Sven-Olof. *Environmental Management Book.* Amsterdam: IOS Press, 1992.

Schmidheiny, Stephan. *Changing Course: A Global Business Perspective on Development and the Environment.* Cambridge, Mass.: MIT Press, 1992.

"The Challenge of Going Green." *Harvard Business Review* 72 (1994):37–50.

Tibor, Tom and Ira Feldman. *ISO 14000: A Guide to the New Environmental Management Standards.* Chicago, Ill.: Irwin Professional Publishing, 1996.

United Nations Environmental Programme. *Environmental Auditing,* Technical Report Series No. 2. Paris: United Nations Environmental Programme, 1990.

U.S. Environmental Protection Agency. *Incorporating Environmental Costs and Considerations into Decision Making: Review of Available Tools and Software, A Guide for Business and Federal Facility Managers,* EPA 742-R-95-006. Washington, D.C.: U.S. Environmental Protection Agency, 1995.

U.S. Environmental Protection Agency. *An Introduction to Environmental Accounting as a Business Management Tool: Key Concepts and Terms,* EPA 742-R-95-001. Washington, D.C.: U.S. Environmental Protection Agency, 1995.

U.S. Environmental Protection Agency. *Life-cycle Assessment: Inventory Guidelines and Principles*, NTIS PB 93-139681. Washington, D.C.: U.S. Environmental Protection Agency, 1993.

U.S. Environmental Protection Agency. *Life-cycle Assessment:Public Data Sources for the LCA Practitioner*. Washington, D.C.: U.S. Environmental Protection Agency, 1993.

U.S. Environmental Protection Agency. *Life-cycle Design Guidance Manual:Environmental Requirements and the Product System*, EPA/600/R-92/226. Washington, D.C.: U.S.Environmental Protection Agency, 1992.

U.S. General Accounting Office, *Environmental Auditing: A Useful Tool That Can Improve Environmental Performance and Reduce Costs*, GAO/RCED-95-37. Washington, D.C.: General Accounting Office, 1995.

Walley, Noah and Bradley Whitehead. "It's Not Easy Being Green." *Harvard Business Review* 72 (May–June 1994):46–52.

Willing, John T. *Environmental TQM*. New York: Executive Enterprises Publications, 1994.

Index

ABOUT THE AUTHOR

VASANTHAKUMAR N. BHAT is Associate Professor of Management Science and Operations Management at the Lubin School of Business, Pace University. He is author of numerous books and articles including *The Green Corporation: The Next Competitive Advantage* (Quorum, 1996), and has several years experience in pharmaceutical and engineering companies.

Date Due

MAR - 1 1999			

BRODART, CO.   Cat. No. 23-233-003   Printed in U.S.A.